PELICAN BOOKS

Dual-Career Families

Rhona and Robert Rapoport are social anthropologists whose work covers a wide field of mental health and family research. Rhona Rapoport was born and educated in South Africa and afterwards at the London School of Economics, where she received her Ph.D. As a qualified psychoanalyst she worked on the staff of the Harvard Medical School before returning to this country with her husband. Robert Rapoport was born in the United States and trained there, receiving degrees at the Universities of Chicago and Harvard. He is at present Convenor of the Family and Environmental Research Unit at the Tavistock Institute's Human Resources Centre. Rhona and Robert Rapoport have written *Community as Doctor* (1960), a book on therapeutic communities. Recently they have collaborated with Michael Fogarty on studies of women's careers in *Women and Top Jobs* (1967) and in *Sex, Career and Family* (1971).

They now live in London and have two children.

Rhona and Robert Rapoport are currently co-directors of a new Institute for family and environmental research.

Dual-Career Families

RHONA RAPOPORT AND
ROBERT N. RAPOPORT

PENGUIN BOOKS

Penguin Books Ltd, Harmondsworth, Middlesex, England
Penguin Books Inc., 7110 Ambassador Road, Baltimore, Maryland 21207, U.S.A.
Penguin Books Australia Ltd, Ringwood, Victoria, Australia

—

First published 1971

—

Copyright © P.E.P., 1971

—

Made and printed in Great Britain
by Richard Clay (The Chaucer Press), Ltd,
Bungay, Suffolk
Set in Linotype Pilgrim

Contents

Contents

Preface

This is a book of case studies of five families in which both the husband and the wife pursue active careers and family lives. We call this type of family, in which both heads pursue careers, the dual-career family. It is one of many types of family structure present in today's complex society. Families are in general much more complicated and variegated than may be realized. Current thinking on the family, both in popular and in professional circles, proceeds as though it were a unitary phenomenon. Modal patterns are taken to be natural; variations are frequently seen either as indications of a change process or as some kind of deviation based on abnormalities or radical tendencies. Variations arouse discomfort, even in a world that values permissiveness in other areas of life such as food, clothing, art and architecture.

In fact, beneath the façade of uniformity, even the modal conventional family of working father, housewife mum, elder son and younger daughter may be more complex than meets the eye. Their patterns of decision-making, authority and discipline, division of labour, communication and evaluation of experiences vary enormously. Dual-career families, which are not conventional, present additional aspects of variation. Little is known about this type of family structure and the present book aims to contribute to understanding how this type of family is evolving and what are its characteristics.

The fact that both heads of the household pursue full and active careers gives rise to a number of specific problems and yields a number of specific benefits. Furthermore the fact that such an arrangement is still highly unusual provides additional elements of both strain and satisfaction. Though many married women work, and their numbers are increasing, the tendency is still for women to subordinate their own career aspirations to those of their husbands and defer their own involvements in the world of work until they have attended to the conventional requirements of child-bearing and child-rearing. There are a number of elements of social change at work which suggest that men and women will increasingly want to alter the conventional family arrangements. However, given the fact that the whole fabric of contemporary society is woven with the conventional patterns implicit, it is not possible for more than a small proportion of those who ideally might like a dual-career family to actually make such a structure work. Very little is known about what kinds of people are able to do this and about how they make it work – with what gains and at what cost.

The presentation of a few case studies, obviously, does not constitute a total accounting of gains and losses of such an arrangement – for society, for the families or for the individuals concerned. However, it does indicate some of the costs and benefits, what kinds of people have pioneered the pattern and what their experiences have been. The people in this study are clearly not ordinary people in one sense. They are highly effective in their careers and at the same time have managed to have intact families which they also value and in which they find satisfactions. On the other hand, despite their characteristics common to many creative and complex, determined people, they are not social deviants or psychological deviants in a pathological sense. The psychopathology that could be seen in their stories is taken to be in common with other people of their type and calibre, and we attach much greater importance and emphasis to the ways in which they have channelled their drives and needs adaptively, even creatively, in forging a new kind of social structure. They are seen, then, as 'ordinary' people who have created something extraordinary. The product is a result of many forces, of which their own individual personalities are only part of the picture, the most important aspect being the combination of circumstances that produced their present pattern of living.

The study of the dual-career families has been carried out as a collaboration between the researchers and the families. While we defined the scope of the study and developed an interview guide for collecting the data, the families themselves not only complied with the request for data about themselves and their experiences but actively worked with us to mould the conception of the phenomenon at hand.

Altogether, sixteen families were interviewed over a period of two years. The families were nominated by the organizations or professional associations to which they belonged as representing intact families with children still at home where the wife was pursuing a responsible career and the husband was also earning at a high level. The last condition was set in order to assure our selecting families where the wife's commitment to work was not because of economic necessity. We deliberately included for contrast three families in which the wife had decided to stop working for an indefinite period while her children were young. The five families presented here represent the range of occupations studied and are all examples of the continuously functioning dual-career families.

When it came to the stage of writing up the preliminary case studies, the families were often very active in correcting and revising the initial pictures which emerged. There are a number of kinds of selectivity that have affected the ultimate cases as presented. In eliciting information based on an interview guide, there was selectivity in the initial formulation; in providing accounts of their lives and relationships, the couples exercised varying degrees of selectivity; and finally in the writing up – both on our side and theirs – selectivity was at work in providing what we could all agree to be an integrative picture of the families. In the final stages, applicable only to those families chosen for presentation here, there was a further stage of selectivity based on limitations on what could be published. There was variation among the families in terms of just how much they felt could be made public, even using pseudonyms and other devices for disguise.

The descriptions of some of the husbands' patterns of work and family participation are less full than those of their wives. Initially, some of the men's reticence followed from their perception that the study was mainly concerned with their wives. When they understood that the study was of the family as a whole, most of the husbands gladly participated in a frank and open manner. Nevertheless the accounts of half the men were less full and vivid. This would seem to stem from two characteristics of the husbands as compared with their wives in contemporary dual-career families. First, the husbands tend to be men who, though competent and often outstandingly successful in their own work, are not themselves pioneers in new roles. They are, on the contrary, people who have facilitated the departure of others (their wives) from the more conventional patterns. They tend, as a correlation of this, to be people who do not seek or attract personal attention for themselves. A second factor stems from this personal tendency. When the write-ups were completed and presented to the couples for review, some of the husbands felt that they preferred to abridge the accounts of themselves and their activities. This was partly because they felt that they were more vulnerable to publicity if they should be recognized (family analyses being seen as irrelevant to their work). The wives particularly were concerned with innovative patterns for young people whereas for the husbands this was sometimes a less salient consideration. Some felt that they did not have much to contribute to young people by making public their life experiences. For various reasons, then, some of the husband's accounts are less full than their wives'. This is regrettable in terms of providing a balanced picture of all elements of the dual-career family pattern. However, it is an inevitable shortcoming of the research process which is striving towards a perfect and complete form that is unattainable. A fuller account in future would involve not only a discussion of the husbands' patterns in greater detail, but would deal with the even greater deficiency of the current analysis, namely the details of the children's developmental patterns.

Nevertheless, we feel that what has emerged is a reasonably honest and accurate account of what it is like to operate dual-career family structures and of the kinds of people who do so. The experiences and personal patterns that characterized these 'pioneers' may not *in toto* face their successors. As young people consider this among other options for family and work life, they will quite probably be able to enjoy the advantage of having had a number of people like those described here work through the barriers and obstacles of achieving such a pattern. It may be more socially acceptable to live in this way, and the support institutions and services that ease the operation of such a pattern may have reached new stages of development to facilitate this among other patterns.

The formation of dual-career families and their establishment as viable and legitimate forms of social structure has been, in our view, a kind of act of creation. Like many intellectual and technological acts of creation, when the times are ripe for the emergence of a new social form, there are parallel occurrences in various contexts. Bringing together in a single volume accounts of several such creative incidents may help to give the social invention that these incidents constitute a public awareness which is part of the legitimation process. To the extent that this contributes to the choice process for future generations of young families, and to the everyday process of living for those already committed to variant patterns of different kinds, this book will have served its purpose.

Acknowledgements

This book is part of a larger study which was reported in *Sex, Career, and Family*, published by Allen & Unwin in 1971 collaboratively with our colleague Michael Fogarty. The study was financed by a grant from the Leverhulme Trust to Political and Economic Planning (P.E.P.) for the purposes of assessing the possibilities and problems, the costs and benefits, of encouraging more highly qualified women to participate in the national economy.

From the outset the study was both multi-disciplinary in character (economist, social anthropologist, and sociologist/psychoanalyst and others) and multi-institutional (P.E.P. enlisted the collaboration of the Tavistock Institute particularly for the family and personal aspects of the problem). It is a tribute both to the Leverhulme Trust and to the members of the relevant research institutes that this collaboration could emerge. It represents a highly modern and adaptive way of combining specialist resources to deal with large scale problems. This is more particularly seen in the overall report. The present book reports on a fragment of the overall study, but one selected for elaboration because it has seemed to many who saw the initial work of the dual-career family concept and materials as broadly useful. An initial paper, published in *Human Relations* in 1969, received widespread attention in the profession and has already been re-published in textbooks on the family in the U.S.A. and on the continent.

Aside from the authors, interviews on couples reported here were conducted by Elizabeth and William Collins; and other couples in the study were interviewed by David Armstrong and Stephanie White.

The greatest debt, however, is due to the families who co-operated and allowed their stories to be told. They cannot be

Acknowledgements

thanked publicly because they are presented under pseudonyms. Though the couples reviewed the family write-ups for accuracy, they cannot in any way be held responsible for our analyses, which reflect our own conclusions only. However, their contributions have been of the essence, and it is hoped that they will feel that the effort has been worthwhile.

Help with data analysis was given by Rosemary Fison, Susan Voorhees and Andrew Bebbington. To all these we are grateful.

Thanks are also due to the Human Resources Centre secretarial staff for their patient retyping of transcripts and drafts. Particularly helpful have been Elizabeth Burrett, Susan Dimond, Joanna Erikson, Pamela Rant, Angeline Agran and Patricia O'Brien.

The Act of Creation

CREATIVE VARIANCE AS A SOCIAL PROCESS

In the field of human relations a quite different attitude prevails from that in the technological fields. In science and technology it would be recognized as nonsense to say that because something has hitherto existed it cannot change. Of course, there are 'laws of nature' which are presumed to be immutable, but the ways in which they manifest themselves may change and the formulation of the laws is continuously open to revision. Thus to say that because man has never been propelled more than thirty miles per hour, it would be contrary to human nature to seek greater speeds, is manifestly absurd; yet this was seriously put forward as an argument against the railways which hurtled men through space at dizzy speeds of sixty miles per hour and more. The history of technology is a history of revision of received principles and the quest for bigger, better, faster, more efficient and above all different ways of doing things than prevailed before. Yet, in the human sciences the arguments that a given pattern is the statistical mode, that all through history the pattern has been modal, that primitive tribes show it, and that animals show it, are used daily to support assertions about the limitations of human nature. Because men have tended to be economic providers and women have cared for infants, it is argued that babies need their mothers and that men need to be the breadwinners. Because the nuclear family has been in recent times the basic form of social organization, it is assumed that it is the form best adapted to modern society. Because more men are ambitious and committed to work in contemporary society than are women, it is argued that this is the way men and women basically are.

In decades gone by, anthropology served a useful function in dislodging ethnocentric viewpoints. Certainly it has been useful to see that there could be many kinds of religious life, that men and women in different countries divided up the work of the society differently, that they had different temperamental modes according to their earlier training and what was expected of them, and that in different societies there were different norms about sexual behaviour, aggression, child-rearing and many other things. However, the earlier view of many anthropologists that a given custom could best be understood in the framework of its own society's values – the doctrine of 'cultural relativism' – is sometimes taken mistakenly to mean that anything was possible and could be morally acceptable if justified in the society's values. The events of the Hitler era gave pause to this line of thought and a search for 'cultural universals' was launched. There has, consequently, been a disinclination to visualize cultures that have not in fact existed. It is as though the anthropologists have said, if there were potentialities for a cultural or societal form to exist, it would have come into being somewhere and be known to us. This essentially conservative view, which may be termed the 'tribalist fallacy', does not take into account the emergence of new ecological conditions, never before known, which call forth new structural forms which have not been recorded or analysed. The urban condition is one which allows for the emergence of new forms which may be masked from view both by the surface homogeneity of social structures like the nuclear family and by the crudity of research concepts and instruments. Most survey sociologists describe urban types in terms of modalities. Newly emergent structures tend to be in a minority statistically, and psychologically marginal to established positions. There are some variants, of course, who are viewed by the majority with fear and distrust – the so-called 'deviants' who show criminal, mad, or destructive behaviour towards all that is valued by those representing the modal patterns. On the other hand, variation *per se* need suggest neither danger nor eccentricity. As Koestler has pointed out, certain types of variation are essential to the creative process. Toynbee has shown historically how creative minorities can arise and provide leverage for subsequent social change. Specific variant patterns provide natural experiments which may be studied for their relevance to the emerging conditions that will affect future life.

Variants whose experiments in social innovation are of interest may, as with the dual-career families reported here, be socially successful and privileged, though also marginal and sometimes under critical fire from their contemporaries. Or, they may be reviled and penalized, sometimes failing to gain a foothold in the social system of their day at all. How does one distinguish between the creative variants who are forerunners of things to come and those that are 'freaks of nature', flourishing briefly in some ecological niche or backwater but not really adapted to the requirements of mainstream development?

This is not an easy question to answer, and no prediction can be certain because of the contingencies that affect social development particularly in short-run change sequences. Predictions, even by people in other ways very gifted, may be far off the mark in the field of social change. The oft-cited comment by Thomas Edison on the airplane illustrates this. He felt that the airplane had no future other than as a plaything for wealthy aristocrats. Nowadays prediction is somewhat more solidly based on social theory, and a more complex and dynamic analysis is possible.

The argument in favour of the dual-career family becoming a more pervasive pattern than it is at present is based primarily on a complex of trends in our society and in the world generally. One element is the trend towards equality of opportunity. This means equality of access to higher education. Given the fact that higher education is increasingly geared to the requirements and opportunities of careers, and that careers themselves are increasingly a primary source of personal satisfaction for more and more people, it is reasonable to expect that women will wish to commit themselves increasingly to the world of work as well as to that of family life. Conversely, as the impetus for total commitment to work is reduced with increasing affluence, men may allocate more of their energies and interests to domestic and community activities of one kind or another.

Social changes usually occur piecemeal. New patterns are often set up by individuals with sufficient determination to break away from an aspect of prior patterns to which most of their contemporaries adhere. When they evolve their new pattern they seldom have an integrated conception of it.

WHAT IS THE DUAL-CAREER FAMILY?

The dual-career family is the type of family in which both heads of household pursue careers and at the same time maintain a family life together. The term 'career' is sometimes used to indicate any kind of work, but in its more precise meaning in social science it designates those types of jobs which require a high degree of commitment and which have a continuous developmental character. The individual develops a career by moving from one job or stage to another, continuously gathering and applying relevant experience for improved performance in a more senior position or in a more expert role of some kind. Careers within large organizations are thought of in terms of a progression of posts leading upwards in some kind of hierarchy. Careers in professions are thought of as proceeding through stages of cultivation and experience, accumulating expertise.

Work, as distinct from career, may involve any kind of gainful employment. Dual-worker families are more numerous than dual-career families which are a special type of the former It is assumed that they have a good deal in common. No research comparable to the kind reported here has been done on dual-worker families generally. The fact that work is sometimes taken by women for economic reasons rather than out of personal commitment does not necessarily decrease the stresses or problems associated with dual-worker families. On the contrary, the rewards derived may be less, so that the exchange that inevitably goes on in human relationships may be tipped more toward the negative side in such instances. On the other hand, in more conventional families certain strains are minimized because of the readiness of one member, usually the wife, to drop her job if the family situation or the demands of her partner's career become too great. This may help to reduce conflict and competition and to ease some forms of decision-making. The non-career type of dual-worker family is more likely to occur among people with lower formal qualifications. Where both husband and wife are highly qualified, the dual-career pattern is more likely to arise, but even here it is only one of several patterns that emerge in marriages.

The research which we have recently conducted, and that of others in related fields and in other countries, shows that highly-qualified women may develop different kinds of orientations to their careers; the patterns may be more varied than that of men graduates because the women, unlike most men, are constrained to reconcile any attitude they take towards their careers with prescribed family norms; these are sufficiently demanding to require major involvements particularly at the family stage when there are small children.

For all workers, men or women, one can discern differences not only of competence and success in a given line of work, but of commitment and motivation and of changes that occur at different points in the life cycle. Both men and women differ, for example, in the degree to which they are personally identified with the work they do and in the degree to which their work is a major source of personal satisfaction to them. Some, particularly in the less skilled occupations, are engaged in jobs with which they are personally not greatly identified and which they perform predominantly as a means to earn the money for other pursuits which they value more highly. Others, particularly in the more highly trained and professional occupations, work as much for the personal as for the financial rewards entailed.

Recently it has been increasingly appreciated that there is a reciprocal effect between the satisfactions and involvements to be derived in one sphere of life and those deriving from another. Aside from the purely practical policies adopted by some industrial firms, such as interviewing wives of prospective managers prior to deciding on a job-offer entailing a move of residence, there are indications that family events affect career decisions and vice versa at various points in the life cycle. A wife's involvement in a local circle of friends, her illness and involvement in a treatment network, children's involvements in school etc., may affect a man's responsiveness to new job opportunities, particularly if it entails moving a home. Our own survey indicates that the mere fact of having children has a very powerful effect on both men and women, though in different ways. For the highly qualified women that we have surveyed, having a child means a drop not only in actual work participation but in ambition as well – at least in the short run. For men, this family event seems to have the opposite effect.

As will be described below (p. 23 ff.), the graduate women surveyed manifest three major work – family patterns. The 'conventional' pattern is where the woman drops her career when she marries or has children and thenceforth concentrates on being a housewife; the 'interrupted' work pattern is where the woman may drop work for a period when her children are small but intends to return eventually; and the 'continuous' work pattern is where the woman interrupts her work only minimally if she has children. All but a tiny minority of men are continuous full-time workers. For women, the pattern is more varied; only about one third of even these highly qualified women are continuous workers, and only a tiny sub-group – 5 per cent of the sample – are full-time continuous workers with small children. The particular pattern adopted will depend not only on the woman and her commitment to career, but on opportunities available, the nature of the work, the facilities or other supportive action that are available on the domestic front – including the attitudes, work and family patterns and personality of her husband.

Within each of these broad categories there are many variations. Women who remain conventionally domestic in their behaviour vary enormously in terms of how much they like what they are doing. The bored or 'captive' housewife is as familiar a figure in contemporary society as is the houseproud, happy wife. Similarly for the workers – interrupted or continuous. Variations are observable in terms not only of the meaning of work for the individuals personally (which follow at least as wide a range as is observable for men), but of the degree to which the individuals are working reluctantly under force of circumstances. It is generally accepted as part of a man's normal role that he must work, and men are socialized for it from infancy. For women, working is more often viewed as an option; and if a particular woman finds herself working, against her personal wishes, because of an incompetent, disabled or disagreeable husband, then her disgruntlement may be greater than that of a man in a similar situation.

The 'interrupted' worker is nowadays perhaps the most generally approved model – particularly for women with special skills or talents. It allows them to fulfill societal expectations about what a 'good wife and mother' does when her infants are small (and many will want personally to experience this pattern at least for that phase of their lives) and, at the same time, holds out the expectation that they will not 'waste' their skills and talents but will use them effectively at a later date when their children do not need them so much. The more 'continuous' pattern, as will be shown in great detail in this book, entails considerable sacrifice and strain but where it is in response to a genuine commitment to work it has its rewards, not only for the woman herself who is striving for self-expression but also for her family, to the extent that she achieves greater satisfactions from work than would have been possible for her at home.

One of the complications which adds to the burdens of those adopting the dual-career pattern is that it is a minority pattern. This tends to arouse disapproval and even envy from some who wish that they were fortunate or competent enough to have adopted such a pattern themselves. The fact that such a pattern occurs with little precedent in recent social history and to some extent in the face of powerful counterbeliefs and indications makes its adoption doubly difficult. It is difficult as a pattern from a sheerly structural point of view – rearranging role relationships, finding domestic and child-care help in a society where these are in short supply, and so on. But the additional difficulty of facing disapproval in one's personal and work environments tips the balance for many families. The legitimation of creative patterns like that of the dual-career family contributes to its social acceptability. Legitimation is, of course, a complex process and to some extent it is rooted in values. However, to the extent that information can be accumulated which is relatively objective and systematic, and that this information points to the positive balance in the cost–benefit assessment that many families make in evolving their particular work–family structures, the research is a contribution to the legitimation process.

The facts, in the context in which this research has been conducted, are that it is difficult for women to rise into positions of senior responsibility once they have dropped out for a substantial period, however unprejudiced the work environment may be and however competent the woman may be. Whatever ambition she may have had prior to child-bearing is often damped down in the experience of infant-care, and there are few with sufficient resilience to overcome not only the strains of re-entry into the competitive world of work but the extra effort required to make up for lost time, missed information and the development of expertise.

Each dual-career family is produced by a particular constellation of forces – personal, interpersonal and social – not only in relation to the woman but in relation to her husband, how they fit together as a couple and the social environment in which they live. The dual-career family is seen as a new and pacesetting structural phenomenon. As will be clear in the case studies presented and the discussion in the concluding chapter, this is not a homogeneous type but one with a good deal of variation both in terms of the forces which produce specific examples and in terms of the patterns which sustain them. In this chapter we shall concentrate on common features in the backgrounds and current circumstances of dual-career families.

WHAT PRODUCES AND SUSTAINS THE DUAL-CAREER FAMILY?

As it has been the norm for men to expect to have careers and women not to, we are led to ask what has produced and sustained the kind of woman who does in fact have a career and what has produced the sort of man who favours, or at least allows, his wife to work in this relatively committed way. These questions are fundamental but the answers to them are not enough. If the dual-career family is to be more than an ephemeral phenomenon, the couple must work out ways of sustaining it – supports and bulwarks of various kinds. In the long run the adaptive props which individual dual-career families have been finding or providing for themselves will have to be woven into the fabric of society and functional equivalents will have to be evolved that are workable in a more broadly-based way than is presently possible.

If the social system, its family norms and educational teachings, incorporated a component of women's roles that prescribed continuous work – as happens for men – the career-oriented woman would be the ordinary woman. In our society one must search for special circumstances that may have fostered a tendency which is different. What predisposes a woman to be career-oriented in contrast to her more conventionally oriented fellow graduates – and what differentiates the husbands of those who actually pursue active careers from the husbands of those who do not?

We have two kinds of data on which the following discussion will be based. The first is a cross-sectional sample survey of men and women graduates from British universities in 1960. This sample of about 1,000 was surveyed in 1968 so that the respondents had had a chance in the intervening eight years to have established a pattern of work and family life based on actual experience rather than on envisioned ideals only. Within that sample there are nearly 400 married women graduates of whom some 200 returned the questionnaire forms filled out by their husbands as well, providing a sub-sample of 'couples'. The graduate wives vary according to their career orientations from the most career-oriented types (who have worked continuously and intend to work continuously throughout the period when they have children and who subscribe to the ideal of women having equal opportunities for careers as men) to the most conventional types (who do not believe that women should have the same kind of careers as men, and who do not intend to work outside the home once they have children). The other data is from the intensive interview study of sixteen dual-career families selected on the basis of the wife having risen to a senior position in one of the organizations which was being studied as a work environment. (See Fogarty, Rapoport and Rapoport, 1971, and Fogarty *et al.*, 1971, for detailed descriptions of these sub-studies.)

A number of comparisons of contrasting groups have been made – between types of individuals and couples within the survey, between the survey respondents and the intensive interview couples and so on. The description provided here is the best integration of this information possible on the basis of areas of broad agreement among these different sources of data. The sharpest contrasts are between the conventional young couples within the survey (i.e. women who do not intend to work outside the home after having children) and dual-career couples (the latter being somewhat older and having translated their commitments and intentions into action).

Comparing the intensively interviewed sample of dual-career families with a sample of twenty-five conventional couples drawn from the survey sample, the first point of general interest is that the dual-career wives are more different from the conventional family wives than are their respective husbands, though the latter are distinctive in crucial ways.

Social class background differentiated the wives but not the husbands. Proportionately more dual-career wives come from higher social class backgrounds than do their conventional counterparts, as indicated by fathers' occupations. Mother's occupational experience and attitudes were also important for the wives, though not for their husbands. Many more of the dual-career family wives had mothers who worked than did the conventional wives, and those dual-career wives whose mothers did not work showed a greater tendency to have been frustrated with their housewife roles than was true for the conventional wives.

There are a number of factors which may be associated with higher social class background that distinguish the women from one another. For one thing, higher social background families tend to be somewhat smaller, and this would account in part for the greater tendency of dual-career family wives to come from smaller families than conventional wives. They tend more to be only children, or first children, and even where they are part of a larger set of siblings they tend to be separated in some way, e.g. by a large age gap. We have, consequently, felt that there is a syndrome which we call the 'only-lonely' child syndrome, which encompasses these different possibilities. It has long been noted that innovators and creative people in various fields tend to have this background of personal loneliness. Added to this, the dual-career wives tended to experience longer separations from their parents during childhood than did their conventional counterparts – sometimes through evacuation in the war, sometimes through attending boarding schools.

Perhaps as important as the sheer size of the family and the position of the individual in the birth order of children is the general atmosphere or psychological climate in the family produced by the quality of interpersonal relationships. Somewhat greater overall tension is reported in the early family backgrounds of dual-career wives as compared with conventional wives, and in some cases there were specific foci of tension, for example with the father, the mother, or between the father and the mother. The general impression in these families is that there was less reason to idealize family relationships or to place full confidence in the conventional type of family relationships as sufficient for one's personal needs and aspirations.

The two sets of husbands, while differing from one another less than their wives – e.g. in social class background, birth order position and general family background characteristics –

did contrast in one crucial aspect. The dual-career family husbands tended to come from families in which, if there were other children, the others were girls. They also tended to have closer relationships, overall, with their mothers than did the conventional family husbands, though this is obscured by the tendency for conventional family backgrounds to be generally warm and close.

Some of the early interpretations of what differentiated career-oriented women from their more conventional counterparts were based on clinical materials from psychiatry and paediatrics and they emphasized psychopathological elements. Women who wished to have a work component as part of their personal identities tended to be seen as frightened of or as rejecting their 'natural' maternal role; or, in more extreme forms, they were seen as 'castrating' women who envied men and took up destructive competitive attitudes towards them in work.

Our studies of successful dual-career families put another perspective on this. Most people can be described in psychopathological terms. Outside of those whose difficulties bring them to the attention of therapists, it is usually more useful to describe them in more positive terms. The dual-career family wives, for the most part, do not greatly fear or reject family roles, but wish to combine them with work roles. Indeed, some of them insist that they are better wives and mothers than they would have been had they been forced to concentrate on domestic roles only. This wish to combine work and family roles is increasing, and our survey materials provided by highly-qualified women indicate that some kind of combination is now the modal pattern. The only issue is how much work and at what point in the family life cycle. While there will always be a minority of women who wish either not to marry or not to have children once married, most now wish to have the satisfaction of family life and work life.

As this tendency becomes more firmly established, it becomes clearer that there is a range of motivations underlying participation in a given combination of work and family activities, for both husbands and wives. The assignment of a typical motivational syndrome with connotations of deviance and pathology becomes increasingly inadequate as a descriptive device, and it becomes more important to see each individual and couple in complex terms of strengths and weaknesses. Taking the women in dual-career families : it is clear from the description given of their characteristic backgrounds and subsequent performance that they may be characterized in different ways. If one concentrates on the loneliness and insecurity of certain elements in the backgrounds of many of them, one gets a picture of uncertainty and a drive for security and self-realization underlying their career motivation. Yet, why is this thought of as deplorable in women and admirable in men? It is only against the background of conventional role expectations that these different connotations are given to the same kinds of behaviour and motivational patterns in men and women. The same is true for the men. The capacity to understand and sympathize with the aspirations of women is, if balanced by appropriate strengths and competences in the man's own world, seen as a point of strength rather than as an aberration. The man who is deficient in this capacity is less adequate as a husband, whatever pattern his wife may pursue.

In fact, dual-career families, as will be elaborated following presentation of the descriptive studies, are not unitary in their composition or in the underlying motivations that have produced them. Husbands varied in their motivations towards their wives' careers from great involvement and participation to relative detachment, encouraging their wives to work to some extent as a compensation for guilt they may feel about their own heavy involvement in their careers. However, leaving aside these variations for the moment, there are a number of themes that run through the dual-career families' stories. Once a husband and wife work out a dual-career family structure, for whatever combination of background reasons, they find that there are ramifications that may or may not be to their liking. In most instances the pattern emerges through a series of accidents which have a cumulative character rather than being guided by a preconceived model. The steps that are taken to achieve a given satisfaction or reward or to avoid a given dissatisfaction may entail costs which become known only as they accumulate. How the costs are balanced out against the gains is a matter that different families experience in different ways. What seem to be overall patterns that emerge in terms of marital satisfaction?

As will be seen from the case-study analyses presented, the kinds of people who evolve the dual-career pattern do not provide simple answers to a question like, 'Is your marital relationship a happy one?' They have complex perceptions of this, ways in which it is happy and ways in which it is not; ways in which trade-offs have been made so that compromise solutions of different degrees of complexity could be worked out and more or less accepted. On the other hand, individuals and couples *do* think of their marital relationships in global terms as relatively happy, mixed or variable or relatively unhappy. Bailyn's analysis of the 220 couples in the survey has increased our understanding of the major patterns that exist. Prior formulations seemed partly acceptable but too simple – e.g., that on the one hand marital happiness decreased with a wife's commitment to work because she could not give the necessary attention to her husband and to her home; or, on the contrary, marital happiness increased when the women go out to work because they then avoid boredom and a sense of being 'captive' or exploited.

It is clear that marital happiness is something that can exist or deteriorate whether or not the wife follows a career. Many women who are highly committed to a career are less likely to experience an idyllic family life whether or not they work, because of their own family backgrounds of considerable tension; this alone tends to predispose against idealizing the family. On the other hand, the evidence now available indicates that on the whole people choose the pattern that will give them a certain level (or in a sample, a distribution of levels) of happiness. If the family is one in which the woman would be miserable not working, she will tend to take employment, shifting the family into the category of a dual-working family with a higher degree of marital satisfaction than if they had remained in the conventional pattern. Conversely, if a woman is reluctant to work and she does not actually have to, she will tend to adopt the conventional pattern and show a higher level of personal and marital happiness with it than if she had worked unwillingly. These choices are not totally open, but depend on opportunities in the work environment, support at home and the personal motivation of the individuals concerned.

What are the effects of these different types of work–family structures? The analysis of our survey data on marital happiness as associated with the different patterns of couple relationship indicates a very high general level of marital happiness among the graduate couples at this stage of their careers; over eighty-five per cent of the couples report that they have a 'pretty happy' or 'very happy' marriage as perceived *both* by husband and wife. Over sixty per cent say that they have 'very happy' marriages. To differentiate the effects of different work–family structures it is useful to look at the '*very* happy' proportions in the different categories.

One thing is immediately clear. Having a wife who works or who intends to return to work is not disastrous for marital happiness in couples of the kind reported here. In the analysis of the data available, a distinction was made among the men as to whether they emphasized career above family life as an area of satisfaction, and among the women as to whether they were committed to the idea of women's careers at all. Combining these variables produces family types in which both husband and wife emphasize family as the major source of their satisfactions (the 'familistic' couples), couples in which both emphasize career ('careerist' couples), couples in which the husband emphasizes career but the wife *only* the family ('conventional' couples), and various mixtures, among them those that Bailyn calls 'coordinate' couples in which the wife has a career orientation but the husband values family life as well as career. The dual-career families in this study represent the latter type. The findings indicate that the level of 'very happy' marriages is not significantly different for any of the couple patterns except for the 'careerist' one, where there is a significant drop in level of marital happiness. This sub-type of the dual-career family is not represented in our case studies and is probably very rare in general.

HOW WERE THE DUAL-CAREER FAMILIES STUDIED?

The dual-career families with whom we worked relatively intensively were interviewed by both of the authors, and in some instances other interviewers as well. Where possible, their children and work associates were also seen and relatively informal discussions were held. The more intensive personal interviews with the couples were tape-recorded, transcribed and the write-ups based on the interview materials were then shown to the couples to be corrected. Before publication, the write-ups were screened again by the couples, for accuracy and presentability. For most of the couples, the idea of participating in this project was both attractive and problematic. They were uniformly interested in the idea of contributing their experiences to the general pool of knowledge about how marital roles might change and what some of the problems were that they as pioneers and pace-setters in this process had experienced. On the other hand, in some instances this was not an entirely comfortable line of territory to go back over, and for most the idea of publication of the findings in paperback book form aroused stronger reservations. They had, in many instances, a reluctance to bring their private lives into public view, even in somewhat disguised form, because their positions often make them highly identifiable. In some instances there was a reluctance to present publicly materials about others involved in their lives, for fear that this would embarrass or harm them – parents, relatives, children. Finally, the reservations of those who cooperated with us and allowed their stories to be presented were won over by their positive perception that using the cases as 'experiments of nature' might provide learning experiences that could be instructive for others.

How were the Dual-Career Families Studied?

In the actual write-ups of the cases and the discussion which follows we attempt to describe the families largely as they see themselves. They are, in many ways, unusual people, but far more they are recognizable as people coping with problems familiar to many others of their generation and occupations. The ways in which they resolve the familiar issues are different – and this is what gives them their special interest here. However, their 'differentness' has usually emerged as a consequence of the combination of personalities, experiences and social circumstances in which they developed rather than particular over-riding unique features of any of these. For all the couples each individual's activities were important in some way for the other partner, and this allowed for the possibility that each developed parts of himself that might otherwise have remained neglected or dormant. Each person enlarges and extends the life possibilities of the other in such a family, though at the same time in some instances there has undoubtedly been a curtailment of some individual developments in ways that would not have occurred under different circumstances. The net gains and losses must be assessed in each instance independently, and this can best be done after a detailed examination of a number of representative cases.

The families presented are chosen to represent each of the five work environments in which the women are involved and have successful careers.

In the Kiley family the wife entered industry as a research scientist, and worked her way up to her present position as a research manager in her company. Her husband has, at the same time, developed a successful career in marketing in another company.

The Bensons are both architects, working together as a team in a private partnership based in their home.

In the Jarret family the wife is a television drama director while her husband is a partner in a large private firm of architects.

In the Neal family both husband and wife are senior administrative class civil servants.

In the Harris family, the wife is a fashion designer, who at the time the study began had built up her own business as an independent entrepreneur. Her business was later absorbed into a larger company where she became design director. Mr Harris is a managing director of a marketing company.

In another publication (Fogarty *et al.*, 1971) a more extended discussion is provided of the specific problems and advantages of career development in each of these types of occupational setting, together with more illustrative materials from families like the five presented here.

The purpose of the present set of case studies is to allow for a more detailed understanding of how various elements of experience add up and are dealt with to produce a whole meaningful pattern of family and work life. The presentation of these case studies, it is hoped, will provide a set of models for the structural properties, dilemmas and resolutions experienced by a range of people who have tried and succeeded at this particular pattern. The picture is presented 'warts and all', so that difficulties and shortcomings as well as advantages are put into perspective.

The basic point of view that we as authors hold is that for a society in which meaningful choices are to be made among available options, there must be detailed knowledge of what the options are. The family, particularly among the kinds of people reported here, is a bastion of privacy and its interior world is not easily known to outsiders. Respectability acts as a cloak and façade behind which the human problems of living, facing crises and experiencing developmental gains tend to be obscured. By sharing some of the 'backstage' elements of their personal, family and work worlds with a larger public, the couples presented here are not being boastful, exhibitionistic or 'pompous'. Many would never have dreamt of doing such a thing except in the context of the goals of this project as described here and presented to them at the outset of the research. They have agreed with us as authors that the potential usefulness to others of learning from the experiences of pioneers such as themselves outweighs their natural reserve against lowering the veil that is normally put around such matters in contemporary urban life.

SUMMARY OF DUAL-CAREER COUPLES PRESENTED

	Husband's Occupation	Wife's Occupation	Number of Children	Degree of Overlap in Work Sphere	Degree of Overlap in Domestic Sphere
Kiley	Sales Manager	Science Manager	2	Low	High
Benson	Architect	Architect	3	High	High
Jarret	Architect	Drama Director	1	Low	Low
Harris	Company Director	Designer and Company Director	2	Medium	Medium
Neal	Civil Servant	Civil Servant	6	Medium	High

The Kileys: A Science Manager and a Sales Manager

BACKGROUND — DEVELOPMENT OF THEIR FAMILY STRUCTURE

Catalogue of Events

Met: End of summer, 1948.

Going together: 1948–1950 during which time he was doing a teacher's training course near London; in the autumn of 1949 she moved to London to be closer to her husband-to-be.

Married: August 1950; that year Mr Kiley started a degree course at London University.

Establishment of a home and residential history: For the first four years of marriage the Kileys lived in a flat. In 1954 they bought a small house in a London suburb. In 1959 they moved to a larger home in a more elegant suburb of London where they now live.

Children: Two sons – born 1954 and 1956.

Major events in child-rearing: As a baby, the first of the Kileys' sons was cared for by a neighbour whom the Kileys were able to pay for this help. When they moved their son was still under a year old. They began to employ au-pair help for the care of the children after the birth of their second son. The Kileys did not send their sons to nursery school. At the age of five the boys started at a local elementary school. The elder son went on to a private school when he reached 7 years and now at 16 goes to a technical grammar. The younger son aged 14 is in a grammar school.

Domestic help: The Kileys relied on a series of German au pair girls employed through the Labour Exchange; the first was employed three months after the birth of the second son; the last domestic help left when the youngest boy was 9.

35

The Kileys

Major illnesses: They have suffered several major illnesses. Mr Kiley was subject to migraines during their courtship and up until quite recently. Between 1959 and 1962 these became very severe and Mr Kiley was treated by several doctors. This treatment seems to have been successful, and with the lessening of tension in his work situation he has found himself free of migraine for the last six years. Mrs Kiley suffered a thrombosis in her leg last year. She is still under doctor's care to prevent a second attack.

Major family separations: None.

THE KILEYS

At the time of the interviews in 1968 both Mr and Mrs Kiley were in their early 40s, Mr Kiley being slightly older than his wife. They live in a residential suburb of London in a detached house, attractively set in landscaped grounds with an extensive garden backing onto a tennis club.

Mrs Kiley is a bacteriologist by training, and she currently manages a scientific research team for a large chemical company. She is a fair-haired woman who gives the impression of considerable determination and 'spark'. Mr Kiley is a dark-haired man of medium build and gives the impression of easy-going amiability. He is a sales manager for a large industrial chemical firm.

The Kileys are both involved in their family lives and in their careers. Neither brings work home, and while they keep each other informed about their work in a general way, they do not participate in any specific way in each other's work concerns. Their two children are boys who were aged 12 and 14 at the beginning of the interviews. The boys are described as 'good friends' though 'completely opposite' in temperament. The elder is more tactful and diplomatic, oriented to getting along with people and getting round them by using indirect and discreet approaches, like his father. The younger, more like his mother, is described as very 'strong-willed' and 'intellectual', accumulating novel information that will allow him to take up the stance of an 'authority'.

In the course of the interviews with the Kileys two themes were impressive. First is the theme of the struggle to rise from less affluent social backgrounds to their present position and style of life as a professional family. They feel a considerable sense of pride in their achievements. Mrs Kiley says :

I would call myself professional class now. I would not hesitate to tell anybody that my parents had not been well-to-do, that we'd lived in a poor district, that I got on by scholarships and I would despise somebody who tried to conceal this sort of background from me. In the area that I came from the speech was very bad, but my mother made sure that I spoke grammatically and with no accent.

The second theme has to do with the way in which the temperamental contrasts within the family have been harmonized. At different stages in their marital career, the Kileys have had to work through not only the implications of having such contrasting temperaments, but concrete issues associated with them. Mr Kiley, though initially trained as a scientist, did not find the actual work congenial, and after experimenting with other training and work went into his present position in sales and marketing. As a consequence, Mrs Kiley was farther along in her own career than her husband, and even with a clear perception of complementarities and a strong wish to facilitate one another's development, this kind of imbalance has been a problem with which the family has had to cope. In resolving such issues, the Kileys have come out with a fairly well-defined set of norms emphasizing sharing and mutual help. They see themselves and their children as having contrasting personalities, but do not regard a particular pattern as superior or dominant; each has strong points and difficulties and each plays a contributory part in relation to the whole.

PERSONAL WORLDS

Mrs Kiley

Mrs Kiley characterizes herself as a person who has had to fight for things all her life, from an early background of deprivation and parental opposition.

It was a bloody battle right from the age of 11 till about 30. . . . I didn't get on with my father and he could have crushed me, but he didn't. If I'd have been a different sort of character I'd have been wholly crushed, but he hardened me and I'm prepared to fight. There's a sort of hard core and I know I am probably quite a hard person. I dress it up more softly nowadays – it used to show much more when I was young. But I don't take so much of a stand on trivialities as I did before. The hardness can withstand a great deal, we've had a heavy battle to fight and we've fought it.

Mrs Kiley, who presents a picture of being a very purposeful and tough-minded person, speaks of the successfully fought battle for establishment in the plural – i.e. with her husband. She clearly sees him as a helping and steadying influence, recognizing that she has a strong temper which she has to control. Her husband, whom she sees as a model of tact and discretion, has contributed to her capacity to moderate these explosive tendencies. Mrs Kiley has, however, two sides to her character – the hard, logical side and the emotional side which does not only erupt in temper but is seen in her intuitive characteristics. She considers that her greatest strength is the capacity to separate out emotional and logical components in work and other decisions, and to realize there can be both types of reactions in a situation. She is able to separate out the two analytically and then decide on what form of integration is appropriate to the situation at hand.

I'm a very logical thinker and I'm impatient with woolly-mindedness. However, if the approach I've got to a problem isn't working, I'm prepared to go back to square one, right to the very fundamental, and argue it through. More than most women I know, I can separate emotion and logic. . . . I might make an ultimate decision based on logic but I am very well aware that emotion can play a big part; I do my best to analyse my approach to something that isn't going easily – what I ought to do, what I want to do, and the likely consequences of each.

Her emphasis on logical thinking with a recognition of the emotional side – sometimes pressed onto her by other people's reactions – is something that is culturally stereotyped as a masculine way of thinking. Mrs Kiley feels that a more emotional reaction is characteristic of women who are not professional in orientation, and many of the women whom she meets in her neighbourhood and social activities not only do not think this way, but do not want to. She, on the other hand, wants to and finds it useful in her work.

In my dealings with people, I'm intuitive and I'm very often right about a person. A person who will be a trouble-maker may be good at the job but they will be an emotional upset to everybody. With many people who have worked with me I have seen that when they get emotional problems the work suffers. We must have the emotions straight, and if they've got an emotional problem, I'd like to know about it. Not that I'm going to help them – I may not – but it will give me an idea of when they're faced with a situation, what way they're going to jump. I'm very rarely wrong, if I know enough about what's going on.

While Mrs Kiley says that she is not the 'motherly' type in the work situation, she has on occasion fought to help people in difficulties if she thought they were basically worth helping. On two occasions unmarried girls who dropped out for a period to have babies were accepted back in the face of colleague-opposition, whose view was based on conventional morality. Mrs Kiley's view was based on the intuitive appraisal of the girls' potential work performance in a value-neutral framework. This value-neutrality, which is essentially a scientific stance, is part of the process of analysing what is fact and logic and what is emotion and intuition.

Mrs Kiley feels that both sides of her character are recognized in her work situation by her colleagues. She is known to be competent and to have a rather fierce set of standards both for herself and for others:

I'm afraid I have a tendency to judge people by their intelligence and the speed with which they pick things up. I would despise a person for being stupid much sooner than I would despise them for being a rogue or poor or anything like that. I'm very impatient of stupid people. I'm very impatient of obstructionist people too. I have no sympathy for the little man who goes by the book because in my way of thinking most rules are there as guidelines and there will come a situation that the rules do not fit and you must use your innate sense. If you try and make rules fit, you will come up with something that won't satisfy anybody.

While Mrs Kiley is not one to suffer fools gladly, she sympathizes with people whose needs for help are genuine, and she relates to people regardless of sex or status on the basis of the individual's competence in any area of interest.

The thing I like most in a person is their ability to be interested in anything different that comes along. Obviously you can't be interested in everything, but if there's something new which you don't know about, how can you tell if you're going to be interested in it or not unless you show some interest to start with and are prepared to talk about it? Things that seem very deadly dull and boring can suddenly come to life if you're talking to someone who knows about the subject.

Where she has been under attack – on the emotionally stereotyped grounds of women's capacities – her colleagues have defended her. Their respect is based not only on her sheer competence, but also on her intuitive qualities.

Mrs Kiley's Personal Background

Mrs Kiley was born in a village in Lancashire, the only child of a junior civil servant. Her father's father had deserted his mother when he was a boy. Her father ran away from home at an early age, finally joining the army in the First World War. He was billeted in the home of Mrs Kiley's mother's family, and this is how they met. Mrs Kiley's mother was the daughter of a 'poor but educated' bookbinder and his wife, a farmer's daughter. Both were Welsh and Church of England. During the period that her father was courting her mother, he showed that he still had not settled down, 'fiddling around at all sorts of things'. Mrs Kiley's mother made it a condition of their marriage that he settle down to a 'decent, regular job'. He sat the Civil Service examinations and entered the Service.

While her mother's family of orientation had been a reasonably happy one, with music and a rich family life, the new family which she formed in her marriage to Mrs Kiley's father became more like his family, which was filled with strife. Although Mrs Kiley's father did not physically desert them, nor did he fail to provide for them financially as had his own father, the tensions that he introduced into family life were a constant irritant. This contributed a good deal to Mrs Kiley's developmental pattern, though not always negatively.

When Mrs Kiley was about five, the family moved to Liverpool because of a promotion that her father received. There they lived in 'a comparatively respectable working-class' neighbourhood. Though her father did not earn a great deal, he had a steady job and this was important because there were times during Mrs Kiley's childhood when many children in the neighbourhood were underfed and underclothed because their fathers were out of work.

Mrs Kiley describes her mother as a very bright, 'social and entertaining' sort of person, 'beautiful' and 'magnetic'. 'She could laugh and was gay and there was life in her.' However, her mother felt increasingly 'trapped' and 'limited' both by the family's general social environment and by her husband.

She didn't care for the district we lived in or the social life. She wanted better for me without being specific about it.

Mrs Kiley's father was very autocratic and her mother felt their social life was too narrow; she wanted a richer and more interesting life meeting and entertaining more people. While Mrs Kiley's father provided financial stability through his Civil Service post, he maintained a very tight control of the pursestrings. There were violent rows over family expenditures, such as holidays, because the money had to come from her father, who preferred to spend it on convivial activities with his friends. He preferred the company of his male mates :

I don't think my father liked women. He was never comfortable with the wives of his friends. When I got older and insisted that one or two of my friends came, he was never comfortable with them, and he was never comfortable with my mother's friends. . . . He thought (that all) women were stupid, unreliable, bad-tempered; think of something bad and that's what he thought they were.

When Mrs Kiley was born her father was disappointed that she was not a boy, and he dealt with this by treating her as though she were one.

My father tried to make me interested in all sorts of masculine things; he showed me how to use a soldering iron and how to make a radio and he wanted me to play golf and cricket. He wouldn't let me be feminine, and I put up with this; this was the way to be friendly with my father but there was an enormous feeling of rejection from him always.

The struggle between mother and father and later daughter and father became a constant theme in their lives. In retrospect, Mrs Kiley thinks that her father may have suffered from an endogenous depression, and that his drinking and consequent bad temper may have been related to this. Father and mother quarrelled continuously, keeping in Mrs Kiley's awareness the possibility that they would split up. She knew that in such an event she would go with her mother.

Though her father did make attempts to teach her, his efforts were inept. She says :

He did spend a tremendous amount of time with me helping me with school-work, geography and history and things like this, although it usually ended in tears because he was not able to appreciate that at 11 you are not an adult. If he'd been able to appreciate that a child starts from nothing and grows, it would have been easier. But he expected me always to react in an adult fashion and to know things. He expected me at the age of 8 to read the daily paper and be able to talk to him about all the important political things that went on. Well I couldn't and I didn't want to, I wasn't interested. I don't think many children at the age of 8 are. And this led to a lot of disagreement between us.

Though he was very proud when she earned a scholarship at a grammar school, he was proud partly for 'wrong reasons' and he had unrealistic expectations of her. However, Mrs Kiley was determined to go on and never wavered in her determination to have a higher education. Increasingly as Mrs Kiley grew older her father felt the loss of control over her that might be entailed if she succeeded in her educational and occupational aspirations. He had exercised the same control over her as he had over her mother, forbidding her to bring her friends home, denying her spending money and only acknowledging her success when it contributed to his own prestige with his colleagues.

As she became involved in the larger educational world of the grammar school these tensions increased.

When I started getting a mind of my own and quoting schoolmistresses and schoolfriends and the parents of schoolfriends and saying, 'but that's not right' when he pontificated (I didn't have the sense not to argue) that was when we started to have trouble and it was all 'don't you think because you're getting educated you're any better than we are', and it carried on from there.

During an illness, Mrs Kiley read *Microbes by the Millions* and became absorbed in the idea of a medical career. She liked science very much – the way one could arrive at a definite conclusion and distinguish between what was a correct answer and what was not. However during this period relations between father and daughter grew worse and worse. A crisis was reached when Mrs Kiley was studying for her Higher School Certificate and her mother was seriously ill.

My father didn't take any interest at all in what happened. I had to get the doctor, I had to cope, to look after her. I had to look after him too. It didn't matter whether I had homework to do. I would be physically ill-treated if I said 'Can I finish my homework before I start?'

When she failed to win a grant to medical school on the basis of her results on the Higher School Certificate, Mrs Kiley was forced to modify her ambition. She was very disappointed about this, and her father's role in discouraging her and preventing her from studying for the examination as much as she would have liked seems to have further embittered the relationship between father and daughter. When Mrs Kiley applied to various universities her father refused to sign the necessary forms giving his permission.

Forms had to be signed and he wouldn't. Whatever I wanted to do, he wouldn't let me.

Finally at the age of 18 Mrs Kiley left home taking refuge with her grandmother.

My father and I quarrelled and quarrelled and quarrelled. Part of my mother's illness was due to this, I was quite certain. So in the end we had an enormous row and I left home. I took his best leather suitcase with me, and the dog. I'd bought the dog myself and I took the dog. He was very cross about that. And I went to live with his mother.

From this new base she obtained a job as a laboratory assistant. In the course of this job, she was encouraged by her employers to apply to the university, where she was able to get a grant on the strength of a commitment to teach when she was finished.

From the personal developmental point of view this period after Mrs Kiley left home was crucial. She was active in a number of sports and hobbies as well as in her academic work. She did well and formed new friendships. Though her ties with her parents were considerably loosened, the struggle with her father continued because despite having a scholarship she needed annual permission to continue in the university and financial assistance for her living expenses. Her father had made it a condition for the initial acceptance that she give him her first year's earnings. Thenceforth, he paid her grandmother for her expenses, and Mrs Kiley lived a very spartan life, with no new clothes other than those she made herself from scraps of material.

I remember this was a squeeze. I ate a cheese bun at lunchtime because I couldn't afford the full 11d. for the university lunch, and I walked instead of taking buses. Costs are different nowadays but in those days I would walk from the station to grandmother's house to save three ha'pence, because it was necessary to do. I couldn't consider the likelihood of ever having a car or anything like that. I was a student, I wasn't contributing anything, I was learning. When I got my degree and I got a good job, then I would have these things, but I didn't believe that the world owed me a living; I was battling madly to keep a footing and proud that I'd been accepted in the university, so I feel very cross with these people who can't manage on £10 a week.

During this university period – which Mrs Kiley considered a challenge that she mastered and was thereby entitled to her subsequent success – she put her earlier relationships and struggles more in perspective.

Nevertheless, Mrs Kiley's departure from the family home was not only beneficial for her but for her parents as well. Without her there to spark off disagreements they seemed to quarrel less, and they shared the anticipation of her visits.

From her mother Mrs Kiley feels she got her high aspirations.

As long as I can remember, and I think my mother had a lot of influence in this, I felt that what my parents had was not good enough for me, and I was going to do better. I didn't know how but I was not going to live like this. I was going to have a car. Of course in those days not so many people had cars. She wanted me to live a happier life than she had and she wanted me to live a more comfortable and livelier life.

Her mother encouraged her to read. Father read only the newspapers, though he brought home all sorts of books that had been left on ships coming into port. Mother not only read them herself, but found in her daughter a willing person with whom to share this enthusiasm, and Mrs Kiley recalls:

My mother used to claim that I would read the label on the sauce bottle – anything to read.

More important, she was the person whom Mrs Kiley could love and from whom she got love. Her mother, frustrated in her own marital relationship, lavished on her daughter a very intense affection and care. They provided for one another an alliance against the father whom they felt often to be tyrannical. On the other hand, her mother was emotional and did not think logically, an essential ingredient in the sort of orientation to which Mrs Kiley aspired.

Her father, in contrast, was seen mostly as difficult and oppressive, and from an early age Mrs Kiley tended to generalize this to all men, as the only other adult male she knew at all well was an uncle who was in her eyes a weak character. Furthermore, she sees in the experience of having had to struggle to get her own viewpoint over in a situation of considerable emotional tension, another source of her current skills at dis-entangling logical and emotional components in a situation. In this her father was a negative model:

I think this has shaped quite a lot of my attitudes, I've been very analytical about a lot of things and I've tried very hard to separate what is the logical thing to do and what is the emotional thing I want to do and what are the likely consequences of this, how fool-ish would it be and what effect on the children. . . . I've tried to look at it from the outside which my father never did. He never thought of the effect of what he did on other people. It's been almost a con-scious attempt all my life whatever he did to do something different.

On the other hand, she did eventually understand her father somewhat more sympathetically, as indicated by her retro-spective account of his suppressiveness:

But looking back, his idea of discipline was to find out what the child wanted to do and to stop her, because he was let run wild as a child and he regretted this when he was an adult. I don't think his attitude towards my education was as negative as I thought it was. Looking back, he wanted me to go on and he was very proud that I could, but I didn't see that at the time.

On balance, in mature retrospect, she sees that she has elements both positive and negative from both her parents:

I was much more my mother's girl, much more like her in tempera-ment, although I can see both of them now. I'm like my father in that I'm comparatively hasty-tempered – very determined to get my own way if at all possible, and I'm volatile like my mother. My mother was a tremendously volatile person; my father was down to earth, very solid. I think I'm a fairly reasonable mix of the two, not as volatile as my mother, not as solid as my father.

Mrs Kiley felt that she was conscientious because of her father's insistence on this virtue.

That was one of the things my father was very strict about. If ever I was given something to do, I did it until I did it properly and it was simpler to do it properly the first time.

Mr Kiley

Mr Kiley is 'opposite' in temperament to Mrs Kiley. He is easy-going and casual and does not like to plan much for the future :

I like things just to drift by. It must be the Irish in me which does this. I don't like to say 'Well, this time next year we'll be doing so and so.'

While Mr Kiley presents a picture of amiability and good humour, he tends to worry. These worries are turned in on himself, in contrast to Mrs Kiley's fighting spirit and buoyancy. She feels that he is a pessimist and says :

When I have nothing to worry about, then I don't worry ... whereas my husband is much more of a pessimist and if the worst doesn't happen (he feels) there must be some good reason it hasn't and it's going to happen next week. This is quite foreign to me. It took me a long time to get accustomed to the idea that if there was nothing to worry about, he'd worry about that because this in itself was an unnatural condition.

Mr Kiley gives the impression of considerable strength underlying his easy-going and acquiescent exterior. Both in relation to his early career experiences and in relation to his domestic situation, a superficial reaction might belie his real drive and determination. Earlier in his work career, he appeared to lack either sufficient motivation or talent to succeed in either of two initial areas of concentration, namely chemistry and teaching; in retrospect it was clear that he did not find these subjects congenial in a deep sense. When he did get into a satisfactory work situation, he not only functioned effectively, but showed initiative and drive to rise so as to make up for lost ground in his own career development. By the end of the interviews early in 1970 Mr Kiley had not yet closed the income gap between his wife and himself but had reduced it considerably and he had found a situation in which the way was clear for him to achieve higher levels.

Mr Kiley indicates that early on in his work he had had to endure the impression of others that he was an 'odd-ball' in being married to a relatively high-powered career woman : he says that when he would describe his wife's work it would stop the conversation dead. This was particularly true when his work associates, as in his last job, were northerners. If a wife worked 'it'd be expected that she'd be in the cotton mills as a machine hand'. Locally, in their residential area they have not felt this discrimination so directly, though the overall tendency is to assume that the male makes the major decisions and the female runs the domestic scene and their family is viewed in a friendly way as a bit 'mad'. Now that Mr Kiley is in a firm that is not only London-based but cosmopolitan and international in its composition, the Kileys find that their social circle includes many more people like them.

Even when Mr Kiley was considered an 'odd-ball' he did not seriously waver from the pattern they had developed. He had the strength to continue with it, discomforts included, rather than to opt out or to try to change his wife's pattern. The Kileys say that they know of husbands who try to prevent their wives from working and think that this stems in part from the male's insecurity.

Mr Kiley's Personal Background

Mr Kiley was born in Wales, the only child of an Irish father and an English mother. He always felt part of Welsh culture but also apart from it. The family was typically working-class 'Coronation Street' pattern with father working for the transport authority and mother collecting payments for a mail-order firm during the hours Mr Kiley was at school. The family did not relate to the Welsh–Irish community because though Mr Kiley's father had been raised a Catholic they were not practising Catholics. Mr Kiley's mother was Church of England and sometimes attended Quaker meetings. His father did not drink with his mates but worked very long evening shift work, and arrived home tired. On the other hand, his mother fitted into what Mr Kiley regarded as the dominant pattern in Welsh family life, namely the wife running things at home. However, Mr Kiley notes that his parents took many decisions together after joint discussion.

Mr Kiley's father was a trade union shop steward. Aside from this activity, which took a good deal of his off-work time, he belonged to the British Legion; his mother belonged to a ladies' social club. Most of his time was spent with his mother and Mr Kiley felt closer to her; he also felt close to his father who was ambitious for him; he did not often see him more than briefly because his work was on a six day rota and the day off varied. Mr Kiley's parents were a bit remote from him because of their ages. They had married late and when he was born his father was 49 and his mother over 30. His mother suffered from a tubercular hip; she could ride a bicycle more easily than walk. This made for companionship between them as they would cycle together, but otherwise there was little physical activity in the family's relationships. On holidays, they went to his mother's family in rural England, which was more fun for him. He had little contact with his father's relatives. In general Mr Kiley's childhood was fairly uneventful with no dramatic changes in pattern of family life or particularly memorable incidents.

Mr Kiley was an average all-round student – he played games, swam and so on; he excelled in science only after he came under the personal influence of particularly able teachers in grammar school. He decided during this period that he wanted to be a metallurgist but his parents discouraged him because they were afraid that this might tie him into the moribund local industries. They wanted him to escape and encouraged him to think of subjects like chemistry, physics or even English. Both his father and mother were very keen that Mr Kiley should have a higher education to escape the drudgery of Welsh industrial work. He was second in his class throughout grammar school, and his father pressed the headmaster of Mr Kiley's grammar school (whom he knew personally) to push him up.

Mr Kiley considered geology, having been attracted to the idea by the romantic image of a cousin who was a geologist-explorer. However, this was not acceptable as the local schools did not offer courses in geology and the universities would not accept students in this field unless they had had a school course in the subject. He then leaned towards chemistry, which was encouraged by a good master.

Mr Kiley's aspirations for a university degree – spurred by his parents' ambitions for him – were deferred by the war. When he left school at 17, he volunteered for the Royal Navy to avoid being drafted compulsorily into the coal mines. In the Navy he was trained as a radar mechanic and served in the Far East, returning to Britain only when he was 21. On his return he worked around a bit and then decided to go to teacher training college.

His mother's disease was progressive and she died when Mr Kiley was 22, shortly before he met his future wife. His father had retired the year before and after his wife's death he went to live in Suffolk with her family. His father died of a cerebral thrombosis shortly after the Kileys' first son was born in 1954.

While Mr Kiley was in teacher training college, he met Mrs Kiley and they went together until he completed his training. Jointly they recognized that teaching was not for him and they married 'with the understanding' that he would go on to university and that they would have to accept the precarious financial situation that this entailed. 'For three years we were going to be right on the edge (financially).'

This was a period of considerable strain. As it turned out, the Kileys not only had to deal with a situation in which Mrs Kiley was employed by the University in a science laboratory while

Mr Kiley was a science student (which did have its positive elements, e.g. their going in together in the morning) but Mr Kiley found that he was not as well fitted for the science field as he had imagined. He also suffered during this period from migraine, and the 'accidental' arrival of their first child added to their problems, though in retrospect they were glad about it. In the end, Mr Kiley failed in mathematics and did not return to complete his degree, partly because he was not that keen on the course and partly because of the pressures on him to begin to earn money : his wife had moved, by this time, into a more remunerative career job in industry.

His first job, calling for the equivalent of a university science degree, turned out to be a fiasco and he was forced to leave it, making it virtually imperative that his wife continue her work despite having the small baby. In this way an interim pattern evolved with Mr Kiley helping at home while his wife continued her career development and he continued his exploration for a good 'fit' between what he really wanted to do and could do well and existing opportunities. Eventually he finally found a niche for himself in sales and marketing. This is a field in which his university training and his capacity to get on with people, to be friendly, tactful and sympathetic, are put to good use.

FAMILY WORLDS

The Kiley family consists of Mr and Mrs Kiley and their two teenage sons. Their home is comfortable but not so large as to require domestic help. They had au pairs when the boys were younger, but they now manage by every member of the family participating in the domestic chores. Indeed, the two fundamental threads that seem to run through their family life from the earliest stages to the present are the enjoyment of the material benefits of their success in their domestic life and the sharing of their domestic tasks. Mrs Kiley describes the latter as follows :

The Kileys

The main rule we've tried to work to ever since we were married is that if there is a job to be done, we do it together so that there isn't one person working and feeling 'there's me slaving over a hot stove and there's him sitting with his feet up'. Unless the person who is specifically doing the job says 'Right, you go and sit down,' we do it together and nobody sits down and does nothing until everybody sits down and does nothing. The children join in this plan and they are expected to work when we are working and we don't expect them to work and us sit down but we all do it together.

The Kileys have a relaxed and casual attitude towards household cleanliness and furnishing, though occasionally things get to a point where Mrs Kiley feels that there is unnecessary mess. She tends at this point to 'blow her top', following which there is a general clean-up. They have two cars and a boat, recently acquired, which occupies them on many weekends.

The conception of marriage that the Kileys share is one in which the members should have time for one another (which was not possible for Mr Kiley's father), that they should sympathize with and facilitate one another's development (as was not true for Mrs Kiley's father), and that they should find happiness in the way suited to their individual personalities. Mrs Kiley feels that this is something that needs working at but can be accomplished with their particular characteristics, given mutual support:

Marriage to me before I married was a very unhappy picture – my parents' marriage was very unhappy. Looking back now I can see causes that were hidden at the time, but most of it is covered up with the feeling, 'what a terrible waste – these two people could have made so much more of it'. I didn't want to get married and my mother's unhappy experience didn't seem to be all that rare. In the north in the working class districts there's a lot of distinction between husband and wife with the man going out to the club or pub. The women would gather together at home and talk about babies and housekeeping and nothing much else. So that didn't strike me as being the sort of life I wanted to live. I wanted to live a more rounded life where there were people of all ages and both sexes together and I would go out with my husband and do things with my husband.

Once she met Mr Kiley and married him they evolved their present pattern which resembles her earlier ideal:

It was nice to have somebody to lean on. I'd been very independent and I'd fought my father over ten years every inch of the way. The thing I enjoyed very much was masculine company and a man who could see what needed doing and say what he thought wanted to be done or altered without being unpleasant about it. We discussed what we wanted to do, where we wanted to go and what we wanted to buy without him saying 'I have decided such and such, you will do so and so,' which was my father's approach. I had very little contact with men, particularly older men when I was young and my father was the pattern, I thought, of what an adult man was and I didn't like it and my husband was so much nicer.

Notions of partnership and sharing are important to the Kileys' conception of their marriage. They feel that their shared experiences have drawn them closer together over the years. Mr Kiley gave the following example of the extent to which the Kileys share all activities.

We do practically everything together. We never go on vacation separately apart from my wife going away for a few days and staying with her old school friends and things like that. We enjoy it too, it's not the case of I have to go with my wife and I'd rather go with the boys or another woman or anything like that; it's just the case that we both prefer each other's company.

The Kileys also feel that communication is an important element in their relationship.

We can talk to each other about anything without having to think first if it's going to cause trouble.

The degree to which Mrs Kiley participates in the major decisions is greater not only than their parental pattern but greater than the prevailing pattern in their environment. Differentiation is based on their different skills. She feels that she is a better manager than her husband, but that he is better at 'seeing the snags' than she.

I don't think we are typical. I think we try to participate more evenly in the major decisions. Most of the women who live round here (talk in terms of) 'my husband decided to buy a new house', 'my husband decided to buy a new car', 'my husband decided this and that'. Well, my husband and I talk a decision over always together. . . . I think we are well matched and very complementary in our marriage. I would honestly say that we haven't ever had a major disagreement on money. We've had some heart-rending sessions of 'My God, where did it all go.' We've never had any quarrel or any ill feeling about 'I save away and I don't get what I want'.

They operate a joint banking account and discuss all major expenditures. Though she earns more than he, they think in terms of their gross earnings rather than the differential entitlements that a 'his' and 'hers' set of accounts might imply.

The Kileys' leisure activities as well as their division of labour in the household are nearly all shared. Other than occasional business or professional meetings that each attends separately, they tend to take most of their leisure activities together. They both 'cut off' from work at the end of the working day, and concentrate on their family life. Discussions of work tend to be of an interest and information kind rather than carrying over of problems to be solved.

The neighbourhood social centre has male and female activity clubs, and they participate in these but not in a major way. Most of their leisure activities are done as a family – gardening, boating, and holiday travel. Differences in activity and emphasis arise from the family members' differences in interest or competence rather than a preconceived differentiation based on sex roles. Mrs Kiley and her younger son are more interested in natural science pursuits – rocks, fish, birds, growing things; Mr Kiley and the elder son are more interested in mechanical things and the repair of household machines and so on. The management of the boat falls to 'the men' of the family but not because of any sex-linked idea of mechanical competence. Mrs Kiley sees that her car is properly maintained by the garage and feels quite at home with mechanical things. Similarly, while Mrs Kiley does do most of the preparation of the evening meal, there are times when Mr Kiley does this and he does the morning meal. Decisions about household management are made by Mrs Kiley because she is considered better at this kind of organization, and he accepts this both on its own terms and as something quite compatible.

Mrs Kiley's management of the domestic scene is not on the basis of her intrinsic interest in this kind of activity but on the basis of being good at it. Mr Kiley says:

> She was never interested in domestic life. She found her two six-month periods at home (for maternity leave) terribly boring. Nobody to talk to except the neighbours, and talking about what the milkman said and the price of fish and whether they would have boiled potatoes or mashed potatoes tonight, and all these things she found terribly boring. When we go anywhere where there's mixed company, she's always with the boys. She doesn't go very much for female company, small talk. She finds female chitchat terribly boring. She'd rather talk about motor cars or boats or work or anything rather than potatoes or babies' nappies.

Parent–Children Relationships

The Kileys' eldest son was, at the end of the interviews, 16 years old. They described him as a 'late developer'. As he did not do well in his 11 + examinations he first attended a private school. He is now at a technical grammar school, which suits him very well. He is agreeable and easy to get along with, and the Kileys say that he learns very quickly how to cope with their moods and tempers; he is diplomatic. The second boy who is two years younger is quite different in temperament. He likes to be 'right'. Mrs Kiley says that 'he will just bash his head against a brick wall and try and test his will against ours' in contrast to the tact exercised by the older boy. At grammar school the younger boy is developing a strong science interest and is extremely bright.

They described their present overall relationship with both their sons in this way:

> I think neither of us is fond of babies. We like children and as they develop I like them better than I've ever liked them before.

They are fun, you can talk to them and show them things in the paper and you can have interesting conversations with them and do things with them.

Mrs Kiley recognized explicitly for the first time that she was not automatically maternal and they were fortunate in having a first baby who was temperamentally agreeable and healthy. When the baby arrived, they took his care in hand in the same pattern of joint sharing of activities as they used for their domestic arrangements generally. Mrs Kiley says:

He had had a difficult birth and I didn't see him for two days until he had gone beyond the stage at which he would learn to suck, so we had to put him on a bottle. There was nothing that only I could do, and my husband decided that he could help also. He was as good at cleaning him and changing him, washing nappies and so on as I was. We took him in our stride because that was the only way.

Mr Kiley says:

When he yelled for any reason and I happened to be there, I would pick him up and find out what the cause was and deal with it on the spot, rather than charging all round the house yelling for my wife. So if it was a nappy change, I would just whip it off and do the change and do the necessary work and put him back again.

The Kileys were fortunate in being able to find a neighbour to care for their child so that Mrs Kiley could return to work. Mrs Kiley described her feelings about this arrangement; though she was not enthusiastic she felt it was adequate and says:

When the first child was born, it was a very difficult time because in those days we really could not afford to have a live-in help and we hadn't anywhere for them to live because we had a flat. We were lucky there. Our next-door neighbour was very fond of babies. She had two of her own and she wasn't able to have any more so she adopted two. When they got to the stage of say two years, three years old she lost interest in them, but babies she was very fond of, and very good with. When it was obvious that I would have to go out to work, I asked her if she knew anybody who would look after a baby and she said she would love to very much. I didn't know her very well, but she was under supervision as it were because she had these adopted children and the health visitors visited, and I thought, well, he couldn't come to much harm.

Both felt strongly that they did not want to have an only child, for both had been only children themselves. Mr Kiley described the decision as one taken implicitly on the strength of this mutual feeling.

After about one and three-quarter years we thought it was reasonable (to have another child). I can't say that we deliberately said, 'Well, right, we will start making a number two,' but we agreed that we were both only children ourselves, and we knew the difficulties an only child can have, so we thought having one, we must have at least one more.... Before we were married I was talking about having six ...

Two was a compromise between his wish for a large family and her not really wanting any. They indicate that his conception of a large family was based on an idealized view of some of his relatives' families with children aged 8–10 or so, not babies-in-arms.

The second child was in one way more easily absorbed into the family life and in another way less easily. More easily because by then they 'knew what to expect' and how to handle babies, and also they could afford to hire help. Less easily because their second son made it clear from the outset that his was a different sort of temperament than the elder. He had a mind of his own and usually it was oriented otherwise:

You know, most children learn to say Mama and Dada? He learned to say 'No'. And he knew what it meant. And then he learned to say 'No like it', and 'No like it Dada', 'No like it bed', 'No like it din-dins', and so on. Whatever there was, the situation, the object, the time, the place – 'No like it'. With his fists clenched, his face red, and stamping his foot, and he could do all this before he could walk!

They say now that one could not have desired a more amiable baby than the first one; he was 'very good, didn't cry, easily trained, ate his food, etc.' But had the second one been first, the compromise on number of children might have stayed at one only. Mr Kiley says that the younger son – despite his interest in food and cooking – has only started eating properly in the last year or so. 'It has taken twelve years to get round to eating without a lot of fuss and frets and cajoling.'

The Kileys' philosophy of child-rearing consists of a balance between encouraging self-confidence and independence in their children while at the same time exercising controls. Aside from the immediate necessity for controls, this gives their sons some structure to grow into, and something to 'fight' against. Mrs Kiley illustrated how they carry out this philosophy:

We take them to various places although we also let them go themselves. We want them to have self-confidence, to be able to go and to decide to go. For example, this football match – we tell them we will give them money for the tickets but we won't give them money for the rosette. I may be wrong, but I think it helps to be a little oppressive like this. It gives them something to feel grown up about and a chance to fight without affecting the fundamental issue.

They also believe in teaching their children the value of money and so tell them how much things cost. The Kileys disagree with the way some of their neighbours handle their children; the way in which children are not taught to do things to contribute to the work of the household, and the way they are given everything and then do not learn the value of money. In handling discipline and permission the Kileys feel it is important to be firm and consistent. They feel they have the same outlook about what is and what is not being allowed, so few conflicts arise in this area. Mrs Kiley says:

I was mostly very firm. If I said 'No', I meant 'No'. We've agreed that when something isn't allowed it's not ever allowed. One must not have a situation where if I'm in a good temper you can be naughty and tomorrow if I'm in a bad one you can't do that sort of thing. I think we've got an intuition about what one of us has said and what the other doesn't know. The one who knows tries to bring it into the conversation so that there is not permission on one side and unknowing refusal on the other. When they are out of the way I'll say that the boy wants to do so and so and I said he could and I said you'd give him the money. I think we have naturally got very much the same outlook and ideas about what they can and can't do.

The Kileys do not make it a point to spend a particular period of time with their children individually. Rather, either of the boys might come to talk to their mother while she is working in the kitchen or around a shared interest. Mrs Kiley says:

The older boy has now reached an age where he doesn't terribly want to spend a lot of time with us. On the other hand he goes to bed later so we've got more time in the evenings than when he was younger. But he is at school all day Saturday. He gets a bit embarrassed if you sit down and have a session. He thinks, 'What have I done wrong,' and goes all over all sorts of crimes . . .

In addition, the older boy now has an active social life and goes off with friends on outings and to parties. In keeping with the general family emphasis on self-help and sharing the chores, he has to look after his own preparations for these things – washing a shirt in the machine and so on. One of the rationales stressed by Mr and Mrs Kiley in teaching their children to participate in all of the chores of the household without reference to conventional sex role stereotypes is that if they want to live at a high standard like that of their parents they will have to expect that their wives may work, and this will involve sharing. The boys have both been taught to cook 'since the time they were tall enough to see over the top of the stove'. The younger one is 'an excellent cook, probably the best cook in the house when it comes to fancy cooking. He makes very light cakes.' This talent emerged when Mrs Kiley was at home ill and he helped to look after her by helping with the cooking. Mrs Kiley describes this episode as follows:

. . . he was looking after me just that bit too well and I was wishing to goodness he would just go away and he couldn't think what to do. I made a few suggestions and then I said 'For heavens' sake go and bake a cake.' So he brought the book upstairs and we went through it and worked out what I could afford to waste, and we picked out a reasonably simple recipe and he went downstairs.

Then he came up again and said, 'Now what do I do?' And I said, 'Read the instructions.' So he went and it said, 'Weigh out half a pound of flour' and he came back and said, 'I've weighed that out, now what do I do?', and so on, up and down; it took about two hours to mix this cake. It really was very good, and fortunately it was successful and he was delighted. Now, any time when anybody is coming, particularly at the weekend, he'll say, 'I'll bake a cake.'

He makes evening meals during school holidays as well, as he is now able to make his own combinations for the meal's menu. Each son makes certain special dishes, but the elder boy's specialities tend to be simpler : 'fish and chips', 'bacon and eggs', things like that. Cooking carries some privileges as well, as the person who cooks does not have to clean up. Mrs Kiley indicates that the young boy uses cooking as a strategy of dealing with the family allocation of tasks at the weekend.

The elder boy wants to become an airline pilot. He likes adventure, as shown in his love for boating, etc. He is good at technical things and temperamentally is calm and collected. His mother is glad that he has chosen a job that is highly remunerative but that he has not chosen it for that reason. The younger boy is orientated towards science, and will probably follow in some way in his mother's footsteps. Aside from his intrinsic interest in naturalistic pursuits, this line of thought was recently given a fillip when, following a remark by his science teacher, his mother sent in some bacteriological cultures for the benefit of the class which were very well received.

He must have been talking a lot in class and I think got this comment, 'If your mother's such a jolly clever bacteriologist why doesn't she give me some bacteria to show the boys?' . . . so I duly sent these cultures and tried to make them interesting for children and wrote out an information sheet for each one and got an astonished and grateful letter from the biology master who was very pleased and had got far more than he expected . . . he's a good biology master because he's got the children's interest, and so my son decided that there's more to this being a bacteriologist. . . . He may be a doctor . . . or perhaps something else to do with medicine . . .

The children have always been accustomed to their mother's working and this is thought to be the normal state for the family.

Occasionally I've been home in the holiday, usually sick leave or something like this, and they've said after I have been somewhat tiresome, 'Mummy, you *are* going back to work aren't you?' They are accustomed to my working, and they have never known anything else. As far as I can judge they feel that they are superior because they have got a mother clever enough to work. When they were five and three or something like that they thought that because the poor woman at the end of the road couldn't drive she wasn't capable of working.

In the neighbourhood the family is considered a bit 'happy-go-lucky' about the way they manage things, according to Mrs Kiley, but there is quite an open and friendly feeling overall with children in and out all the time. They are thought of as being less 'odd' as a family than formerly, partly because at the stage of family life in which most of the neighbours now are, many of the wives are beginning to go back to work, at least part time. The attitude within the families is not always like the Kileys, however, even aside from the fact that none of the women have such high-powered careers. To give one example, Mr Kiley describes a couple where the wife is a teacher but the husband does not really make any concessions to her having this career:

Her attitude always is that she can't go out any evening when there is a working day following. She's got the house to clean, the garden to dig, the car to clean and everything has to be done.

Unlike the Kileys this family has the attitude that their social life is the one thing that has had to be sacrificed to the wife having a career. The husband does not help in the house other than with traditional male maintenance jobs. Mrs Kiley says:

One begins to wonder how much the man's sense of security in some of these couples depends on their wives not being successful at work. One of them, in particular, seems to see it as a personal affront that his wife is successful and to feel that he himself is diminished in some way because she can do something – which I think is terrible.

The Kileys themselves have arrived at a feeling that what each does enhances not only himself but the other as well, this being the key to their feelings of having accomplished a lot :

It's only been in the last five or six years that we've had what we wanted. It's wonderful. I feel a great sense of achievement. We started, both of us, with pretty well nothing ...

To understand how they arrived at their present situation from the family point of view, it is necessary to review the background of their marriage.

Background of the Kileys' Marriage

Mr and Mrs Kiley met at a student hostel in 1948. Mrs Kiley says :

I was going on holiday with a girl friend. We went youth hostelling in South Wales and he was the assistant warden of one of the youth hostels we stayed at, as a holiday job, and that's how I met him.

Mr Kiley says :

The final summer before entering college, I decided to give myself a couple of months off so as to recuperate from this ghastly job that I took immediately after leaving the services. A friend of mine was warden of a youth hostel and he was having difficulties and screamed for help. I said, 'Okay, I'll help you,' and I went up there and acted as his assistant. I wasn't paid, just fed. We had a whale of a time. She and a friend of hers were two of our customers. That's how we met; we just met and were attracted and that was it. She'd just finished college, I was about to start college, and we were both gay, free, no responsibilities.

They were attracted to each other immediately. He says that very early on they knew they had met their future mates and decided that they would someday marry.

We met on 12 August 1948 and about a fortnight later we decided we were *the* two people, we'd both known a lot of other people

before, but we were *the* two people. . . . It was a two years' engagement, but it was all decided within the first couple of hours.

The Kileys postponed their marriage for two years so that he
could complete his course at teachers' training college. When
they decided that he would go on for a university degree after
the teaching course, they felt they did not want to wait any
longer and got married in 1950.

Their early marital years were taken up with the management
of their educational and early work situations. Mrs Kiley had
completed her M.Sc. in the north while they were engaged,
and her husband was doing the teachers' training course. Then
she came to London and took a job as a research bacteriologist
in a teaching hospital for the second year of their engagement.
They got married, and he started immediately on his university course while she continued in the hospital job for
another year. During this period, they enjoyed the companionship of travelling to and from work together, but there were
financial problems. Mrs Kiley showed some of her drive and
persistence in her dealings with Inland Revenue about these
problems :

One person I must give a lot of credit to for our success was the
Inspector of Taxes. When I got married I applied for allowances and
they said 'you can't', and I wrote back and said my husband was
a student and they said, 'students on grants know this counts as
income'. I wrote back that he doesn't have a grant. But they wrote
back 'students on grants counts as income'. So, we were getting
nowhere but I thought I should be entitled to some allowances. So
I went along to the income tax office and saw the man at the
counter and explained. He said, 'Yes, but you see, with husbands
that have been in the forces, their grants count as income'. I said,
'but he's used it up on the teachers' training course, which was
not successful. . . . I'm not satisfied, I want to see somebody more
senior'. So somebody more senior came along and was told the
whole story. After I'd been there three quarters of the morning,
somebody went along and told the Inspector himself that they'd
got a very awkward customer here and they weren't going to get
rid of her and perhaps he'd better see me, so he did. I explained the
situation to him; I was getting this really very clear by all the

number of times I'd explained it. He considered this, and said, 'I don't see why you shouldn't have what allowances your husband would have if the sexes were reversed.' . . . He grasped the problem at once, and he put out an eminently just solution to it. This really helped enormously to get us through.

Mrs Kiley's relationship with her husband's father was not very good at the outset. Whereas Mr Kiley's parents would have wanted him to become a teacher, having completed his educational qualification, she supported the idea of his going on to university because he was not really happy with the idea of teaching. Mr Kiley's relationship with his wife's father was easier, and her father withdrew his initial protest to the marriage on the grounds of religious differences once he actually met Mr Kiley. Mr Kiley recalls :

I got along with him amazingly well. I never had any quarrels with him. I think he had missed having a son and he appreciated this opportunity of having a fully-grown son without the bother of bringing one up. It was more of a son and father than son and father-in-law relationship.

Mrs Kiley's difficult relationship with her father only improved gradually thereafter :

When we married my father would still lecture me about how to spend our money and about what we were doing wrong. He would lecture me; he never lectured my husband. As far as my father was concerned I was never more than seven, and it was hard for him to accept that I was grown up and independent. If he thought that I was at all cheeky he would want to slap me. Then I told him very firmly that my husband wouldn't permit him to treat me like that, and we didn't have any more trouble.

In retrospect the Kileys feel that the arrival of their son at what then seemed like a most inopportune time because of their unstable financial situation had several fortunate elements. Firstly, it catapulted them into family life which they might have found themselves too old for if they had waited much longer. She feels that to have started a family in the late thirties or early forties would have 'driven us dotty'. Secondly, their circumstances tipped the balance against any possibility that she might have left her job – something which she would later have regretted :

There was a very strong feeling against a mother working when I started and I did it not from choice but because there was a tremendous financial compulsion. I think I could easily have fallen by the wayside if it hadn't been the choice of I worked or we starved, at that time. I've always been very grateful for this happening to me because I think I could have fallen to the social pressures.

The Kileys have come through two major crises in which each was helpful in his own way to the other. The resolutions of these situations have consolidated the basis for their relationship.

The first major family crisis emerged over Mr Kiley's long-standing problem of migraine interventions. When Mr Kiley was a child, he suffered from stomach cramps which his present doctor thought were precursors of his subsequent migraine. By the time he was in his teens he began to have attacks which lasted for about sixteen hours, during which he could not cope with any kind of activity. As one of the symptoms of an impending attack is a narrowing of vision, he could not drive a car during these periods. He was relatively free of these attacks during his time in the Services, but while he was courting his wife he began to suffer more intensively, nearly every weekend after seeing her. At one point they attributed the attacks to something about his relationship with her :

It happened with my wife at weekends which caused tension between us; she was quite sure I was allergic to her and that I had some horrible feelings which I was trying to bottle up and which came out in a migraine. But I discovered by doing some sort of statistical analysis of what I was eating, drinking and consuming that it was the fact that I would give her chocolate at the weekend and eat some myself, and chocolate I discovered was one of the worst triggers possible for causing migraine. We figured out the chocolate probably about 1956.

Initial medical consultations were not helpful. Mr Kiley felt that one of the prime sources of tension arose from his feeling of inadequacy because his wife earned more than he did.

There was a feeling, I suppose, of inadequacy. A man likes to be the provider of the family and he thinks that he should be paying in more to the general funds than his wife. But nowadays it has evened up rather more than it was then. And when one pools incomes and deducts tax it helps to hide the fact that there is such a gap. This of course is one of those things that we never really discussed, it was just something we accepted.

The situation reached a point where Mr Kiley refers to his impairment as taking the form of a semi-breakdown. Mrs Kiley describes her own involvement in turning the tide of events as follows:

I tried to make him talk to me and I tried all sorts of things from being tremendously sympathetic to being fairly unsympathetic, to being positively provocative. Every so often I could get through to him and make him so mad he would talk, which helped quite a bit to see how he felt.... I could see the physical effect but it took a little while to appreciate the ability he has got for worrying.... He had migraine headaches and he also had a sort of subjective headache which was not the same thing. It seemed to be a physical manifestation of an unquiet mind.... It got to the stage where he was taking so much aspirin that I thought he'd do himself some physical damage and it was getting me down. I went to the doctor because I was fed up ... and he said, 'Send your husband along.' So he went along and told the doctor a pack of lies: 'I feel fine, I'm not worrying about anything.' Things got worse so I went to the doctor and said, 'Look, I don't know what he told you, but I can guess and the situation is quite different.' I then said to my husband, 'I've told the doctor you've been telling him a whole lot of rubbish and if you don't go I'm leaving ...' He thought I wholly meant it, so he went. Having got the doctor knowing the right questions to ask, he realized that this was a much worse problem and that my husband had not got the right sort of treatment. We weren't really that close to breaking up. It is one thing to say firmly, 'If you don't do something I shall leave you'; it is quite another when you start thinking of the financial complications. We own the house and everything in it jointly, and when you sit down coldly to think how you would divide this, it wasn't worth the trouble.

The migraine episode was resolved by a combination of factors. The Kileys' research on his diet and the doctor's help with medication were brought into effective play by his wife's forceful confrontation. Mr Kiley indicates that he had very few people to turn to by way of friends or relatives, that initially he had had poor success with medical help, but that he had succeeded in dealing with the problem because his wife 'rode along with it. It could have wrecked our marriage'. She did ride along with it in her own direct way, and in the aftermath there ensued a working through of the social psychological problems that affected her perception of the situation as well as his. As a consequence they arrived at a re-formulation of their life values that was mutually acceptable to both of them, allowing them to move on to the next stage of development of themselves and their family.

In their re-formulation the Kileys came to look at their careers in a new way. Mrs Kiley decided that she wanted to work even if there were no financial necessity to do so, for she found housework tedious in contrast to her career. Therefore they decided that they would try to eliminate as much housework as possible with the help of labour-saving machines. Mr Kiley explains:

That was when she decided no matter what, she was going to carry on working. Even if we were millionaires or if someone left a large fortune to us, she would still carry on. She found housework very tedious and boring. She does something if it has to be done, to get it out of the way and do something more interesting. As we have become somewhat more affluent we tried to get rid of some of the chores in the house by getting machines. There isn't a great deal of difficult work that is necessary, apart from decorating.

The Kileys now agree that if both work, they can maintain the standard of living that they would like at less cost to the health of each other. Both expressed their feeling that the extra worry and responsibility of an administrative position and the consequent risk to one's health was not worth the higher salary, particularly when a so much higher proportion would go in taxes.

The second crisis, the resolution of which had a formative effect on their marriage, occurred more recently when Mrs Kiley's father died. Mrs Kiley describes the support her husband gave her at the time of her father's death and the positive consequences for their relationship in the following terms:

We've had a very few rows. Mostly upsets have come when I have felt in some way that my husband was being like my father. It was particularly bad when my father died. But my husband understood this and he let me talk about all the difficult things that had happened. I think his death brought back all the feelings that I'd had as a teenager, and instead of coming one incident at a time, as it did when it happened, it all came back – phoomph. I had felt rather cross with Father. He came to stay with us for Christmas and he coughed and spluttered a lot and he wasn't very co-operative. He got annoyed with the children around and I was a bit niggled. Then he became ill which was rather inconvenient. We didn't have a very nice spare bedroom; it was the sort of spare bed you only really wanted to sleep on for a couple of nights, and I felt a bit bad about him being ill in there and me working and two children and the German girl (who spoke only a little English). Then when the doctor came, he had him straight off to hospital and then he died. I believe it was about seven weeks later, and oh it was all muddled up. I felt I had every reason to hate him but I felt guilty that I did, and I didn't really. It was all wound up and I just talked and talked and talked it out with my husband.

Mr Kiley says:

I realized what was happening and I felt that the only thing to do was to let it work itself out. I felt that any outside interference either from myself or from medical psychiatric treatment or anybody would aggravate it. It just needed to be off-loaded somewhere and I was the nearest shoulder.

Mr Kiley helped Mrs Kiley in his characteristic manner – providing calm and patient understanding while she sorted out her thoughts and feelings. During this time she realized that her father – always seen as very stingy – had been saving money which he left to the Kileys. Also, she began to appreciate, as a result of some of her father's conversations about her mother, in which he indicated that he had had no idea how unhappy he had made her, that he was simply behaving with lack of insight and not in a fundamentally malevolent way, characteristic of his conception of men of the times. This was similarly true of his treatment of Mrs Kiley where he was thinking of trying to avoid the undesirable consequences of too much permissiveness, but in carrying out his policy without much insight or control over his own needs it was experienced as oppressive. She also realized, at this time, that her father may have suffered from the concomitants of a psychological illness, such as endogenous depression.

In any case, one important consequence of working through all of these thoughts and feelings was an easing of her relationship with her husband, because to some extent some of the tensions in this relationship, as she indicates, stemmed from an unresolved transfer of feelings belonging to her father onto her husband.

WORK WORLDS

Mrs Kiley

Mrs Kiley is in charge of a research unit in a large chemical and pharmaceutical company. She has been with the company since she left her job as assistant lecturer in a teaching hospital in 1951. The industrial job was better paid and had more potential for career development; at the same time it allowed her to work in a medically-linked field of research, something which was important to her from the outset. She began on a development project to translate some initial experimental findings into chemical substances that could be produced for pharmaceutical marketing.

Initially Mrs Kiley was concerned about whether the industrial setting would provide difficulties in the way of sex prejudice.

When I came to have my interview I asked what the prospects were there and how far could one get because by this time I was aware, quite considerably aware, of sex prejudice. Anyway, this man said, 'the sky is the limit, we make no distinction between men and women at all'. He, as I realized later, was concerned to staff his department with a lot of young women graduates, particularly attractive ones, who would get married and leave and then he could start with some more, so he wouldn't need to promote them. But the only one that he took on that was married not only stayed but had two babies and still stayed and he was stuck with me for sixteen years.

For several years Mrs Kiley has been involved in the project described above. During this period the success of her work together with the general policy of expansion of the company has led to her running a fairly large research unit with about twenty people and a large budget.

Mrs Kiley's job at present – given the growth of her laboratory – involves her in tasks which remove her from the excitement of actual experimental work which gripped her in her early years of research. Much of her time now goes into management, negotiation with company administration, support and consultation with her staff, writing reports, giving papers, and so on :

You may very well need a degree in a scientific subject when you start on this kind of a career, but when you reach my stage what would really do much more good would be a degree in English.

Her laboratory's work is related to commercial market conditions in so far as the research board of the company that commissions work internally is responsive to market investigations. However, once in hand, the work goes on according to the criteria of experimental method, and the same interest is present in it for her as if she had been working in a hospital laboratory. There is considerable staff support for supplies, maintenance, and so on in relation to the physical elements of laboratory functioning, and she has a library and computer facilities available.

As she has risen in the hierarchy, Mrs Kiley has experienced some of the loneliness of high status, with a large private office, segregation of senior staff into their own areas and so on. These are balanced, however, by the greater perquisites of the job – not only higher salary, but greater latitude in spending money, greater freedom to attend meetings, and so on. Over her years with the company she has developed a network of relationships that make life manageable for her. Within the larger context of the firm as well, she has made direct personal relations :

I've made quite a point of getting to know people who are in various situations so that when I want something done, I know the person whom I have to ask.

Mrs Kiley has known since the age of 11 that she wanted to do medical research and she is deeply involved in and committed to her work.

In relation to the larger profession of bacteriologists, Mrs Kiley feels that she has attained a position of greater responsibility working for a commercial concern than she could have in a medical research laboratory.

I have financially very much greater responsibility but not the same sort of responsibility for somebody's life or treatment as I would have if I was in hospital laboratory work. But I wouldn't be able to be in charge of a hospital laboratory, not being medically qualified. I have done better in commerce than I could have hoped to do non-commercially.

Mrs Kiley feels that she is respected by her colleagues and superiors both for her opinions and for her willingness to stand up for them even when to do so was not 'politic'. She described how their estimation of her was established by several 'rows' in which she was fortunate in that she always chose the right subject to have a row about and was in a strong position.

Though the company Mrs Kiley works for is open to women rising in their careers, and indeed there are a number of women in senior scientist positions, the battle for establishment has nevertheless been severe. Mrs Kiley has felt that she had to do a bit more, do things a bit better than her corresponding male colleagues, if she wanted to have a chance competitively, given the stereotypes about women. She points out too that for those who wish to make a career in a large company, paralleling her own career:

It is almost impossible to make a compromise between family and work, of the kind where the woman works for a few years, takes some time away, say ten years, to get her family to school age, and then wishes to return to full-time career employment. My company has a formal structure of salary and grading akin to that found in the Civil Service; the grades are related to the age of the employees. We do not normally take on a person who is, say, ten years older than others in the grade appropriate to qualifications and experience unless driven by serious shortages of staff. Thus the choice between family and career must be made early. In more academic jobs, I do not think this arises so much.

Now, running a major research unit within the company, she directs the work of a team with a large budget and with a research output that can involve the company in very high expenditures.

Sometimes papers she writes go 'off into the blue' and are never heard of again; sometimes they come back with comments from various interested parties and with the request to collate them with a recommendation for the Managing Director, and sometimes one sees direct and massive action resulting. She has had to learn to be very cautious in this kind of situation because 'incautious expressions of enthusiasm, enthusiasm expressed too soon ...' could set in motion actions which the researcher might not feel quite prepared to sanction. This could be alarming. On the other hand, the traditional hedging statements of the academic researcher are unacceptable to management:

If I write that sort of report (too many 'on the one hands' and 'on the other hands') he slings it straight back at me and says words to the effect, 'I will not have you sitting on the fence!'

Sometimes she is sent 'open-ended' requests:

He sends this stuff to me and says, 'test it and find out what you can about it and tell me what you think'. This is a very tricky situation because if a person is over cautious and says it is no good, throw it away, probably nothing more will be heard of it. On the other hand, if the researcher says it is good and it turns out later to be no good, they are back onto you with, 'Who said this was good!'

There is no question but that Mrs Kiley's main satisfactions in her work have come from the actual experimental work. She has enjoyed doing the experiments, thinking about them and seeing if the ideas she evolves have any substance. When asked what the most enjoyable aspect of her work was, Mrs Kiley said:

Thinking, I wonder if I would get a certain effect if I did a certain thing, trying it and finding that I do. This is almost like a shot of heroin to a drug addict.

Now that she is more remote from the day-to-day experimental work she misses some of the immediate satisfactions. However, there is still a great deal of thought which finds expression in the work of her staff, and there is a new kind of thinking involved in the communication and presentation of her results. She says about her new role:

I shall have to stay with this because – I know it sounds bigheaded – of the people in my unit I know the most and can organize the work best and I can spark off ideas better, and indeed this is what I am employed to do. I would be wasted working on the bench. Somebody would have to do what I'm doing and there isn't anybody around that I think could do this particular job as well as I can.

She now has the additional task of presenting discussions and results of her work to conferences, of doctors for example, and also to present more technical aspects for journal publications. These tasks present challenges which she is currently confronting.

In her relationships at work, Mrs Kiley has come through as the sort of person described; who is disinclined to 'boot-lick', somewhat hot-tempered, and a fighter for people and things she thinks ought to be supported. She recognizes that it is important to put effort into establishing good relationships at work, because, as she says:

If there is grit in the relationship the job won't get done and I will not get satisfaction from it. It will be irritating and frustrating.

She therefore works on making good relationships and some firm friendships have developed in the work situation :

Some people I like very much, some people I can't stand and a lot of people I think we waste our time to employ – they've been around for a long time. I have several close friends, not because they first attracted me but a lot of them are people that I had to be on good terms with or the job would fall down. It would be bad for the job if I didn't get on with them – so I must find something I like in this person. And I have found that when I have to try hard to like someone, surprisingly these are often the friends that last.

Mrs Kiley distinguishes between her work personality and her home personality. She says she tries to hang the former up with her white coat when she leaves work, though occasionally she is her authoritarian work-self with the children.

The Kileys commented on this together :

Mrs Kiley :

I wear a white coat at work and I do try to hang my working personality up with it. I'm very authoritarian at work. Well, I have to be. Looking at myself through their eyes, I'm probably at least ninety years old and fierce. I'm not really, but when I say I want something done, I don't mean next week. I want it done now.

Mr Kiley :

I have called on a semi-official basis on my wife's company, not to see her specifically but other members of the company. I've met her in the course of this, and it is not the same woman. It is not my wife – a tycoon; she cracks the whip and they are efficient. I mean, you have got a very good name amongst your colleagues.

Mr Kiley

Mr Kiley has just moved from being a district sales manager for a very large British chemical company with headquarters in the north, to being sales manager for an American chemical company, based in their London office.

The kind of work he is doing is very similar though there are differences in mode of work and in career prospects that have improved his situation appreciably. In addition, he has had a substantial pay rise which has reduced the gap between his wife's income and his own.

The nature of Mr Kiley's work in the previous job might be called creative sales activity. Rather than working in the field to sell a prepared product, his work had a developmental character to it. He described this as follows:

Our philosophy (was) to lead by utilizing our know-how to open up new fields rather than say here is a firm making good profits from substance X, let us undersell them. ... We relied to a very large extent on close collaboration with our customers. There was, in most cases, a great deal of two-way passage of information between supplier and consumer. Both sides benefited from this attitude.

Mr Kiley's stock in trade was his knowledge of the company's products, their properties and their uses. He gave an example of the way in which he employs his knowledge in making a sale:

A company which makes plastic tubes and that sort of thing has a problem. The plastic is in a semi-molten state and it's squeezed out through a hole which is shaped to the sort of material you want to produce. They were having trouble with the material sticking to the orifice, so instead of coming out perfectly smooth on the outside, it was coming out with lines on it. Now, could we help them? We said we could. We suggested that they use two or three of our materials – they'll get samples in a few days' time, they'll try them, they'll come back to us or I'll go and see them, and they'll say, 'Well, fine, a, b and c work beautifully, so how much is it and when can you start delivery?', or they'll say, 'None of these things are any good – now what can you do?'

Mr Kiley operated on his own, making his home his office, and covering the south of England for his firm – as 'manager, representative, coffee-maker, everything – almost freelance'.

He was responsible to the Sales Manager of the company, who in turn was responsible to the Sales Director. He had the use of a company car which was maintained by the company and was allowed a liberal travel budget. He had the backing of the large research and development and technical services of the parent company to work out specific problems put to him by client firms, and this provided him with considerable assurance of being able to deal with the problems that arose.

The job had many advantages from Mr Kiley's point of view. He was able to regulate his work very flexibly because of his relative isolation from the headquarters, and was able to cover domestic crisis situations at home. He enjoyed the work and the relationships he made through it. The professional satisfactions he attained in bringing together scientific information with practical problem requirements is described when he talks about his participation in professional societies:

I'm a member of two or three professional societies. One has technical meetings once a fortnight. ... We listen to lectures and have a couple of pints of beer. Another is more of a club; it's just a boozing organization where they all get together and let their hair down. Then there is a third that I don't attend regularly. The company pays the subscriptions; it's a good idea to join such an organization and meet people. If you've bought a man a glass of beer and you see him next time in his laboratory, you'd be more friendly than if you'd just come in and he said, 'Well, I'm ... who the hell are you?' You gain knowledge from lectures and from talking to people informally; you learn things they probably would never tell you in business hours. Round the bar, or having a sandwich, you might get an idea which you can put together with other ideas. ... Suddenly some quite trivial little thing can just suddenly click.

Mr Kiley's main satisfactions came from seeing his personal negotiations fall into place:

The satisfaction is in negotiating either technically or economically with a company, and eventually having a letter come through to say that they're going to buy several tens of thousand pounds worth of stuff a year. You feel a bit elated about that. I feel if it wasn't for me, nobody would even have heard of them. It's public relations work in that respect. There's a completely open virgin field, say a quarter of a million pounds worth of stuff which has never been sold before, and you've found somebody who wants it. You've got it, they want it . . . you get together and haggle about price and when you fix the price, you carry on.

On the other hand there were aspects of the job with which he was not entirely satisfied. The very largeness and remoteness of the main part of the organization made him feel anonymous, subject to computer management in a highly bureaucratic system :

It's like the Civil Service, it doesn't matter what you do, it's what your tag is and how many years you've been on that tag. It's almost blindly operated by a computer, you could say.

Mr Kiley felt that there was not much chance of advancement on the basis of merit because there were a great many people of similar age and experience as himself who had trained and entered the company following the Second World War, creating bottlenecks. His attitude was that advancement would be a matter of sheer luck :

Most of the people of any responsibility are all much of an age; they all started working just after the war or in the late 40s, early 50s; there isn't much hope that the old men are going to die or retire and everybody's going to move up together and it's just a matter of the luck of the draw that one person will be a manager and another will be an assistant.

At the point of amalgamation of his smaller company with a very large group of companies, Mr Kiley was in fact offered a chance for advancement if he would move to the north of England. After considerable discussion, the Kileys decided that it was better for them as a family to stay where they were as Mrs Kiley would be unlikely to get as good a job opportunity in the north as she now has. They also felt that attitudes in the north towards women having careers were less egalitarian. The resolution of this dilemma reinforced their basic philosophy of sharing the family resources and involvements :

Neither of us has got any tremendous ambitions to become top

dogs in a company ... better to split the responsibility into two
rather than put it all on one person's back ... we reckon that now
we are adequately paid for the sort of life which we live. (Once
you get into the surtax brackets you gain very little by striving
for rises.) You get caught on the slippery slope of taxation. This
is my attitude, if we're going to stay in Great Britain, we might
as well work as much as we can to get the standard of living
which we like, and that's it. We're happy to have Ford motor
cars rather than a Rolls Royce.

Still, at some level the situation continued to rankle, and
eventually Mr Kiley responded to an advertisement that looked
as though it were written for him. The age limit for the job was
30 to 45 rather than, as with many technical jobs nowadays,
much younger; it was a well-known American company with a
London office and they wanted someone who had experience in
dealing with chemicals for prime producers of various industrial
substances. After interviews with various members of the headquarters management team, Mr Kiley was hired and given a
sales position with a substantial increase over his former income.
In addition, he now feels that his chances for advancement in
the management hierarchy are vastly improved as he is directly
in touch with them and they are a very flexible and expanding
group. He contrasts the general atmosphere of this firm with his
former one by describing the former one as follows :

My former company was quite nice, but terribly paternalistic.
They liked to tell you what to do and they had lots of people
around to tell you exactly what to do at all levels. I think they
even had people to tell the chairman what to do. All up and down
the line it was a pile of faceless men.... It's so big, like a government department ... it's all right if one happened to be a cabbage,
but I like something where one is personally responsible. If one
makes a success, fine, and if one makes mistakes, one is close
enough to the top to get the ha'pence and the kicks.

Mr Kiley no longer works at home, but has an office at the
headquarters of the firm in London's West End. His wife says,
somewhat teasingly, that he now has a very attractive secretary;
and he says that the whole atmosphere of being on first name
terms with his bosses and colleagues and going out spon-

taneously with them to lunch is a new and very agreeable experience.

He likes a number of elements in the new situation in preference to his previous one – other than the increase in pay and the increase in informality. First, there is a sense of being in touch with big and important developments and transactions.

The British company is a very small part of the whole organization. They have a tendency to concentrate only on the important work and not to worry about the unimportant things, they'll come along, and they do. They don't worry about the small firms who might buy £1,000 worth of stuff a year – just concentrate on the half-million boys, the large clients, and the little ones, they just come along, and if you lose them – what the heck, lose them, gain them – not to worry about the small people. This means that in the selling section there are only a few people but nobody below managerial class. They don't have any Indians, they're all Chiefs . . .

Second, there is a sense of flexibility and increased creativity in matching a client situation with a science-based industrial solution in a rather more dynamic way than previously – though the elements are similar :

We also have to keep close contact with our own research in the United Kingdom which is more or less day-to-day work, and the same with our company on the Continent. We keep in close touch with them, and also with the basic research going right back to academic work centred in the U.S.A., where they go all along the line from bright ideas right the way through to hard plant production; and they expect to be fed all the time with some sort of guidance on which way they should go. They obviously don't want to waste their time on developing a substance which is never going to bring in any profit to the organization – so they're open-ended and open-minded as well. If one says that there's a possibility of doing something rather than the idea they had in the first place, then they're quite happy to forget about their own idea and take it on the basis of what you've found out.

His feeling of having some influence on company policy is also found in his immediate situation :

It's not only that I have to do the field work, I have to go back and discuss with the higher-ups what is to be done with the problems, whereas before it was very much a case of writing a report and just forget about it. Now I write things down and then see that things are actually happening and sometimes I think 'Oh my God, what have I said, what have I done?' Top management seem to have such a childish faith in their underlings.

His mixed feelings of delight and apprehension at the degree of trust and delegation he is receiving are clearly slanted to the positive side, and he says about his future :

There is no reason why I shouldn't go right up the management ladder.

He already takes delight from the informality of his relationships with top management, and the easy first-name contact that the situation provides with directors from the U.K. and other countries in which the company operates.

Another element in the work situation that affects the Kileys' family and personal worlds is that the people with whom he now works do not consider it such an 'odd-ball' situation to have a wife who has a high-powered career, unlike the people higher up in his last firm, many of whom were from the north and had more conservative ideas than are to be found in the more cosmopolitan metropolis. This means that for the first time in some years his work friends as well as his wife's are more open to the possibility of becoming family friends without the kind of awkwardness that had prevailed previously. Aside from the fact that his present associates are more cosmopolitan in orientation, the fact that they are more senior, with the corresponding higher educational level and diversity of interests, seems to be important. Mr Kiley says that the kind of work colleagues that they would meet in the ordinary course of their lives in his former firm were 'mainly Indians, not Chiefs. Some of them were some rather rough-cut diamonds.' Some of them, he says, had 'never shaken off the Coronation Street attitude' and as Mrs Kiley says, 'they disapproved of us', in a way that people left behind tend to do with people who have been socially mobile.

Now, Mrs Kiley says 'it's entirely different. They're more our sort of people.'

INTEGRATION OF PERSONAL, FAMILY AND WORK WORLDS

The Kileys have different occupational specialities, they have different employers and their career styles and pathways have had different patterns. Nevertheless, there are complementarities that make for an integration between their personal, family and work worlds with only minor areas of overlap.

The overlap arises from the scientific training which each has had. Though the Kileys used this training in different ways, Mrs Kiley's involvement being on a more specialist technical level, they are able to communicate with one another about their work interests in ways not available to people who do not have this minimum basis for sharing. Their discussions are only 'marginal' in a truly technical sense.

Mr Kiley says:

I don't think that we can be of any constructive help to each other apart from just airing things and seeing if it is intelligible to somebody who is not quite au fait with the subject.

But Mrs Kiley elaborates:

Stating the problem, putting it into words is sometimes helpful, just having a receptive ear that at least can understand what you're talking about. ... I feel that if I can put an idea over to him, or he can put one over to me, then we can put it to others ...

Links are created between work and family worlds in various ways. It has been mentioned, for example, that Mrs Kiley produced some bacteriological cultures for her younger son to take to school. The effect was to make the son feel more that his mother's work related to his own interests and had some value in that way. Another example, more related to a potentially disintegrating element found in all situations where the wife pursues an active and successful career, relates to some of the measures taken by Mrs Kiley to head-off any tendency for her work relationships to become split off from her marital relationship. She says:

I've always made a habit when I have made a man friend at work

81

to invite him and his wife to my home so that everything is (understood). I mean, this is a danger. I would hate to get into any sort of involvement of that kind and I would hate anybody to think that there was any such involvement.

Perhaps the most important element in the integration between the Kileys' work and personal worlds is to be found in the complementarity they experience in their personalities. Each feels that they have needed and benefited in their careers from being married to the other. Mrs Kiley says that in discussing the cost to them of having her undertake such a demanding career :

We came to the conclusion that the cost would have been greater not to have done. For me personally this was almost the inevitable way, and fortunately I married the right sort of man. If I had married a man like my father it would have broken up, I think. I've got twenty people now working for me. I organize their working day and then I come home and I've got a husband and two children. Well, imagine all that energy concentrated on my husband and two children, the poor things couldn't stand it.

So, organizing and managing the family – while desired by all concerned up to a point – might, in her mind, have become intolerable had some of the determination behind it not been diverted into career channels.

For both of them, the value of their complementarities to them as individuals and in both work and family worlds has been driven home through their experiences with the crisis situations described above. When Mrs Kiley helped Mr Kiley to work through his difficulties surrounding migraine attacks, she also helped him to work through the difficulties which were attendant on his accepting a situation in which her career advanced for the time being more rapidly than his own. When Mr Kiley helped Mrs Kiley with her feelings of bereavement following her father's death, he also helped her with her general problems of relationships with male authorities. The stabilization of a 'we' feeling in the family out of a diversity of personal and work styles has become possible partly on the basis of having weathered these crises. Now that it exists, it is the core on which the diverse activities are hung. The Kileys protect this core partly by their practice of not bringing work home, and partly by setting up spheres of influence for each. Also, they cultivate a sense of fun and good humour in the family so that tensions are less likely to develop around everyday domestic issues.

The Kileys have discussed the question of whether it has all been worth while, and she sums up their consensus of opinion as follows:

It has been very rough at times, but worth it. We feel that we've learned a lot, suffered a lot, but worked out something that has been valuable for all of us. I always advise young people who come to me and ask how I've done it to go ahead and try, but to recognize that it's not easy.

The Bensons: Architects

BACKGROUND — DEVELOPMENT OF THEIR FAMILY STRUCTURE

Catalogue of Events

Met: 1947 when he was a fourth-year student just returned from the war, and she a second-year student.

Going together: During 1948 and 1949 when he was doing his year in a planning course in London, and she was in her fourth year in the north.

Married: 1949 when both finished schooling and entered their first jobs with a public authority in 1949.

Children: Three children born 1954 – boy; 1957 – girl; 1964 – girl.

Establishment of a home and residential history: Lived in his two-room flat in Bloomsbury at first; then moved to a small Chelsea terrace house with a bedroom floor, a work floor, and a basement which they 'let off'. (ca. September 1953); then to their present larger terrace house which they bought outright (ca. 1961).

Domestic help: Two types – a 'daily' and a 'live-in student'. The first is more permanent – had one for eight years. The second was an 'annual' up until recently when they turned her room into a boy's bedroom.

Major events in child-rearing: The boy went to a local primary school, and is now in comprehensive school. The elder girl went to the same primary school and now goes to the same comprehensive school. The youngest daughter was still at home at the beginning of the interviews, but had entered the same primary school by the end.

Changes in household composition: The household was limited to the nuclear family until 1956 with baby-sitting from tenants in the basement flat. Domestic help added after 1958, and a residential student in 1960.

Major illnesses: None.

Major family separations: Working trips abroad for site visit – children left with Mrs Benson's parents. Where feasible children were taken on study trips. None of the children are school-boarders.

THE BENSONS

The Bensons are a husband-wife partnership at work as well as in the family. Mr Benson is in his mid-forties and his wife in her early forties. Their three school-aged children live with them in their five-storey home which serves also as an office (lower three floors for office and work, upper two for living and family).

In the early stages of the interviews in 1967, one of the focal concerns for this couple was that of creativity and spontaneity. They were preoccupied with how to preserve their creative approach to life and at the same time avoid the constrictions of too heavy commitments in work and too regimented an approach to family life. Their concern with 'happenings' in their life, and the importance placed on them reflected to some extent the hippy movement which was reaching its heyday. They emphasized the degree to which their lives are controlled and organized by their commitments so that 'happenings' have to be prepared for, and space has to be made for them in a very tight schedule. In the later stages of interviewing, this couple focused their concerns on modernity and conventionality, i.e. whether they were now, in their mature and established phase, still avant-garde in some sense, or old-fashioned and passé? The concept of the dual-career family as an advanced structure intrigued them, for in their concern with the generation gap and their relationship with younger people, the Bensons are as much impressed with what they see as their own conventionality compared with the younger people in their field, as with their obvious modernity of spirit.

The change which occurs in the focal concerns of Mr and Mrs Benson can be seen, perhaps, as resulting from the resolution of some of the tensions under which they were functioning. At the outset of the interviews the strains were more pronounced than later : their work situation was relatively uncertain and they had recently experienced a number of frustrations; they were not yet certain about the value of the research interviews, which were demanding; and their youngest child was still at home. By the end of the interviews their work situation had improved, all the children were at school, and they had gained confidence in the reliability of the researchers. The final interview sessions were much more relaxed and the impression gained of the Bensons' personal characteristics was somewhat different. In addition, by the time of the final interview, Mr and Mrs Benson had experienced a change in the main area of preoccupation in their lives. This related not only to their own maturational processes but also to the concerns which the social environment has imposed upon them as individuals.

PERSONAL WORLDS

Mrs Benson

Initially Mrs Benson was somewhat removed from the interviews. She spoke rarely and in a slow, soft voice. The interviewers felt that she was somewhat depressed. She characterized herself as 'tense' and described her whole parental family in the same way. In subsequent interviews, however, she participated more actively and emphatically. By the end of the interview series she was ebullient, and indicated that the early impression was partly a phase phenomenon, in that she does have quite marked ups and downs, and partly a reaction to specific immediate difficulties both with domestic help and in their working situation.

Both Mrs Benson's mother and father came from large northern families, each with a well-developed family folk-lore :

'There was always someone around who had a good memory and a full set of photographs.' Her father's family stemmed from a rural town culture with a strong sense of the need for teamwork; her grandfather and great-uncles had trained with the intention of forming a partnership of engineers. Mrs Benson says about her father:

He's one of these very quiet Yorkshiremen. You never argue, no argument was ever allowed in his home.

Mrs Benson describes her mother as a gentle person who 'never says anything that upsets anybody else ... and worries socially terribly, whether people have enough of everything'. Mrs Benson illuminated more of her mother's character when she compared her to herself. She sees herself as 'running her head into trouble', in contrast to her mother who always avoided it. On the other hand, her mother was 'good at everything ... a good swimmer, a good tennis player, an excellent pianist', none of which Mrs Benson can do or particularly wishes to do; her mother has a good turn of phrase and sense of humour, 'where I've got absolutely no repartee'. Given their differences of temperament the relationship that developed between mother and daughter was described as one of 'antagonistic cooperation'.

Mrs Benson's mother was a student at a school of art where Mrs Benson's father was teaching. Since then, to varying degrees, she has been involved in his work. This background participation is described as follows:

... (Father) was already a teacher there and there were several people in her year that were interesting. ... She was the sort of generation that Barbara Hepworth and Henry Moore are. But you know, it's never been dead in the North. It's been feeding the South with talent, so that she knew people and was always in touch ... father had to run an enormous span of evening classes, right down to Women's Institute level, particularly during the war ... and he was also in charge of the arts of the whole town. He used to go and teach at the grammar schools, not only to see what was going on but because there wasn't staff to go around, particularly during the War. She (Mother) helped because you have to think of ideas,

'Oh, what'll I set today?' There were exams, small test subjects and exam markings. They used to do it before the War more and she would help on that ... spread it all out on the floor and mark it. She never actually went down town and taught but with all the hundreds of backroom jobs there's always something going ...

During the period in which Mrs Benson was growing up her father was an art teacher and therefore remained at home while most of the men in the town, which was chiefly comprised of inter-related seafaring families built up from fishing days, were away in the merchant navy.

Like any of those kinds of work in dangerous occupations, like the coal miners, people depend on working with a team that you can trust ... if a boat was lost you had to support each other.

The result was that Mrs Benson's family felt that they were 'outsiders', and that their position was particularly difficult in the context of such a tight, local community. This seems to have created an anomalous situation because:

You couldn't open your mouth about art or anything.... My parents just stopped talking.

Mrs Benson characterized their position in the town as being almost like that of alien minorities. She says:

... it's a very odd business, not being able to get on with people, finding yourself culturally different. It was almost like being a black child entering a community of white people.

To some extent, Mrs Benson feels this 'marginality' orientation has persisted through the Benson's innovative period in their contemporary life.

She felt that during her school days, the kind of people with whom she should have been friendly and shared values were quite alien to her, and those that she liked were so different culturally that a sense of belonging with them was impossible. Although born in the middle class she felt more of a common bond with the working classes.

... you see, I went to a private school and I think that I got the worst of all worlds. I think that in spite of the terrible dialect one would have been stuck with, a primary or elementary school would have been better. The working class were much kinder. When I went back to do a year at grammar school, they were much jollier girls than I had ever known, and there was no catty back-biting and whispering in corners. We used to stand around as a 'year' in the playground, and they all had to work so hard. One wonders what happened to them all.

Because he was in education, Mrs Benson's father was employed by the local councillors and he seems to have been engaged in a continuous cultural struggle with them over attempts to develop programmes of art education.

... it was a strange society, because all the councillors are those militant politicians who talk about *Culture*, but at the same time they stood out against the Burnham Scale for teachers' wages. It was incredible. It would have been a joke if it weren't so serious.

Mrs Benson was an only child and her parents did not employ a nanny or other child-minder. They had a daily maid until the War, as did most other families in their neighbourhood, and her grandmother had a housekeeper until about 1942.

During the War, Mrs Benson was evacuated first to an aunt on a hill farm in Yorkshire for a long summer, and then to her grandmother in Edinburgh for about three years when she was twelve. Both these families were important to her and she spent many holidays with them. Mrs Benson sees in herself some of her grandmother's traits and she feels that they are more alike in character in many ways than she and her mother are.

I run a household much more like my grandmother's. My grandmother's house used to drive my mother up the wall. (My mother) used to go around wiping up flour, saying, 'Mother, you've made a terrible mess. Mother, that's enough.' My grandmother's entertaining used to curl my mother up. She'd put a cake on the table she'd had in the tin for ages. It would be hard and she couldn't even cut the crust off, and my grandmother would carry it off with talking and laughing. It was the people that mattered. I'm not as confident as her. Our entertainment is more likely to be that you're offered an olive and a flag to fly, but with my mother, everything had to be right.

Mrs Benson said that when she was a child, her father did not have any time for housekeeping and cooking ('he did a bit of gardening and in the wartime built a shelter but it nearly killed him'), but her parents 'always did the house decorating together'. Since he has retired, however, he has done more around the house.

Decision-making, even in areas recognized to be the province of one of the parents, was interactive. Though Mrs Benson's father would leave all of the domestic issues to his wife, she usually referred any decisions to him.

. . . it was always slightly surprising how my mother didn't take the whole decision herself . . .

Both the decision to evacuate her and the later decision to send her to architectural training were decided jointly by her parents. However, the initiative for the latter came from Mrs Benson herself.

A number of points seem to emerge in Mrs Benson's conception of herself :

First and perhaps most pervasive is her feeling that she is living in a world in which there are very powerful forces – largely irrational, generally hostile and against which one has to struggle continuously to carve out something that is right and good. This feeling, which is also fundamental in her creativity, is reflected in almost every stage and aspect of her life, beginning in her conception of the relationship of her family with the society in which they lived when she was small where what her father did seemed to be pushed on him from people from outside. This quality is perhaps most apparent not only in her discussions of her and her husband's early experiences in establishing themselves professionally, but also in topics about which she still writes during periods between architectural projects. The creativity which arises from Mrs Benson's struggle with these outside forces is released adaptively into the Bensons' practice which is staunchly independent. Within this haven of an independent practice, their emphasis is on the way in which creative work emerges by taking into account the societal forces around the architect and his clients.

A second theme in Mrs Benson's self-characterization is the personal constellation of traits which she refers to as the marginality orientation. This has previously been described in relation to her feelings towards the society in which she was raised, and her feelings of a kinship with the various minority groups in society. She also has a fear of going into some situations – for instance she does not like to give lectures. These feelings seem to stem from this marginality orientation.

A third theme is related to a cluster of family traits which Mrs Benson thinks she possesses. Like Scots and Northerners generally, she sees herself as being tough, having a lot of persistence in the face of adversity, and choosing a path and sticking to it even if it is a 'tough road'. Her mother seems to have seen her as aggressive and Mrs Benson has taken over this conception of herself with its consequences.

I probably reminded her (mother) of her sister. It's very difficult to put my finger on this. Aggressive, I think. I mean one does say things and get slapped down.

She also feels that she has a 'missionary spirit' but she is beginning to feel more and more that risks are to be shared by others and not all taken on by oneself.

A fourth aspect of her personality, which is in contrast to her tendency to choose the tough road and be aggressive, is that Mrs Benson sees herself as 'almost unable to fight any opposition ...' 'I just feel I'd give up, can't get through.' She feels that she often knows what she wants but is unable to take a firm enough line at the time, with the result that the decision may go in a different direction. She then feels remorse, is unable to drop it or forget it, and continues to worry. When she was younger she feels she had greater toughness to push through decisions than she has now.

The next two themes in her character are related to the issue of sex-identity. Mrs Benson had two or three major female role models in her childhood – her mother and grandmother, and to some extent her aunt in Yorkshire – who appear to have presented contrasts for her. Mrs Benson feels that she does not accept her mother's way of life and has failed to fulfil her mother's expectations. 'I was a disappointment to her. I think this is (partly) the business of only children.'

Mrs Benson runs her household like her grandmother did. Something has had to give in the requirements of work and family life in their household, and as her husband also has a casual attitude about social niceties such as entertaining, this choice of her grandmother's or aunt's attitudes over those of her mother has made sense in the Bensons' situation.

In general there are very few things that Mrs Benson feels that cannot be done equally well by either sex. Personally she dislikes having to do anything with machinery, including cars, and so leaves this all to her husband. But she indicates that this is a point that she holds on to in defining the demarcation line between men and women only because she feels 'there must be some difference'. She has a very strong sense of being a woman and she respects men who have a definite masculine presence : 'I can't stand the first whiff of a reversal situation.' She wants men to have something she does not have, and not to allow themselves to be dominated by her.

Mr Benson

Mr Benson reacted to the interviews in a quite different manner from his wife. From the beginning he was interested in making contact and interacting with the interviewers on a personal level. He has a somewhat sardonic manner but at the same time communicates warmth. Although he was very expressive and articulate in the interview situation, he often dodged direct answers to questions put to him, digressing into interesting side discussions.

Mr Benson was born in a small northern town. His father's family had come from rural origins and he describes them as follows :

My father's family are quite interesting. I think that he was probably rather slow ... but they are all, in that country-postman kind of way, extremely interesting. Emotionally I tend to identify with them. His uncles (my father's father's brothers) were still in the country, in villages or on farms, and it seemed to me that they were the sort of people who should really have stayed in the country ... their whole tempo was geared to small town life.... My father's father lived out the first part of his life in the country and would then do business in villages and so on, travelling about getting orders.

His father's business was also related principally to rural and industrial villages and this seems to have had a significant influence on the family.

It kept them both a bit more countrified – they thought the pleasurable thing was doing nothing in particular. That is also what I like doing. The only way I really relax is doing nothing special but I prefer not to be in London when I am doing it. The town puts pressure on you.

Mr Benson's father was a commercial traveller but he was away only two nights a month on work, and did all his travelling by train or bus : the furthest he went was about fifty miles. He would always be back at about 5–6 p.m., having left at 8.30 in the morning. He also worked Saturday morning and often took his son along.

I didn't actually see what he was doing, but thinking about it, he must have been paying in his week's takings. They collected bills as they went around taking orders. Then we used to go and have ice cream. I saw quite a lot of him. On holidays he used to take me with him.

He describes their local community as made up of 'artisans or drivers, of a kind of upper working class, and milkmen and this sort of thing.' Although there was widespread unemployment during his childhood Mr Benson recollects that his father worked steadily through the depression, which is an important element in his early environment.

Mr Benson's mother came from a family of industrial working

town people. She was a school teacher and 'stronger than my
father in the sense of knowing what she would like things to
be like and so on – not energetic, not opinionated – but quite
disciplined'. Having been a teacher and having a rather purposeful bent of mind, she was the one to coach and encourage her
son with school work:

...I imagine she was ambitious for me. She would be the one to
help me with things ... neither doting nor particularly pushing or
anything, just what I now see as a fairly normal motherly role.

Mr Benson was an only child. 'I was kept well cleaned and
well organized by my parents ... and I was dead average in
school ... always nineteenth in a class of thirty-five ... I was too
fat for athletics but ordinary team games I always enjoyed. I
got on well with the other boys and had no real problems.' While
he was happy in his pre-school environment and not unhappy
later on, he sums up his family life with the following reserva-
tion:

I didn't actually enjoy my parents much in childhood. I think that
life was really a bit too hard for them, and in a sense it still is. It
has to be running your way for you to be fairly outgoing to
children. It's cruel to say it but the fact is that I did have friends
whose parents seemed more relaxed ...

Mr Benson does not feel that the tension was due to personal
or interpersonal difficulties in his family but to the background
of primitive Methodism in his father's family, with its puritan-
ism, strictness and emphasis on self-improvement. He enjoyed
the relaxation of pressure when he was in his friends' homes,
but at the same time appreciated how much his parents did for
him. This is most important in relation to the crucial decisions
they made concerning his education, which pressed for his improvement occupationally. The parents made decisions inter-
actively though his mother was more forceful in those decisions
which concerned her son's development.

When Mr Benson reached school-leaving age, both of his

parents cooperated in the decision to send him to architectural school. At grammar school he wasn't particularly distinguished in academic subjects but was good at art and physics and generally acceptable in a range of other subjects. Then came the decision point at school-leaving:

... there came a situation where my parents had to decide what to do. That sounds dramatic, as indeed it was, because the time I was leaving school was 1939. When the war started everybody anticipated being called up into the army at eighteen or nineteen, therefore they had to decide whether I would start on a vocational course straight away or stay longer at school and get more subjects in examination. They decided that it would be better to start straight away and due to the war circumstances it was possible to start at the architectural school at sixteen.

When asked how his parents had worked out the actual choice of fields (as he himself had not any specific career formulations at this time) Mr Benson describes it as follows:

There was one architect in the town whom my father had been at school with. Therefore he knew what architects were and I think that he thought of it. It's a traditional, safe thing for people who can draw, and at the time we'd just been through the depression. If you're an architect you can always get a job with a local authority but if you're an artist it's too insecure. Therefore they would tend to say ... 'we'll send him to some sort of tech school' rather than an art school ...

From then on, the most important parental decision with regard to his training was when his parents decided to stake their savings on providing lodgings for him, to avoid his having to commute.

Mr Benson's conception of himself shows six main themes which seem to represent three basic dualities:

First, he sees himself as a creative, artistic type of architect and attaches importance to the fortunate experiences of having become 'famous quite young' in his profession. At the same time he has an explicit conception of himself as an ordinary person and is always surprised when treated as an unusual person. These are the first and second themes.

Another duality is introduced by Mr Benson's feeling that over his professional lifetime he has had the confidence and optimism to go the way of his convictions in contrast with the vast majority of his colleagues who are more conformative. He has usually contended that things would work out, and that they could carry over periods of no project work into the next phase where something good would turn up. On the other hand, there is a certain feeling of doom and pessimism when Mr Benson says: 'four out of five of all the things we do turn out wrong'. Thus it would seem that when the creative path which the Bensons have chosen turns out to be particularly thorny, he feels a sense of despair and concern about whether their optimism and self-confidence were justified. These are themes three and four.

Mr Benson sees himself as a disciplined person, which can be considered as a fifth theme of his personality. While he developed this sense of discipline late, he feels that this is one of the most important values in his life, not only because it distinguishes him from many others in his profession, but because it serves as a common bond with his wife. He feels that it has required a great deal of discipline to take the unorthodox path chosen. And he also feels that it is crucial that they continue to develop their work towards their specific goals in a very detailed self-controlled way regardless of immediate public approval. Thus they go on making their plans, entering the relevant competitions, even when for long periods they get no immediate rewards. Mr Benson stresses the importance of working continuously towards putting into practice the ideals he has.

A sixth theme is that of self-indulgence. This seems to operate in counterpoint to his feeling of spartan discipline. While he attributes his doggedness to the non-conformist Protestant tradition and feels that he and his wife take on a totally dedicated, near monastic way of life, at the same time he likes beauty, fine objects, aesthetic experiences and comforts. This makes him worry about whether he is being self-indulgent, which he considers to be a negative attribute. This even spreads into a concern that if he is enjoying the disciplined way of life, this too may be a form of self-indulgence. Because they have a very comfortable car, an aesthetically pleasing home, a house in the country and enjoy foreign travel every year, he feels that recently there has been an 'inversion of sensibilities' where he has become more concerned than his wife about comforts whereas earlier he had disregarded these things. This concern with self-indulgence is perhaps due in part to having come from a humble background and not wishing to put too much emotional distance between himself and his parental family. He would feel 'exposed, a fraud, a deserter' if he were to adopt what he sees as an ostentatious way of life, which is now open to him financially. This is also part of an interplay between the wish to be different but not 'too different'.

In comparing the parental families of Mr and Mrs Benson as well as their early backgrounds and experiences many similarities are apparent. Both Mr and Mrs Benson are only children, born in the North. Both have mothers who seem to have been more decisive than their husbands and therefore played a bigger part in setting the pace for family decisions, although ostensibly this was a joint activity. Both had fathers who were in stable occupations at home at a time when either there was widespread unemployment, or when a majority of men were away at war. Both Mr and Mrs Benson have had positive relations with female figures in their early life. Both their fathers were interested in them and took them places and showed them things, though in her case the content of these activities relates more closely to the Bensons' present line of work and interests than it did in his case.

There are obvious differences in their family backgrounds as well. Her separation from her mother and father during the war was one.

Although there was a clash of temperaments between Mrs Benson and her mother, it appears that Mrs Benson's parents both actively supported her in her desire to become an architect and they are now gratified by her success. On the other hand, although Mr Benson's parents facilitated his entry into the profession they have not shown any intrinsic interest in architecture *per se*, and have not been particularly moved by his professional success.

FAMILY WORLDS

This is a family with an extraordinarily high inter-relatedness between its internal and its external life. The organization of family activities is greatly governed by work considerations and vice versa, as both areas are salient to both of the Bensons. The structure they have evolved reflects this twin salience, and they place relatively little emphasis on the basic age and sex structure determining activity patterns : children participate in the adults' world; wife in the husband's world; husband in the wife's world; husband and wife can interchange many, though not all, activities in both worlds.

Though their family structure is very 'modern', in that it is based on an equalitarian conception of husband and wife roles, the Bensons see themselves as rather old-fashioned. They liken their way of intermixing work and family activities to the pre-industrial revolution craftsman's studio arrangement, and refer to themselves as being like an old-fashioned family firm or farm family, with everyone lending a hand.

The Bensons have both been keen observers of the trend among young people to form communes. Some of their friends and colleagues have had children involved in communes. As mentioned previously they were intrigued with the idea of the dual-career family being a pattern for the future, but are not sure whether young people are in fact oriented in this way. They feel that the rebelliousness of many young people against their parents extends to the institution of family life generally, and they indicate that many avant-garde polemicists are negative about the future of the family. The Benson family's view is a libertarian one within a rigorous framework : to let people work out their own forms but to recognize that it involves hard work and considerable skills of management to make a new structure a viable one.

Current Structure of Activities

The present household consists of the Bensons, their three children (son sixteen, daughter thirteen, daughter six) and a housekeeper who comes in five days a week for three hours. Until 1970 they had a student baby-sitter who lived in. However, it is very difficult to separate this domestic structure from that of their office because the two are to some extent interchangeable. As the Bensons work in their home they often deploy the available manpower in both. For example, the secretary may be called upon to baby-sit in the daytime or to do the food shopping.

In their family life the Bensons do not feel that they have a routine or typical week. Variations relate to what's going on in the work situation, who is in London from their professional networks, and what the help situation is at the moment. Though these things do not affect the basic framework of the day, they do affect the content of their activities. Mrs Benson says :

... You get a typical day when we're actually doing architecture and a typical day when we have to do something else, and we catch up on stuff during that period – doing theoretical projects or writing, or just getting organized for the next stretch when there will be no time.... Some things are constant. We get up very late and we always eat at about the same times and run out of energy at the same time in the evening. If we do anything like going out to a lunch or a meeting, the whole thing (energy) has to be very consciously redistributed ... that's the most critical thing, to keep the energy ...

To give an idea of some of the Bensons' activities during a week in which they do not have an architectural project 'on', they made the following diaries :

The Bensons

Mr Benson

THURSDAY 18 MAY 1967

9.00	Get up; read mail at breakfast.
10.00	Own design work in office.
1.00	Lunch at home with baby.
2.00	Work with assistant on his problems.
2.30	Own design work in office.
4.00	Japanese architect to office for tea.
4.30	Own design work in office.
7.00	Drinks with ex-lodger in Piccadilly.
8.30	Fail to get into film 'Zorba the Greek'.
9.00	Supper at home; children already fed by baby-sitter.
9.30	Read technical journals.
10.30	Bath.
11.15	Read newspaper in bed.
12.15	Lights put out.

FRIDAY 19 MAY

8.30	Get up.
9.00	Breakfast and read mail.
9.45	Do Rapoport diary. *Morning:* Working in office on revision of project drawings.
1.00	Lunch with baby.
2.00	Visit exhibit at RCA with wife and baby.
3.45	After stop for postcards of railway trains.
4.00	Office design work as morning.
7.00	Dinner with architect from Stockholm at Indian restaurant. Afterwards to critic's house.
11.30	Talk. Bed.

SATURDAY 20 MAY

9.30	Get up. Straight out to market with all children. Afterwards to camping shop to get tent pegs and gas bomb.
1.00	Lunch with children.
3.00	Park with all children to launch re-constructed model boat.
4.30	Tea.
5.30	Read book on country of future project.
8.00	Supper with children.
9.00	Finish reading book on project site.
11.00	Bed.

SUNDAY 21 MAY

9.30	Get up; breakfast and Sunday papers.
11.30	Rapoport diary.
11.45	Drawing work for Monday.
12.45	Lunch with children.

1.45 Drawing work in preparation for Monday.
3.30 Visit to architect to work on furniture competition. Took eldest daughter with me.
8.00 Supper; reading newspapers and bed.

MONDAY 22 MAY

8.30 Get up; breakfast.
9.30 Personal clothing; shopping in King's Road and to bank for cash.
10.30 Telephoning Rapoport.
10.50 Diary.
11.00 Design work.
2.30 Meeting with heating consultant.
6.00 Supper and bath.
8.30 Reading wife's manuscript.
11.00 Watched television, bed.

TUESDAY 23 MAY

Morning: Correct wife's manuscript.
Afternoon: Sort out materials filing system with assistant.
8.00 After supper help son with revision of geography papers for his Common Entrance examination. Read book on Egyptian furniture.
11.00 Bed.

WEDNESDAY 24 MAY

8.30 Get up.
Morning: Drawing work.
Afternoon: Discuss chair design with technical man from chemical corp.
5.00 Tea; afterwards
6.00 Discussion with chair designer friend about a book.
7.45 Dinner out with chair designer friend and editors of a magazine.
10.00 Films by chair designer friend privately projected.
12.30 Bed.

THURSDAY 25 MAY

Morning: Drawing and discussions with assistants.
Afternoon: Visit with wife to two projects sites and drawing and discussion afterwards. Dinner at home with children.

Mrs Benson

THURSDAY 18 MAY

7.55 Remind son of time (watch left at cottage).
8.45 Eldest daughter speeded since; nightdress to

stitch up; turtles to clean out of sink.

9.15 Two foreign letters require action; organize a party; ask secretary for typescript; prior to editing for Primer make our bed, put away maps of Great Britain, day's laundry, prepare Whit maps.

9.45 Go to shops, laundry, chemist – thread, plant, fish, buns, felt pens, polish. (Takes ages since baby trails and observes other people.)

11.5 Office coffee; plant plant; phone call re tonight; hang out day's laundry; carry food to house top.

11.40 Work finally started.

1.5 Lunch.

1.40 Polish shoes on way down stairs.

3.10 Bought geraniums; then stroked street cart horse; hung out second sheet wash and spun woollens of handwash. Geraniums planted – just in time for Japanese visitor in meeting room.

3.55 Tea in garden with Japanese; next week's party discussed; clothes brought in and toys.

4.55 Telephone re chair designer friend's book.

6.45 Out for appointment (after changing and washing hair).

8.50 Return with pizza.

10.30 Bath; design party invitation.

Eldest daughter

4–9 Tea with youngest daughter; tidy bedroom after youngest daughter; change for brownies; wash out small turtle tank, feed turtles; wash all house hairbrushes; brownies; supper with student; bath with youngest daughter and yack to student.

Son

5–9 Lettraset on boat; varnish (last stage of complete reconstruction of yacht found in bin in Kensington Gardens ready for visit of Norwegian scout); supper and yack with student, bath.

FRIDAY 19 MAY

6.55 Again wakened – jets?

8.48 Remind son of time.

8.50 Breakfast; eldest daughter cleans out sink, wiping turtles.

9.45 Draw out invitation card.

10.50 Invitation for printing; hang out wash; son talks to cat in garden; check letter to Japan.

11.00 Office coffee in (too cold out).

12.00 Change to warmer clothes and put wool socks and cardigan on youngest daughter; pay gardener.

1.00 Bring washing out of rain.

1.45 Read to younges⁺ daughter; both get ready to go to exhibition; put toys away; make two telephone calls: (1) engineers; (2) this evening's arrangements; edited book; coloured party invitation express to Germany (after confirming colour of flag).

6.40 Prepare to go out; pick up Swede; proceed to Indian restaurant.

9.30 Visit St John's Wood.

12.00 Sat in Ebury Street in car.

12.20 Looked at plan for centre of Stockholm and new town in Finland on pavement in Ebury Street.

Marks & Spencers; old postcards of 14/18 war and LNWR; Bacernsfather drawings to add to Old Rio and Sèvres pottery on 1871 Siege of Paris bought in Kensington Church Street yesterday at least six times as expensive as six years ago. High Holborn camping shop – tent pegs and blue bomb; Shaftesbury Avenue/pages for twelve glasses for red box for next Saturday; and food.

1.00 Home via decorations for Chelsea cup play.

1.20 Lunch.

2.10 Three of us colouring invitations (1st expressed to Germany).

3.50 Rain cleared and go out to launch boat; typing; supervising colouring of invitations; telephone re chair designer friend's visit.

4.50 Tea.

5.20 Typing/manuscript and colouring of invitations.

8.45 Late supper.

9.35 Typing manuscript. Bath with book on caravans.

SATURDAY 20 MAY

9.45 All up, straight down Portobello Road Market for weekend food and

SUNDAY 21 MAY

9.55 Son got papers; Olgid here; went swimming;

breakfast and papers.

10.20 Daughters go to friends for Sunday school.

11.20 Typing manuscript; lunch; typing manuscript; eldest daughter's knitting to cast off; final sewing up to supervise.

5.00 Tea – son and youngest daughter only.

5.20 Typing manuscript.

6.00 Son switched TV off to do revision; chicken in; scrape potatoes – put on; son in bath; typing manuscript; jig-saw with son; eldest daughter and husband return; supper; found geranium in borrowed book.

9.20 Typing manuscript; cut eldest daughter's hair; son drying his hair.

MONDAY 22 MAY

8.25 Typing manuscript; son off.

8.45 Breakfast; type manuscript; day's laundry to hang out; other clothes to air, put away, etc.; youngest daughter locked basement door but back door open so that I could get in via garden into the house again;

housekeeper not here; assistant not here; husband got son's birthday 'T-shirt' while out shopping; corrected 'Indian'.

10.50 Make two telephone calls – appointment after Whit; Assistant's been to the airport.

11.10 Office for tea; vegetable order.

11.30 Manuscript; telephone; youngest daughter colouring at table.

1.10 Same table; lunch.

1.55 Box for project; start to read for Whit visit; book revisions being typed; telephone re Studio Vista Contract.

4.10 Tidy eldest daughter's room; housekeeper rings; library; shop for lettuce; telephone re chair designer-friend's visit (second call).

6.45 Supper; son's history revision.

7.40 Daughters bathed; set out Tuesday's work.

10.45 Type manuscript; talk over book manuscript; watch end of Olivier on TV.

TUESDAY 23 MAY

8.45 Unload dish washer; type manuscript; no

housekeeper; look for two lost dresses; put away documents; basement, pick up blocks; find heaps of sweeping to clear; no paint rep; brushed cellar area; office coffee; looked out for project line drawings.

11.45   Lunch; shopping in rain; ICI men; read book for project; Office tea; no to eldest daughter for pictures with another child; eldest daughter to sew and watch TV.

6.15   Supper; youngest daughter bathed.

6.45   Youngest daughter to bed; eldest daughter to read in her room aloud to student; on ground floor making her supper; typing manuscript; break for hot milk for son finished test; washing in from garden.

10.20   Read for Whit trip.

WEDNESDAY 24 MAY

7.00   (approx.) Son up after seven to send off cereal corners for model and eats long breakfast; youngest daughter in our bed.

8.40   Breakfast; type manuscript; air clothes upstairs; iron dolls clothes made for daughter's birthday: office coffee; cut out nightie for eldest daughter's birthday; telephone call re book contract; telephone re friend coming tonight.

1.20   Lunch; out in pouring rain.

2.30   Shop at Boots, and for stockings, blouses, cake for tea and buns for the kids; call eldest daughter's school to see if all is OK; project papers; chair-designer friend arrived late; eldest daughter unpicked doll's dress for washing and putting on new doll, then TV; son doing tests; do nails while awaiting chair-designer friend (having done face earlier); fall-back holiday reservations.

8.10   Dinner.

10.10   Films; New York World Fair; puppets; Smithsonian; music of 50s; deaths of 50s; discussion in car outside; (1) Ritz; (2) House.

THURSDAY 25 MAY

9.10   Breakfast; sew button on; washing linen.

11.10 Clear work table and eat
piece of tart left from
tea with youngest
daughter; telephone re
Saturday; office coffee;
correct side plan;
telephone re chair
designer-friend's films;
lunch; take hem of coat
up; visit project site
with youngest daughter

3.50 who got her feet wet.
Wash hair; make eldest
daughter's broderie
anglaise nightdress
present, and final models
of my clothes as dolls
clothes utilizing cut-off
hems; eldest daughter at
brownies and friend's
house; supper.

In the Bensons' activities within the family, flexibility has been a keynote. The emphasis is placed on different activities as demands change. Within this apparently flexible pattern, although there doesn't seem to be a stereotyped masculine–feminine division of labour, there is no question that there are some things that he alone does, and some things that she alone does. In many cases these coincide with the cultural sex stereotypes (though not for that reason): e.g. she does not have anything to do with handling the family finances or with machines; he does not worry about household cleaning supplies; she tends to worry about what the children are wearing. They see this division of function as having developed naturally rather than having been imposed by cultural norms.

The Bensons see their domestic help situation in relation to the energy consideration, in that without good and reliable help, energy is wasted. Mr Benson says:

I'm sure you're going to find that the whole business of women working is dependent on other responsible women who deal with children.

About domestic help generally, Mr Benson indicates their policy as follows, which relates to the fact that they work at home.

Another aspect of working at home is the whole pattern of employment of the people who look after you. I don't want to have someone whom we have to eat with; and that means there are only two solutions – you either have a proper servant's wing in which they are absolutely separate in the old way ... or you have to accept what other people accept, the kind of nanny who is now a social equal.... That would mean that you would have to spend the whole day with work people of some kind. I'm just not prepared to face this. I feel at least we need the evenings without having to make conversation. To unwind, not talk.

When the Bensons first moved into their house, they rented out the basement flat and their domestic help pattern began through using these people as baby-sitters. They also made use of young architectural students who were around but they tended to want to go to the same professional functions as the Bensons and it had to be asked each time as a favour.

They also had a housekeeper whom they employed for about eight years. She was in many ways their 'ideal' domestic helper as she had what Mr Benson terms 'proper natural housewife's instincts' and did not need much instruction or supervision. Since this woman has left the Bensons have had less satisfactory arrangements and they are thinking of changing their arrangement.

We're going to try to have two household helps because paying a bit extra most of the time might save us when the crunch comes ... but it's very difficult. There just don't seem to be the people who want to do it.

Mr and Mrs Benson prefer student baby-sitters because they can rotate them once a year and be tough with them about rules. They also like the security of a living-in baby-sitter, although Mr Benson would personally prefer not to have anyone living in :

It's terrible to have the emotional insecurity of a person coming in to baby-sit ... these girls or chaps tend to be not blindingly useful, and they have their own students' problems.... But it's more important to feel secure about the children than it is to actually have things done for them.... You can't be thinking clearly if you're at the same time wondering about whether the children are safe. They (the students) are a nuisance part of the time but you don't have to worry about them in another sense.

The two eldest children get themselves up in the morning and ready for school. Mrs Benson helps the younger daughter and then the three of them breakfast together. The routine of events at this time, according to Mrs Benson, as follows :

The older ones get up between ten to eight and eight o'clock. If they aren't getting up, I go in and say 'Well?' ... they then make their breakfast and go off, and it means it's more relaxed. It just suits everybody better. ... A friend calls at about eight and sits on the doormat for some reason until twenty-five past – and then off they go. Then the little girl gets up between that time and quarter to nine, when she really must get up, and we breakfast about that time, instantly, and she goes off at quarter past nine.

The preparation of the children for school is part of, and reflects, the larger patterning of interrelationships in the family, where there is a lack of emphasis on 'servicing' one another but rather an emphasis on individuals looking after themselves; in a way it fits the general ethos. She says : 'I expect them to do things for themselves, encourage it . . .'

At bedtime, the older children are relatively self-sufficient with bathing etc. The baby-sitter is drawn on particularly in this period to take up all kinds of slack – playing with the children, talking to them and doing things with them if necessary between supper time and bedtime. She will actually gauge her activities according to whether the Bensons are there or not, as well as what she as a person likes to do.

As far as school holidays go, Mrs Benson says :

There's no trouble there. They are here or we are somewhere else with them. They always have enough ideas, the spare time they have is never enough. There is never any problem of what to do next.

Mr Benson indicated, though, that the children get directed quite a lot in their activities, and there is a tendency for both of them to take off more time from work during the school holidays to do things with the children.

Daily routine food shopping is done by either Mr or Mrs Benson depending on whoever is going out at the time, or sometimes their secretary will be sent out. This pattern is basically possible because their food preparation is not elaborate and the shops are nearby.

Usually at meals they have a couple of options so that they and the children too can choose what they want. In their meals, they stress simplicity in terms of time for preparation but not in the quality of food, and the emphasis is on on-the-spot preparation.

Mrs Benson usually makes supper but Mr Benson may do so and the children are also good at helping, especially when guests are coming. They say that all architects are like this, due to the conditions they experience during their training. They often work alone for long hours at the drawing boards and people prepare meals when they can. When guests are expected they do plan ahead but they tend to spend more time and effort in how the food will be presented than on the food itself.

Special household purchases are made jointly and this is a very important aspect in their lives. Mr Benson says :

... We make most decisions together because it's very loaded for us, with all the design decisions ... when we were first married it was impossible to get almost anything. Almost everything was horrible, so we did without everything, like Berthold Brecht living in New York with a couple of bricks because that was the only nice thing he could find. We were in that situation but we have now acquired things ... and made things, and now we've lots of objects, but it might take five years to decide to buy anything and then it probably isn't there. If necessary we do without it, or import, or go to the country where the nice works are and bring them back. Those are important strategic decisions to us, they kind of impinge on our whole mode of life ...

These purchases are reacted to and thought about as part of their general creative aesthetic ethos which emphasizes creating the kind of environmental texture that they want.

Cleaning the house is done primarily by the housekeeper. When they don't have help, everyone participates and Mr Benson says :

They (the children) have been taught to treat house-work and meal preparation as perfectly normal. . . . If we don't have anybody, we all share the work out, and boys or girls vacuum stairs and do whatever is needed.

Household maintenance is something that the housekeeper cannot do and Mrs Benson does not like to do, so Mr Benson does the minor repairs (changing fuses, putting up shelves, etc.). Sometimes their son helps and the assistants in the office do bits for 'light relief'.

They divide gardening into two types which they see as traditional – 'women's gardening', planting; and 'men's gardening', cutting the lawn, killing the weeds. Mrs Benson will not mow the lawn because it involves a machine. The car, also being a machine, is something that is entirely in his domain. Mrs Benson does not even like to drive and all she does, in her words, is to 'pass cheques' on her driver's licence. Because she does not have anything to do with the car, she has arranged a pattern of living that does not require her to use it, and she does not mind that this is different from the pattern of their friends. Mrs Benson says:

This I'm very much on my own in. All the professional women I know, maybe bar one or two, drive and often they are two-car families. In some cases the women take over the major part of the driving like Japanese women . . . A lot of women really don't know how I manage without driving. They say 'How do you get around? How do you get everything done?' Partly, I think, having the schools so near and the shops so near . . . they're only 200 yards away. Some people think it is infra dig to be seen carrying heavy weights, or it's tiring, the strain and so on. But with me, to find a parking place in inner London would drive me up the wall. I couldn't bear to have a car and to have to take it up to the city.

Holiday planning is related not only to their children's vacations but also to their clients' demands. Mr Benson says:

We've reasonably successfully managed holiday planning, with the exception of taking things rather seriously. We've been hit in the last two years by government planning – it's been appalling – they've said 'We want you to hit the ground on such and such a day'. We've made a very tight working-drawing programme, and sticking to the targets in this has meant that we really couldn't go away. We then discovered that they haven't the money. They are not ready for it. And we had to make a sacrifice to achieve these targets. But ... in a sense ... it hasn't been worth it. Sometimes we've been let down by other people's malplanning.

Recently they have returned for three consecutive years to the same beach hotel which the children now feel belongs to them, and where they have built up sufficiently trusting relationships with the staff to leave the children while they take side-trips of interest to themselves.

The Bensons do no formal budgeting though they regulate their expenditure informally so to keep things going. They work on a very long time span, accumulating capital and living at a rather high standard as a result of a major project. In between projects they also live at a rather high standard on the assumption that before the capital is depleted it will be replenished. They have not had to worry about this so far nor to cut back on their standard of living.

Mr Benson handles the cash flow almost entirely, giving his wife money for incidental expenses every week. The work–family budgets are completely interpenetrated. Mr Benson says:

I always go to the bank. I give her the money. I take it out of my pocket. There is no separate office account. What is not paid by cheque comes out of petty cash. We have a joint account and from that account the office set-up is included. It is budgeted to give us an income: that is, we have what is left. The normal way profit partnerships work is that they pay themselves a salary, which is part of the overheads, and what it left is then split up, which seems to us to be a rather middle-aged household way. We don't pay ourselves a salary and I try to calculate so that we get more than the assistants do, but over a long period it really means that my wife has no financial independence, which would normally be thought of as the main independence a woman could have within marriage.... All the money we earn is joint ... if we have a tight year we both suffer, whereas if we had different jobs, she might be making £4,000 a year regularly, while my money was going up and down. A wife in that situation would want to use a large hunk of that for clothes and so on and would have to handle it.

The Bensons feel that their own situation is tremendously dependent on good health, which fortunately they and their children enjoy. He says:

I don't think that we're particularly fit or anything but we're never ill in any serious sense. I think that we attach more importance to that one fact for our survival capacity than anything else.

Hard work, willpower and determination are strong elements in the Bensons' cultural backgrounds, but the topic of energy is one that has come into their awareness from their own experience. They continually relate things to energy. A leitmotif in this family is the rational organization and expenditure of physical energy. Aside from their rhythmic pattern of work and leisure and their recognition of the 'energy-run-down' pattern in daily routines, they feel that their great expenditure of energy on work, particularly when project pressures are great, sometimes keeps them from giving the children as much as they would like to, and they have to make special provision for this when possible.

Beneath the superstructure of the Bensons' family and their relationships, both internally and externally, with the work and family worlds is the core husband–wife relationship upon which everything else has been built. To understand their present marital pattern it is important to look at the background and development of this relationship.

The Personal Experience of Family Development and Current Husband–Wife Relationship

Mr and Mrs Benson met when they were both students, at the same school of architecture in the North. He entered before she did and had gone off for a tour of duty in the Services during the Second World War and they met after he returned. They went out together when he was doing post-graduate work on planning at a London architectural school but shuttled between

London and the North where he was a teaching assistant and she a fourth-year student. He indicates that his attraction to her was based on her personal qualities:

... she was really the only interesting girl in the school ... in the same sense that she was different. There is a slight age gap, which was then exaggerated by the fact that I'd been away and she hadn't and therefore she probably seemed young and I probably seemed much older than I was. I had a reputation that I came back to, and she probably would have liked to have met me. She dressed eccentrically, like art students do ... there's usually one in every class ... consciously trying to make themselves different in some way.

However, the 'differentness' was not at the centre of what attracted him to her but rather a sense of devotion to the discipline and to the kinds of values in it which they shared.

... the people who saw the discipline as a discipline stood out a mile and I saw that in her and maybe she saw it in me ... a person who knows what the discipline is, is likely to be more interesting to be with and also is likely to be more interesting for all time.

Mr Benson visited the North during the week of her final exam. Subsequently they were both offered separate jobs in London by one of the final examiners. They took up their posts in September 1949 after having had a honeymoon in Italy. After they were married they spent their evenings working together on competition projects. They won the third competition they entered and both resigned from their jobs and set up an office in their flat.

Mrs Benson says that marriage was always important to her. She 'would have died if she hadn't married'. Not marrying would have meant 'there would have been no success at all'. But Mr Benson seems to have had a different attitude and his decision to marry did not come easily.

I was terrified of being married for all the conventional reasons – being tied down and so on. But in fact some part of you accepts very ruthlessly if you're going to find yourself in a married situation, you're not going to marry someone who's dumb, because you can see a lifetime of boredom ahead of you. So you steer miles away from that sort of person ...

Mrs Benson wanted very much to set up a home and begin a family, but because of housing shortages in the early post-war period they had great difficulty in finding a suitable house and began to work together in a small flat and postponed having a family. The tension created by this situation took a long time to work out. She recalls:

It was a most pressuring experience for me not to get a house. Absolutely everybody I ever knew got a load of wedding presents and a house when they got married – and a bedroom suite and a living-room suite and the lot.

However, Mr Benson was not of the same frame of mind as his wife. His model was Le Corbusier, whose explicit views were that having children interfered with the creative life. After they moved into a house Mrs Benson persuaded him that they should have a baby. She continued working and he found that he enjoyed the pattern of working together at home that had evolved. He says:

... there wasn't a question of domestic help ... the baby couldn't be looked after, and that's how the pattern started in fact. We found that drawing, in a sense, providing that you were prepared to work hard, is very much like writing a novel, and you can do quite a lot of work at home and fit things around each other; that is the pattern that has grown. After three or four years we had domestic help.

Following their first successful building, they became part of an international set of innovative architects and they began to plan their lives in relation to international meetings. They would have liked to have had their second child one or at the most two years after the first, so that the children could be 'better company' for one another, but their plans were postponed for a year because of an important international meeting. Therefore the age gap between their first and second child is three years.

At the time the second child, a daughter, was born, the Bensons entered a major international competition which involved working for about eighteen months. They describe this

as a relatively 'carefree' period : the money from their first
building had paid for their house; they used basement-tenants as
baby-sitters; they could work on the coming competition while
earning small amounts of money through teaching and minor
jobs; and the children were around while the parents worked.

In having the third child, another girl, they had more discussion than with the previous two. He says (to her):

I remember that you felt that there ought to be another child. You
get into some very tender areas with these things.... A lot of these
things with children are like insurance policies against one of them
being killed ... that's a very real feeling but it's not a thing you
can easily talk about.... The baby had an easy ride compared to
the others ... very little pressure has been put on her, and she is
happy ...

When asked about ideal total family size, Mrs Benson indicated that she has always wanted a very large family, no specific
number. He indicated that 'a very large number would be
brain-shattering ... four or five children ... you can hardly
keep tabs on them ... you know, they're racing about when
they're small'. In general the Bensons say that they are not fond
of children *per se*, though they like most of the children of their
friends. The Bensons have developed a sense of 'couple identity'
to a very great degree. They are listed in the telephone directory
under both their names; their secretary answers the telephone
giving both their names and people have an image of them at
work as a couple.

Their conception of marriage is inextricably tied up with their
work. A concern for their work pervades their lives and they
both feel it would be a bore to be married to someone who did
not share this central preoccupation. Also there are a number
of areas in which their individual personalities and value systems
complement each other. Mr Benson finds it easier, for example,
to sustain 'chummy' external relationships than she does and
so he does most of the family–work relationships of this kind.
It seems that she is more impulsive than he and he counters
this by providing the kind of 'doggedness' that seems necessary
to force a project through. He sees her impulsiveness as valuable

in throwing up fresh perspectives and regards it as a female trait. In addition, Mrs Benson has a 'vigilance' which he considers both very feminine and very useful to him professionally and to their situation. He says:

This is the secret, perhaps. I know I will be stopped before I do anything wrong or disastrous. You know, there is this complete surveillance, which covers the whole office ... not letting each other get away with rubbish.

Mr Benson seems to provide technical follow-through for her inspirations and works this through with the others involved. He says:

If she makes a rotten drawing. I manoeuvre it so that her draft gets superseded but it is done in such a way that you don't hurt the other person.

While similar interests can encourage stimulation, it can also make for conflict, and in a situation such as the Bensons, it is obvious that tensions which develop in relation to work affect their husband–wife relationship very much. Consequently they have developed some mechanisms for avoiding or reducing conflicts.

The Bensons recognize the importance of criticism to maintain standards. In the more orthodox architectural practice this is done by colleagues and the situation at work is segregated from the love relationship. However, in their case, the work relationship is the same as the marital relationship and therefore when criticism is necessary they feel that it should be made not as a fundamental attack, but 'with love', constructively, and with help to find the way to better solutions.

When stresses are high within the partnership, due to their pattern of ups and downs in work, there is a tendency to review past decisions and raise doubts about whether they were right. The Bensons are very aware that if this takes the form of blame, it is a hazard, and they see it as something explicitly to be avoided.

Because of the overlap between work and family life in the Bensons' situation, there is frequently a very tense situation when work stresses spill over into the family. They recognize that this causes tempers to be short and have tried to learn to tolerate this expressiveness, even to see it as cathartic.

Because both the Bensons are strong-willed and competent, they recognize that each has sometimes to give way when something is seen as important to the other. This stems from a recognition that there are limits to the degree to which they can complement each other, and there are some instances in which their wishes will not correspond.

Mood swings, ups and downs, high and low pressure periods have become part of their lives, and they have in the past tended to see them as something to be met and dealt with. More recently they have sought ways of cushioning the ups and downs. One of the lessons they have learned, perhaps retrospectively, is to close ranks in the face of external work difficulties rather than taking out the strains on one another. If problems arise with a client, not only is it better for the marital relationship, but usually more valid as well, to recognize that the blame lies somewhere in the complexity of events and decision-processes outside themselves.

It is interesting that the marital relationships of the Bensons' friends are not characterized by a stereotyped division of labour according to sex, and they are very much aware of it. There are wide variations in pattern, according to the situation, and the impression is given that all the families have definite ideas about the kind of life they want to lead and the conditions under which it is best to be led. They all value the creation of an aesthetic environment and the maintenance of joint interest in aesthetic things. While this is highly 'object-oriented', it also includes conversation about these objects, historical perspectives and cultural perspectives – all shared between husband and wife, regardless of whether or not they work together.

Parent–Child Relationships

The Bensons tend to encourage the children to look after themselves within a framework of rules and under Mrs Benson's supervision. They are very interested in their children but do not think that the child-centred family ethos is for them. Mr Benson says that their situation is in some ways comparable with his own parental one. In his case his parents did not have much time to give to him because life was hard for them, now the Bensons find that they are tremendously involved in their work and they do not always have energy to give time to the children. However, Mrs Benson says that she is always thinking at the back of her mind about the children and the organization of their activities.

They have a sense of a 'family culture' and very close involvement with one another, so much so that 'we don't really see each member very distinctly from one another ...' In a general way the children are very 'mixed up in' the lives of their parents 'to an extent that you'd hardly believe'. Mr Benson says:

They are in and out of the office, or in and out of other people's offices. I don't know why but we are either not good at it, or we worry too much about leaving them with strangers, therefore they tend to be just around. Sometimes it's extremely embarrassing ... it's conditioned the kind of work we can accept and the sort of organization we had to build ... you have to accept the work and build the organization in which this behaviour is tolerated.

They see this closeness partly as a matter of enjoying being together and partly in terms of maintaining responsible child care patterns.

The Bensons have tried to keep their children young without spoiling them; they try to preserve their sense of fantasy which they see as a precious attribute of childhood. 'You know, we all still believe in Father Christmas.' Mrs Benson says:

They're emotionally a couple of years (behind others). I mean they're unsophisticated ... no kind of attempt to divorce them from fantasy ... because looking back retrospectively, the pleasures start disintegrating once the fantasies start disintegrating. So that you keep it going as long as possible. So that, though they're practical ... (they are not like) these sharp kids who know everything ...

In keeping with their general emphasis on spontaneity, ordinary family rituals such as reading to the children before bed and meal table rituals are not stressed. They do, however, emphasize cultivation of visual, aesthetic and historical interests into what they consider amounts to an 'object cult'.

Though the children are taught to participate in household activities, practical things are not the main emphasis in what the parents try to teach them. They encourage the children to do things carefully and well. Mr Benson says :

... Doing a good job and not telling lies are really the things we are trying to teach them.

The Bensons seem to do most of their disciplining by emulation. They do not believe in interfering with the children's formal school education but they give them 'a visual education' by taking them around to sites with them, etc.; and they admire things that come close to home, e.g., the joiner who is doing a beautiful job of fixing a panelled playroom in their home.

Mr Benson makes an interesting comparison between children and buildings. He says that children are so much more complex than buildings that although he has the notion of controlling inputs with them, he could never feel the same kind of total responsibility for the outcome of their development as he does to a building. He said that as he grew older there was diminishing pleasure from the building activity *per se* – partly because with larger-scale projects there is a longer time scale between any input and the feed-back from the work.

The length of time of the operation almost removes the sense of achievement ... however, you can get almost instantaneous pleasure from a child.

However, this was truer for smaller children than from the children as they grow older and develop outside interests and a collective life of their own as 'the children'. For all this he indicates that he probably gets more satisfaction from his family now than from his work. He might have had even more enjoyment from the children earlier when they were younger, but at that time he was engaged in his earlier architectural projects which had greater significance for him and this diverted him somewhat from family involvements.

There are some things that they do separately for the children. Mr Benson says (talking about their activities in the country where they have a house):

It's more or less traditionally split. She organizes indoor house games and drawing sessions and all that, and I do the cabins in the trees, chopping the wood and all this sort of thing.

In keeping with the Bensons' outlook on the development of their life patterns as a series of 'happenings', they interfere minimally in setting the children's aspirations. They see this as taking form much later in the educational process. However, Mr Benson thinks that their son 'would be mad not to be an architect, simply because he has had no other thought'. However, he recognizes that the son could have experiences that might change his whole life pattern ... 'You just can't tell.'

The eldest daughter is still at a fantasy level of career aspiration, and they don't discourage it. He says:

She wants to go into a flower shop but that is because she has seen *My Fair Lady*.... This puts the flower shop into a very good light. She thinks all the marvellous things go with it.

The children seem to have a varied attitude towards domestic helps in that they treat each person as an individual according to their behaviour. The family ethos is that the housekeeper's job, just as any other kind of job, merits respect if done well; if not, the same disapproval or disdain would go with it as to any other form of shoddy work.

The Bensons think that the children enjoy the student baby-sitters, have fun with them, and that a rather playful quasi-sibling relationship tends to develop – and everyone enjoys it. Mr and Mrs Benson like to make use of students because they can turn the going-to-bed over to them. The children enjoy this as the students are more relaxed about time, whereas the Bensons may have an appointment or work to get back to. With the babysitters they can 'rush about, bang, make a noise', and so on.

Mrs Benson feels that all small children have a stage in which they are anxious about what is happening and who is around them, and that night time brings on this anxiety. Given this belief, she says that she always has

an enormous conscience about leaving them. I will only go out if it is work as well as social. . . . When we all go out, we all leave two or three messages.

One effect of this anxiety is that the Bensons rarely go to the theatre or cinema, as 'that is not necessary'. Similarly when it is necessary to go away to a conference without the children, she feels that she must 'work all the time'. Mrs Benson feels she could not go on holiday without the children.

External Relationships

Outside their family, Mr and Mrs Benson do not have extensive kin relationships because both of them are only-children, and there are no siblings or siblings' families.

While Mr Benson feels rather close to his parents and also feels a sense of gratitude for the early sacrifices and help they gave him, there does not seem to be very much current contact : his parents have not shown much interest in their work and have not seen any of their buildings. They are now very old and still live in the house in the north in which he grew up. Other relatives – whom he rarely sees nowadays – are more rural and many who were important to him in childhood have now died. A girl cousin lived in his parents' household when he was between the ages of five and fourteen and though he still has contact with her, they do not see her often.

Mrs Benson's parents now live in the south and her mother is still very active. They show a great deal of interest and pride in the work the Bensons do. Her parents are available for help in an emergency, and will look after the children either in their own flat or at the Bensons' house; and 'if the weather is nice, they (her mother and father) come up here because they quite like it here . . .'

Apart fom these kin relationships, the Bensons' friends tend to be involved in architecture or associated professions; many are from other countries, although there are a few neighbourhood and service people in their social network. There is little persistence in their lives of earlier friendships. Mr Benson had been particularly friendly with a boy in grammar school whom he has seen every few years. Mrs Benson has not retained contact with earlier friends and she has lost contact now almost completely with all but one fellow student from architectural college.

Neither seems to have sustained previous serious cross-sex relationships. Since marriage they have tended to develop new relationships on a couple basis. Most of their friends have older children, and are a very important reference group for them. The Bensons relate much of their style of life to this group rather than to people of other occupations and other generations. They are interested in their assistants, not only as 'personal' disciples but as a way of keeping in touch with trends in life style among the younger architects.

Mr Benson says of their friends:

They are either architects or art historians or structural engineers – it's very professional. I suppose in any job ... friendships seem to be based on work.

Within their general friendship professional group, there seems to be a smaller group of devotees particularly orientated to them. She says:

... there was a cult at one time of people who called their kids after us and then it moved on. ... There's a German architect who called his kids after ours. ... The children fit into our international set to a certain extent.

The children are also friends of the children of their families and visiting, including international conferences, takes place with children as whole families.

On the other hand, while they feel part of an international colleague community, they feel that they have been discriminated against as a couple by some senior local colleagues, especially early in their career. Mrs Benson expresses the situation as follows :

Usually we have to put a face on it – both go to committees. In the normal partnership only one person goes but somehow we are both expected to appear. Yet there is a terrific resistance to the pair of us. I think if my husband had been on his own, he would certainly have got jobs passed to him. For some reason, they don't pass it to a couple ...

This general feeling of being discriminated against still seems to exist, despite their having achieved considerable recognition. In addition, the Bensons now feel under attack by and critical of many of the younger architects, who regard them as establishment.

The Bensons' participation in professional associations is complex and can best be understood in two sections – one related to the British scene and the other to the international scene. As indicated above, their major focus of involvement is international, to which they have contributed what is seen by colleagues abroad as a specifically British approach.

The Bensons left the RIBA '... because it had died on you, and somehow at some moment you discover that you had no relationship to it, and it seemed a dead thing. Therefore the logical thing was just to leave.' They think that many others would do the same if they could.

WORK WORLDS

The Bensons, working as a team, have chosen a type of architectural practice that takes on only projects that fit into a set of ideals which relate to major social and aesthetic considerations permeating their personal and professional values.

They prefer working in small face-to-face groups, six-eight people, with whom they feel a common sense of purpose. The assistants and secretary who form the central working core with the Bensons identify personally with them and are the kind of people who are able to be turned to academic-type pursuits between high-pressure building jobs.

The office is organized as follows: the house has five floors, the top three of which are primarily 'home' and the bottom two primarily 'office', though there are some overlaps physically as well as in function. The Bensons themselves do much of their own discussion and draughting work on their own floor, descending into the lower two floors where their assistants and secretary work to issue instructions, give guidance and so on.

Ordinarily there are about three assistants ranging from recent architectural graduates acquiring first-job experience for a year or two, to someone with more specialized experience taken on for specific project requirements. While either Mr or Mrs Benson may relate to any of the assistants over specific tasks and may issue instructions to them on behalf of the partnership, there is a tendency for Mr Benson to be the one mainly felt to be 'in command' of the office. Mrs Benson's contributions are directed more into the collaboration with him in formulating plans and strategies. He feels her special contribution to be in her critical and imaginative capacities. He says:

... women are more radical and inventive and creatively truthful because they chuck out things which men would be terrified to ...

Financially the Bensons are accountable only to themselves. They run their home and office all on one budget, drawing from income or capital for expenses and retaining the surplus as profit.

Their income fluctuates considerably. They accumulate capital when they have jobs on hand and eat into it between jobs. Over the years, they say that their average income has probably been about that of 'a G.P. on the low end of the scale'.

It is difficult to talk directly about perquisites in this work situation, as the Bensons' principal yields come from the way they themselves organize their work. Their pattern of expenditure on personal things is so tied with their pattern of running their professional practice and life associated with it that they must include, in their annual accounting to their accountant, a full listing of household as well as office expenditures before the two can be appropriately sorted out. The principal perquisite that seems to accrue from this situation is a flexibility in the handling of things so that the domestic situation and the work situation do not conflict too much.

The current general philosophy, goals and values of the partnership centre on ideals of creative innovation in architecture. They seek opportunity to review prevailing conceptions of architecture, which they regard as rather rigid and formalistic, in terms of bringing about a better functional relationship between buildings and the cultural patterns of behaviour and values of the society in which they exist. They consider the role of architects to be important in providing a creative nucleus of thinkers who combine aesthetic, technological and sociological considerations, and bring them to bear on major construction efforts. They think and act on an international level, and feel frustrated not only by the conventions of local architecture thought and work, but also by the difficulties of actually winning building contracts.

The Bensons relate to specialist colleagues of a wide range as necessary for the work involved in their projects, and relate to a wide range of professional colleagues, local and international, who participate in events of professional interest and visit them. They also sustain a network of friendship relations with people in allied fields which concentrates on the more intellectual and philosophical aspects of their work. In addition, they belong to an international study group which meets in the country of one or another of its members where they discuss developing philosophies, projected plans and aspirations. While the wives of all the study group's members are in related fields and are actively involved in their work, it is only Mrs Benson who is a full female member of the group. Indeed, Mr Benson describes her participation in terms of her vigilance :

... it tends to fall apart if she relaxes ... this has created something of a matriarchal situation ...

Within their practice, the Bensons function as equal partners, each recognizing the distinctive contribution of the other and both feeling that they have evolved in the specific partnership a 'creative framework'. Descriptions of their work which have appeared in the press or in architectural write-ups indicate that there is no point in trying to separate out the contributions of each. There are divisions of labour that have emerged but at the most important level of design strategy they function by attempting to maintain a free give and take of ideas and by acceptance of constructive criticism from each other.

While the division of labour is partly dictated by 'what bit has to be done', the Bensons recognize differences in talent between them which have evolved over the years. Thus division of the work is, whenever possible, allocated along these lines. When describing the nature of their team collaboration they mention differences in their areas of specialized competence. To some extent these are along general talent lines. Mr Benson sees some of their differences as sex-linked traits :

... Both of us can't do certain things and it happens quite naturally. ... It's no good asking me about planting – there's a big band where we know that we're not even trying to learn – e.g., I handle most of the plumbing and structural hardware and she can do things that I can't do – like thinking in colour continuously, which is very rare and she tends therefore to deal with tasks of designing interiors. ... You're getting a lot of basic male and female things; I am fairly abstract but some of the assistants are even more so and you get a very rarefied male thinking. It's all broken down into mathematical terms. I've never met a woman who can think like that. Even a woman engineer tends to be a non-theoretical engineer ...

To some extent their differences of involvement relate to their personal developmental pattern. Recently Mrs Benson has become much more active in relation to the external world and she feels that this is not merely a result of her children all being in school but relates to her increased capacity to deal with people in the profession.

It is important in understanding how their partnership works to recognize their own view of it, namely, that it just 'hap-

pened' – evolved as the result of piecemeal decisions and circumstances. They are very much aware that their working
relationship has not been directed by convention. The winning
of the competition which the Bensons entered jointly and the
subsequent building catapulted them into a set of attitudes and
relationships that gave their joint career its special character.

For the five years after their first job they worked on con-
solidating their expertise and lived mainly on capital – actually
'putting money into architecture'. Mr Benson says about the
way they organized their work:

... there has been a huge gap in our thinking between the strategic
and the tactical ... all the logistic is missing, you know, all those
staff officers ... (we are) all generals and corporals ...

At this time the Bensons established their pattern of working
on only one project at a time, totally committing themselves
to it and expanding or contracting their staff to meet immediate
requirements. Because they found themselves in the project style
of life, and also because they were what she calls 'save paper
minded', they evolved a way of working at home that has persisted. In setting up this pattern, the obvious personal convenience elements have been supported by a rather elaborate and
detailed set of rationales that allows them to continue their
creative development. They feel that two of the more prominent
patterns that exist in many practices do not suit them: the
entrepreneurial one, where individuals borrow or accumulate
capital and set up an office that can assure enough work-flow
to cover ongoing commitments, doing creative work on the side
or on top of it; or the bureaucratic one where an organization
is created by a private firm or a government department, put in
charge of a manager who hires creative architects as employees.
They feel that the first pattern ties one down to commitments
for cash flow that may over-ride creativity, and the second
pattern may stifle creativity in the employed architect through
a feeling of being 'run by' the more political-managerial types.

While neither of these modes is congenial to the Bensons they
recognize that for many types of projects on the scale to which

they aspire, one needs both larger-scale organization than the small domestic-based unit and more political-managerial skills than they personally possess. Their solution has been to work towards larger-scale projects gradually, accumulating the skills they lack and learning to use extended forms of organization as required without becoming tied to them permanently. In doing this, by keeping overheads very low, working on plans and projects personally with a minimum of delegation, and concentrating all of their resources on the next project, they have created an unevenness of the work loads in their office. When a job is 'on' they are totally involved in it; when a plan is pending, as in a competition, they are in total suspense; when a job is 'off', there is a void. Fluctuations in work flow have been endemic in their situation and, having chosen this pattern, a major task for them has been the management of these ups and downs in their work.

By keeping our overheads low we are able to survive a slack period such as the last eighteen months. We can pay the assistants' salaries but not giant overheads. . . . This last year we've turned the heat on to old documents and my wife published a novel which she'd been working on for about ten years . . . but you need the energy to finish it, get a publisher, sit on his chest for three months while he argues you can't do this when you've got to work on buildings because to get them successfully out you've got to keep bashing . . . things like that (the novel) drift because the buildings are central.

The non-project periods, or 'dead-spots' as Mrs Benson calls them, have been used for the productive, non-remunerative side involvements that interest them as very active and imaginative people. Mrs Benson turns to creative writing and Mr Benson writes academic and intellectual papers expounding the philosophy underlying their professional position.

In the conceptualization and production of actual architectural plans, it seems that there are several important processes. To arrive at a plan of what they are trying to do and how to do it, the Bensons exchange ideas freely between themselves (and with their close friends and colleagues) and emerge with a product. At some point, the ideas seem to them to 'take on a life of their own' and various things must be done to follow through the implications of each conception. Each of the Bensons plays the role of constructive critic *vis à vis* the other.

In the past the Bensons' work has followed an uneven pattern. Because of their chosen style of concentrating on one major project at a time, and not taking on projects that they do not feel to be important in the social-aesthetic sense, there have inevitably been periods in which a major project was completed with no suitable new one in hand. In the past they saw this partly as a matter of maintaining standards in the sort of work to which they would be willing to commit themselves totally, and partly a matter of ethical management of clients : they did not want to undertake discussions with more than one client, knowing that they would want to consummate only one project.

However, having accomplished several substantial building achievements the Bensons have come to feel not only more secure financially but also more at ease in the management of client relationships. Because of this sense of security the Bensons are willing to entertain a number of possible prospective projects rather than as in the past only one, without feeling that they would be letting someone down if they were only able to consummate one.

For Mrs Benson specifically, this recent stage of development has signalled a personal relaxation of tension that has allowed her to be more active in relation to their professional environment. Mr Benson discusses it as follows :

... our work pattern is changing ... I think that she has been getting more aggressive ... we have been facing the possibility of a big job overseas and it is one of these jump-points ... I thought she was quite bold in her whole attitude towards it, setting out the conditions under which we were prepared to accept it or not accept it ... there is this new confidence in not really caring if the situation doesn't work out ...

The Bensons seem to maintain a very complex position with regard to the architectural profession in Britain. They are well known for British and international architectural developments and they stand for a very special kind of work which, while it is creative, is not harmonious with the mainstream of British architecture. As a result it seems that they do not sustain general relationships with the profession in Britain, although they do work with colleagues on specific projects or interests.

Recently however the Bensons have found a new feeling of professional acceptance which was lacking earlier in their external relations.

It's so nice now that one is getting one's age group as an active age group ... this business of sitting around the table and trying to get a communal building knowing that you're all of an age group and it's so easy to talk, you are all on the same accepted basis. ... Also, when you go around meeting people looking for a site, people are falling over themselves to help because you are suddenly greyhaired and they are willing to trust you. This is the age group that they want to work with ... you are neither too old nor too young; you are just right. ... When you're forty, the road slopes away and it's easier from then on ...

This feeling of acceptance and security is experienced by the Bensons with a certain amount of ambivalence. While they enjoy the sense of colleague acceptance, they feel also that to make themselves part of a group practice that is too communal in nature would be contrary to the creative framework within which they have developed their distinctive partnership. Mr Benson says:

Probably the younger people would find group operations ... more acceptable than we do but one regards that as very personal insofar as ... we have rationalized our position *vis à vis* society; many of the wellsprings of our energy come from feeling outside, being an outsider. As soon as you are in a collective structure you are an insider ... therefore it wouldn't work for us I don't think, but it's so personal ...

The Bensons in relation to their career perspectives, seem to have a life plan which involves a sequence of projects, each more important in some ways than its predecessor.

At the back of both our minds is the fact that we are consciously working towards a bigger project; that is, training ourselves to do something that is probably either forty or fifty acres of some city or part of a new town, which is a very big technical deal. It requires setting up a big team to do it; this can't be done in the way we now work, one would have to have a separate project office to run it in. How exactly we would handle that I can't tell you, because one regards the work we now have – if we get through that successfully, we will know certain techniques, mostly of handling people, how to work with the forces through which buildings come into being . . .

Along with the greater sophistication and know-how that goes with maturity and experience, the Bensons know that if they want to work on larger projects they will need help and consultation; the changes in architectural technology make them more dependent on specialists. Their capacity, as a home-based family firm, to handle projects of the magnitude of their aspirations is limited increasingly. Mr Benson sees this as manageable, however, and says:

. . . I think one gets more skilful in handling the outside world. That's how one's techniques develop as one gets older. You get less skilful at the technology of the thing, that it, we positively need a large collection of consultants who are outside our office . . . acoustic people and all these things . . . but we also need assistants who are good at handling the basic materials as architects.

The Bensons have given considerable thought to the nature of partnerships generally, in the performing arts, in business and in the professions. They tend to view some of the processes that characterize their work relationship as endemic to partnerships. They consider that the stability of working partnerships, in spite of the difficulties that may emerge between the individuals concerned, is due to the fact that it is more difficult to give up a working relationship, however bad, to face the uncertainties of something else. Mr Benson says:

I think that all good working partnerships are like marriages. It's the only way you can explain the relationships. Something works between (them) and on the whole they've decided . . . that though there are rows and frictions, it's still better than they can imagine in other frameworks.

Like marriages, not all partnerships run smoothly. One of the hazards of a couple relationship where both persons are in the same profession is competitiveness; however the Bensons feel that the fact that they are husband and wife eases the normal strains of a partnership:

... (competition in the partnership) is avoided by being of different sexes. We are less jealous of each other because it is a man and a woman. I think that we avoid professional jealousies because we do have a partnership here that an ordinary one-sex partnership lacks.

In their case, they feel that the fact of their being of different sexes provides part of the advantage, but another part is provided by the fact that they are married, making for a double structural bond holding together their involvement with one another. This means that it is doubly difficult to break up the relationship if one were so inclined in times of stress and difficulty.

One often thinks that it is all falling apart. We have periods when neither of us seems to work well together, and then suddenly it will all come back again. This is where the organization carries you a bit ... working not only with each other but through other people ...

The Bensons' conception of themselves is that of a particular kind of architect which has many facets. They consider themselves to be on the artistic end of the architectural continuum and they see their work as closely akin to artistic creations. Because of this they want to remain in personal touch with each piece of work.

They think of their work not only as intellectual, searching continuously for the ways in which their buildings could express the 'ethos' of their times, but also of themselves as innovative leaders helping to determine trends and public opinion, often against opposition from various members of the establishment. However, in their more recent work and interaction with professional colleagues, they have been reassessing this position. Now that they are accepted and in some sense 'establishment' themselves they have had to take a somewhat different orientation to themselves as innovators, stressing more enduring values. They have come to see modification of one's position not as erosion of values (which would follow from their earlier conception that purity was associated with self-abnegation and conflict with the established positions) but as a state arrived at through maturation and experience.

They do not see their life as simple : risking financial insecurity by holding out only for special projects; continuously struggling with others rather than accepting the prevailing view of professionals or the view held by their clients; and setting up a form of partnership and mode of functioning that arouses resistances. They attribute this complex way of solving problems to a regional physical type belonging to 'Northerners'. Mrs Benson says :

We're both Northerners and I think that Northerners and Scottish people have this fanatical sticking at something, and taking such a rough course for themselves. You read about these people (e.g. Scotsmen in India, or the Industrial Revolution) and you wonder why they make it so tough for themselves rather than just going on and working out quietly the simple, rational, non-strain way out of it.

This awareness of how tough their chosen way is and how much of a strain it is 'having to switch your brain on to inventing another task' is Mrs Benson's principal argument against Mr Benson's feeling that their way of life may be self-indulgent. He says :

It's probably purely self-indulgent – you know, doing it this way which is the way we like doing our work.

She counteracts this tendency in his thinking by reminding him that the course they have chosen requires concentration, stress, 'putting ourselves in a vulnerable position'. She thinks that it is like George Stephenson – 'knocking himself out to make the railways because he wanted to do that and could only be happy doing so, though it meant working extremely hard'.

It seems that the Bensons are recreating in the present pattern of life several of the positive elements in their earlier lives. In their present work–family situation they have created the kind of folklike environment that he sees as positive in his father's family background. He liked being home with his mother in his early life, and the sense of discipline, but at the same time he did not like the tight supervision. Mrs Benson provides a sense of discipline (in a somewhat different sense) but at the same time she is casual about household regimens. They are casual towards the bourgeois elements in many professionals' domestic values, but in a sense their casualness is more apparent than real because they place a very high value on tidyness and good organization.

While they are creating a cohesive environment for them-selves, they are also creating a situation of considerable tension which also repeats elements which were present in their back-grounds. Mr Benson mentions the religious ethos and the economic uncertainties at the time; Mrs Benson mentions the temperamental clash between her own aggressive tendencies and her parents who were more restrained and the feeling of being at odds with the whole outside environment. He felt quite normal while he was being brought up and he seems to have been a late developer; he realized only during and after the war that he had any special gifts or powers. However, she felt dif-ferent. One of the springs of her creativity may have come from a sense of rebelliousness in relation to her early environment.

The work sub-identity of this couple is central in their lives. They not only work in their home but they are able to hire individuals who accept their way of organizing the work to take children's rhythms into account and help with them.

Mr Benson says:

I think that one of the advantages of working at home is the flexibility. After eight o'clock things begin to quieten down and if there's a piece of work you need to do with peace and quiet, it can be done. . . . Most men in the office lead an equally fragmented and broken up life as the wife in the kitchen with the kids all around them . . . there are so many people coming in and going

out and by the time you have had lunch and coffee and all the
ritual aspects of it, there's half a day gone and nothing's achieved
... but I reckon that in fact when we have it well controlled we
only get about six interruptions in a morning...

Their tri-weekly trips to the country are considered therapeutic both for them in relation to work pressures and for
the children's health. Aside from routine retreats, like their
country cottage, the Bensons are able to arrange participation
in conferences and site visits in such a way that the children
can often come along with them.

We have a choice of when we go for a site visit, and if we want
to take the children, we bend the programme to fit into the school
holidays.

When they go to a conference on the Continent, for example,
they take the children along:

When we go to conferences in Europe we generally take them
because we're all with friends, and we find someone to deal with
them during the daytime.

Because their whole work–family situation is seen as one
life space, they tend not to see divergent demands as conflicts,
and they have been able to plan for work far enough ahead to be
able to work in family events harmoniously, thus avoiding many
work–family conflicts as well.

Although they did not begin their partnership with a firm
idea that it would be permanent, the alternatives to not working
together have never been very appealing. He is clearer about
having chosen their current pattern as against the other options
open to him, but he seems to feel that the current one is a
meaningful creative framework. They do recognize that some
women, e.g. in public relations or advertising, may earn £3,000
to £4,000 per annum, but he jokes about this by saying that
'she couldn't earn a penny outside of this family'. On the other
hand, for this couple the idea of her not working is virtually
inconceivable. Mrs Benson's working not only gives her a more
interesting and satisfying life, and him a more interesting partner, but they feel that the children benefit through the informal

'education' they get by participating with their parents on visual excursions into the environment.

INTEGRATION OF PERSONAL, FAMILY AND WORK WORLDS

In this family there is the greatest overlap of personal, family and work worlds in the study series.

The Bensons joined their work worlds in a partnership. The fact of a partnership in itself makes for certain characteristics in work – of close working together, mutual interdependence and trust. In this particular partnership there is a strong element of complementarity in work style within which their common goals are pursued. In addition, their emphasis on the creative productivity of their work partnership is something that gives it still further solidarity. Once such a creative combination evolves, it takes a definite action to make the parties to it want to break it off.

The fact that the Bensons also have a marital partnership reinforces it still further, they feel. The reason they give for this is that unlike some partnerships, even creative, productive ones, the success of one partner is less likely to arouse in the other feelings of envy and loss. To the extent that the pair have strong 'couple' sense, they are able to feel that benefit accruing to a part helps the whole.

These elements of interpenetration provide a highly overlapping form of integration among the Bensons' personal, family and work worlds. In addition they have chosen a physical arrangement which enhances the interpenetration still further – namely, their office and home in the same building and they use many elements of space, personnel and other resources in common to all of these systems.

The key to how well this form of integration works seems to lie in how two issues are handled – the issue of compartmentalization and the issue of flexibility through the life cycle. Unless there is a degree of compartmentalization introduced at certain points, there is a danger that disruptive events in one system will have too great an effect on the other systems. An example mentioned by the Bensons is that they have learned through the years not to take too immediately and uncritically into their personal and family worlds the blame for difficulties encountered in the work worlds. Similar points could be made about the diffusion of untoward influences from personal or family worlds into the work situation. Flexibility is important in another way. While it is imperative at some stages to have stable functioning, it is equally imperative when there is a transition from one stage to the next in any of the component life cycles – personal, family or work – that there be sufficient flexibility in the other systems to accommodate the change, otherwise the whole interpenetrating structure is endangered. An example is when Mrs Benson felt that she did not wish to attend certain international meetings. This reflected a personal shift in value and emphasis associated with her own development. Had the work partnership not been flexible enough to accommodate this, tensions might have mounted precipitously at this point thereby endangering the work. On the work level, specific goals also alter in different phases in the developmental cycle of the enterprise. Thus, the example given is their readiness now to take on large-scale projects which will not be able to be handled in the cottage-industry style. Once again, the high interpenetration of the systems makes it imperative that this requirement of the work situation be flexibly met in personal and family situations. In the Bensons' case, they have only allowed the work development to reach this stage in its cycle when personal and family cycles were ready to accommodate it.

A highly interpenetrated form of integration such as that observed in this situation potentially provides very great advantages for flexibility because the same people control to some extent all the systems. On the other hand it may provide hazards or rigidities if there is insufficient flexibility in any one of the systems to meet the requirements of the other systems, each of which changes to some extent autonomously in response to forces outside the areas of overlap.

BACKGROUND — DEVELOPMENT OF THEIR FAMILY STRUCTURE

Catalogue of Events

Met: 1931 when he was 17 and she 11. Their brothers were college friends.

Going together: On and off for 15 years during which time she was away in the U.S.A. and he married briefly during the war years before her return.

Married: 1946.

Children: One boy, born 1953.

Establishment of a home and residential history: Lived in a central London flat while he worked with colleagues to establish a group architectural practice. They were offered a flat in her parents' house and lived there until they built their own house in 1950.

Domestic help: Early infant care was assisted by nannies. For the first 2½ years there were two very satisfactory continental women, with a succession of au pairs and dailies later. To assure stability of help, and coverage during school holidays, the Jarrets have constructed a self-contained flat adjacent to their house, in which domestic help is accommodated.

Major events in child-rearing: Son went to nursery school then a day school. He went to a boarding pre. school when he was 8, and following that to a progressive boarding school where he was a student at the time of the interviews.

Major illnesses: Mrs Jarret was seriously ill the year preceding the interviews. Mr Jarret underwent surgery a few years ago. In both instances there was an increase in strain and overload, but domestic management patterns were maintained. Their son experienced some early difficulties which have since dissipated.

Major family separations: The son is at boarding school, but spends holidays at home at which times programmes are arranged around his interests.

THE JARRETS

Mrs Jarret is a senior television drama director. Her husband is a partner in an architectural firm. Their only son is a teenage student in a progressive boarding school. The Jarrets live in a small purpose-built house in a suburb of London, with rural surroundings and garden. They have built as a self-contained attachment to their house a cottage for domestic help. The impression that they give as a family is one emphasizing the individual integrity of each member and the privacy of the family unit.

Both the Jarrets are slim and youthful looking in relation to their ages – Mrs Jarret in the late forties and Mr Jarret in the early fifties. Both are attractive, highly articulate and cultivated people. Temperamentally they present a picture of considerable contrast, with the son showing a blend of the two.

Mrs Jarret describes herself as having had good fortune all her life, having been sheltered, economically comfortable and occupationally lucky. She says that she is by personality a 'temperamental' individual, who is rather volatile in expressing her feelings.

Mr Jarret, in contrast, is described by his wife as relatively restrained and quiet. She talks about him as a terribly nice person who has virtues of patience and understanding aside from his considerable gifts and creative ability. Mr Jarret indicates that he has tended to be rather shy and retiring. However, it is clear from the entire pattern of his life – both at home and at work – that he is a person with a strong and positive personality. It is accepted between them that he is unequivocally the dominant partner in the marriage, and in his professional work his qualities of purpose and leadership are very marked indeed. He says that he is the kind of person who thinks and acts rather more slowly and deliberately than his wife, whom he feels to be someone who thinks rapidly and goes quickly from one thing to another. He tends to take a long-term view and to mull things over before taking any action, whereas she is more likely to react immediately to things and then try to put them into the larger picture afterwards. Though patient and not easily roused, Mr Jarret has very strong feelings about things that are held to be important and he says that when he is disturbed he has a very strong temper.

The Jarrets' son is described by his father as an individualist. From the time he was an infant he has had a very determined sort of personality 'when he sets himself a goal which he wishes to attain'. However, this is tempered by the fact that he is, as his father says, a 'realistic character'. His mother indicates that he has a 'sweet and generous' side, like his father, but is also somewhat 'temperamental' and 'alive to atmospheres and emotions'. Like both parents, he has a strong temper.

The Jarrets have known one another since childhood; this fact is an important element in their relationship which has passed through a number of phases and withstood numerous strains. The depth of their knowledge of one another provides a basis for security in a world that has provided many changes for each.

The fundamental element that seems to characterize the orientation of each towards his work and life generally is a rather uncompromising set of aesthetic standards. The value of creativity is a paramount one for both, and each respects the other's total absorption in work that has an important creative element in it. For Mr Jarret the creative element is sometimes obscured by the burdens of operating a large scale private architectural practice, and he seeks respite in his hobbies. For him the aesthetic side of his work, important as it is, must be viable not only as an enterprise but also socially significant and useful.

For Mrs Jarret, the aesthetic side of her work is less burdened with the tribulations of ultimate financial responsibility, as she is a salaried employee.

When they decided to have a child, Mrs Jarret gave up whatever aspirations she may have had for a more individualistic and creative type of career in drama – e.g. in films, or the theatre – in favour of this sufficiently creative and more stable type of career. She is able to enjoy the sense of participation in an exciting and socially significant form of creative venture through her husband's work, to some extent as a more conventional wife does, while at the same time having her own somewhat less enduring but still rewarding form of creativity.

In interviews, discussions tended to centre on one or the other of the Jarrets as individuals. Despite their appearance of couple solidarity, they seem highly individual. Mrs Jarret never felt that chance factors might have determined whether or not she would continue to work when she had a child. Working was as much a part of her personal identity as eating or sleeping, and marriage to a man who would find this antithetical would be unthinkable. For Mr Jarret the idea of his interfering with this wish was alien as well, not only because his conception of his wife included that element of her personality and behaviour pattern but because, he says :

The idea of 'letting' (a word used by the interviewer) your wife go out to work infers an attitude of mind which would be foreign to the kind of world I live in.

On the other hand, he does not take a particularly active interest in domestic life, other than in the conventional masculine areas of building, maintenance, etc.

Mr Jarret is characterized by his wife as a person who has always had 'an extremely clear idea of what is important in the world and where he is going and why'. He sees himself as someone who, having been shy in his youth, felt a misfit in the spartan atmosphere of a conventional boarding school. It took him many years of professional practice and considerable professional recognition to develop a firm sense of self-confidence.

The Jarrets come from somewhat different backgrounds –

his family being of upper-middle-class British stock; whereas Mrs Jarret's family was an American one, although living in England. The inevitable differences seem to play little or no part in their current lives. The things that do grip them seem to re-volve around three major themes – social idealism, aesthetics, and the enhancement of each individual member of the family.

Each of the Jarrets holds very strongly to the view that the meaning of marriage is in the mutual enhancement that each person in the couple can provide for the other. This entails the recognition, in their case, of the importance of the work and its intrinsic rewards for each of them. The emphasis on individual enhancement is, however, within bounds of a rather strong couple-conception – it is not totally individualistic, nor is it familistic in the sense of being child-centred. The parental couple exist primarily for themselves and to enhance one another, rather than for the purpose of launching a new genera-tion. The new generation, once it was decided upon – and this family is interesting partly in terms of the limitations they place on the size of their desired family – was something to be handled as well as possible for the enhancement of that individual, while at the same time preserving the individuality of each member of the family.

The Jarrets have built themselves a very personal house. They designed it together to incorporate their ideas of how a pro-fessional couple can function with a child, without submerging the interests and tastes of the adults. The presence and stability of the adjunct family who provide domestic service has been important to the management of the household, particularly in relation to the Jarrets' son, who at the time of the interviews was in his mid teens and away at boarding school, but home intermittently for visits and holidays.

The Jarrets' home and its management incorporates many of the labour-saving devices associated with the modern dual-career family – underfloor heating, open plan of main rooms, some use of man-made fibres for clothing and sheets, etc.

When the Jarrets met, their friendship flourished partly on the basis of a shared interest in the theatre. Each also felt a very strong sense of complementarity between themselves as persons. He values her expressiveness while she values his gentleness. They share adult interests and do not enjoy, as do some of the couples, entering the world of children. When they had a child, they shared the difficulty surrounding the absorption of a child into their lives. Both have been distressed at some of the problems their child experienced when younger because of this, but feel more sanguine about their relationship with him now that he is a teenager to whom they can relate more on their own terms.

The absorption of an infant into this very sophisticated and individually self-sufficient family atmosphere was not an easy process for any of the parties concerned, but what seems to have emerged in the family is a trio of individualists among whom there are various complementarities.

PERSONAL WORLDS

Mrs Jarret's Personal Background

Mrs Jarret is a highly cultivated person. She has had a privileged educational background and has enjoyed a whole range of activities and interests associated with privileged status in society. She recognizes that this background and situation has both advantages and hazards. The advantages are more apparent, in the good luck she feels that she has enjoyed throughout her life. On the other hand, inner pangs of unhappiness seem sometimes to be associated with the fact that she has been protected from the really rough and evil aspects of the world. Because she has felt that there is so little that she personally could do about these things, she has tended to pursue her own interests in the best way possible and to count her blessings:

I have been very lucky in this horrible world with my friends and my husband. I have missed all wars. There was no war for me in the States: a little shortage of coffee and a little shortage of gas, but that was nothing. I have always been in work except for five weeks in my life. One appreciates that. But one has seen such a horrible amount of suffering, one feels that one should always be doing something about it, but I find that I don't, I think about it but I don't do anything because I don't really know what to do. It isn't so often that a thing is clear enough actually to go out and do a specific thing about it.... I don't think I am a person who will go out and carry a banner.

Thus, while Mrs Jarret's idealism does not take the form of tangible products or good works in the social sense, she is very much aware of the importance of this dimension of life and appreciates her husband's effectiveness in this way as representing them as a couple. Her own pursuit of her interests is then able to centre on the more creative and aesthetic aspects of living. However Mrs Jarret's standards are very high, and her annoyance is very marked at anyone's attempt to pass off a piece of work or rise to a given position on grounds other than competence and merit. She wants the same standards applied to herself :

I want my work to stand for what it is and to be employed for my work not for who I am.

The emphasis given by Mrs Jarret to standing on her own feet and being evaluated in terms of her own performance seems to stem from a number of elements in her personal and family background. She was the youngest of three children in a socially active professional family. She was separated from the others by a gap of several years, experiencing her early life as a 'lonely-only' child, with parents at some remove and an intervening pair of siblings who were quasi-parents who had separate pre-occupations and activities. Also, being in the care of a nanny gave her a life that was somewhat on her own, though not in the extreme sense that she was socially or interpersonally deprived. Her nanny left to get married when she went to school, at six years of age, and after that she was very much alone.

The greatest regret of my childhood was being shut up in the nursery while there was fun going on downstairs. I remember hanging over the bannister and listening to them talking and laughing. My parents were either giving dinner parties or they were out.

I was alone in the daytime. I was put out into the garden. It was quite rigid. They would say, 'You've got to go out for two hours,' and I was not allowed to come in. I used to go and talk to the gardener.

As she grew up she felt that she would like to discuss her own ideas about life with her parents, but she came to the conclusion that open discussion was not really possible in their family framework:

One just didn't have rows at meals. Then I would storm up to my room after dinner.

On the other hand, there was much about her parents as individuals that Mrs Jarret did admire, and many aspects of their relationship with her that did encourage her development as a person to be reckoned with intellectually and later professionally. Her father's emphasis on learning and her mother's vivacity were ever-present sources of stimulation, though her feelings of closeness were more for her father than for her mother.

My mother was a very gay, bright person ... but she had a quick temper. I got on reasonably well with my father, but I got on badly with her. We were unable to talk to each other.... My father was very devoted to me. I was the one that was going to do this, that and the other thing. It was a terrible burden for a child to have to bear, because you always think, 'Oh, I've got to live up to this.'

On the other hand, though being pushed on to achieve greater accomplishments, particularly academically, there was no specific focus on what ultimate form the achievements would take.

My father believed very much that everybody should lead their own life and think their own thoughts. He was rather idealistic, I suppose, and he believed that if you left people alone they would come to believe in the good and right, whatever it was, so I was never forced into anything at all.

There was some assumption she might one day be a writer, but primarily it was just the generalized idea that she would do 'something'.

The elder brother was very important in Mrs Jarret's early life. Like her father, he was particularly indulgent towards her and she remembers him as 'very sweet' and 'marvellous' in helping her, behaving almost like a little father.

She was pushed ahead quite rapidly in school because of her academic ability, and by the time she went to secondary school – a day school which emphasized academic achievement – she was working with children two or three years older than herself, finishing school when she was fourteen. Retrospectively she thinks that she might have been better off having gone to a boarding school because that sort of schooling might have provided a more all-round developmental experience. She says :

I didn't want to go to boarding school because I was scared to, and my brother hadn't the sense to insist on it, but it would probably have been much better.

As it was, she was a high achiever in academic life, but didn't develop close friends in this period and feels that she didn't 'grow up' as a whole person in that period as much as she ought to have. Because she was so much alone she became very much a self-contained individual.

Mrs Jarret's completion of secondary school came at a time when there was trouble brewing on the Continent. She had hoped to study at the Sorbonne, and had in fact at this point spent a year in France, but when she actually entered university it was decided that she would go to the United States, where she gained an honours degree, attended drama school, following the director's course, and subsequently worked for the U.S. Government in the economic field. This was therefore a period which was extremely stimulating for her, in very mixed ways. It was during this period that she laid the groundwork in many ways for both her subsequent work career and her marriage, both of which flowered only on her return to England.

Mr Jarret's Personal Background

Mr Jarret is the second son of a professional family whose life in a village outside London seems to have been unexceptionally conventional. His father was a professional man who commuted daily to an office in London where he was a partner, and the internal family life was comfortable and fairly united.

The grandparental family, on Mr Jarret's father's side, seems to have been typical of a certain kind of Victorian family, with three sons following different paths in rebellion against the rigid norms of the time. Mr Jarret's father was the middle son, and the most stable one.

Mr Jarret considers that his father was a frustrated man because he appeared to suppress considerable creativity which, apart from life-long work in the amateur theatre, had insufficient outlet.

Mr Jarret feels that his father was fundamentally a very 'nice man' who 'tried hard'. His mother was more conservative by nature, and was conscientiously religious. She sang in the church choir and played the piano a little. Her main interests, however, were in the management of the house and garden.

We had a couple of servants and a gardener, very conventional ... acre and a half of garden, two cats and two dogs ...

Indeed, there were also two boys, and the contrast between them was rather significant. The elder brother was four years older than Mr Jarret, and both were born when the parents were already fairly advanced in age – late 30s. Like Mrs Jarret, Mr Jarret had a particularly close relationship with his elder brother, who stood somewhere between himself and his parents. Also, like Mrs Jarret's family, the presence of servants and the general ethos of life in this kind of upper-middle-class family was such that there was not very much closeness between parents and children, inforcing whatever common bonds and loyalties might develop among the siblings.

The closeness between Mr Jarret and his elder brother was based in large part on the differences and complementarities between them, rather than their common features. In contrast to Mr Jarret, his elder brother was a scholastic success, and from the start it was clear that he was an academic high flyer, whereas for Mr Jarret school was a rather awkward and painful experience, partly because of his being a shy person, but mainly because he had no interest in athletics and little in academic pursuits.

Mr Jarret describes his brother as being the one who expressed their feelings of rebelliousness against middle-class culture. His own style was different:

My brother was a very much more outspoken, sharp-tempered person, whereas I was always playing things in a soft key. When he was about fifteen, he made a great statement: 'On this day I no longer go to church.' I don't say that mother wept, but she was upset and there was a great scene. It was rather characteristic. As far as I was concerned, I didn't do any of that. I just didn't go and no one ever really quite noticed that I hadn't.

Broader than their joint rejection of their mother's religious attachments, Mr Jarret and his brother rejected more generally the values and way of life that their parents typified – the complacent, conservative bourgeois form of life which seemed to them to be a persistence of Edwardian society into their own times.

On the other hand, the rejection of these values did not involve the personal rejection of their parents, particularly their father, to whom they were both tied by their shared love of the theatre.

He (father) regenerated and started a village amateur dramatic society with two or three friends so that our main social life probably came from this. They did rather traditional amateur work, not cultured particularly, because it wasn't a very cultural village society. He was a pillar of the British Drama League and entered competitions. Later when my brother and I ran our own theatre he acted for us.

The interest and excitement in the theatre became a focal point for the entire family.

The theatre is the great common bond that runs through my family and crosses over to my wife. My father was (I think I am not exaggerating), for his time, a superb amateur actor. This was his real love and when he was young he did a great deal. He was a comedian – a basic character actor, and when we were very young, he took it up again.

Outside the father's deep involvement in the theatre, Mr Jarret does not remember his family as being very 'social'. Apart from their involvement in community activities, they did not devote a great deal of time to entertaining their friends and he feels that he is rather like them in this respect.

From all this the emergence and stabilization of Mr Jarret's character makes sense. He sees himself as a liberal but rather steady and sensible-minded man, who has always been clear on what he has wanted and never wavered in his pursuit of a particular type of architectural career. Like Mrs Jarret, he feels that the way in which his early life and educational experiences were handled had the effect of retarding his emotional development in many ways. He was very introspective and retiring in the public school situation, feeling it a sort of prison.

When he entered student life, there was a major change in his whole outlook and way of living. Whereas he had felt before that he was imprisoned and subjected to meaningless tasks, he now felt a sense of excitement and purpose. The school had spawned some early English pioneers in architecture, but just prior to his own entry group, it had become somewhat more conventional. His own group felt the mission of revitalizing it very strongly – 'our generation set the place on fire again'. However, these professional experiences were put into a different perspective because of events of the period. Mr Jarret recalls how the students in the 30s came to feel themselves as a distinctive group, and how they became welded together in certain emotional ties that have persisted to the present:

Those of us who were students in the thirties have much in common. We experienced growing up in a frightening period, very different from that enjoyed by those a few years younger who became students after the Second World War, and different again from those who are young and worried now. We who came from secure middle-class homes found ourselves exposed to the intellectual and emotional ferment generated amongst young people in universities and colleges as Hitler came to power. Most of my student years were marked by events in history as Hitler strengthened his power and moved to war.

Mr Jarret seemed to speak of the friendships established during his university days as most important to him in his career. His partnership was formed with friends from this time. Teachers were not an important influence in the same way.

It was while a student in London that Mr Jarret joined his brother to establish their own private theatre.

For three and a half years we ran this private theatre, he producing and I spending all my spare time designing and building for it. This was the focal point in my life and his between the ages of 16 and 19. At the time I was a student and it was almost stronger (as an interest) than architecture.

During this period Mr Jarret met Mrs Jarret, when he was 17 and she 11. They met through their elder brothers who attended the same university. Over the next five years, while Mr Jarret was a student in London, they became friends.

Mr Jarret said that he was still very young (22) when Mrs Jarret departed for America, shortly before the outbreak of war. They corresponded until a point about a year later when he decided to marry someone else whom he had known off and on for about four years. This marriage was rapidly dissolved, but not without contributing to his development. Ultimately, it made his marriage to Mrs Jarret more solidly based. The wartime period was difficult for each of them, filled with experiments of life and personal relationships which made them feel certain about their compatibility when they met again after the war.

FAMILY WORLDS

The decision to marry, as indicated above, occurred after the prelude of an earlier adolescent relationship between the Jarrets and the interlude of a brief first marriage by Mr Jarret. Their wartime separation and experiences with others seem to have confirmed in the minds of both of them their suitability for one another. When the Jarrets met again after eight years separation they just naturally seemed right for one another.

They soon realized that at 24 and 30 years old their relationship was 'no longer a naïve one'. Mrs Jarret describes her feelings at the time as follows:

Because I knew him so very well, I wouldn't even say that we decided it, it seemed quite inevitable, when we met again we didn't even really think about it.

Mr Jarret too had changed. On the one hand he felt that he had grown in the experiences of war, but on the other hand, he felt that he had missed a lot of the fun of youth. As a consequence he was resistant to settling down in marriage:

Apart from my first marriage, there was the fact that my generation lost their youth. One looked forward to the period after a long studentship, of having a free and slightly gayer period in which you earned something, although it wasn't much. That was cut right out, so that at 30 one had this business of making up a lot of time.

In the context of all these changes the Jarrets felt their meeting after the war was a home-coming one. They got together immediately and were married a few months later.

While they deliberately did not have children during the first years of their marriage, both because of their involvement in their work and in order to catch up with the developmental experiences that they as a couple had missed due to their earlier life circumstances, they reached a point about seven years after their marriage when they decided to have a child. Mr Jarret describes the process of decision at that time as follows:

There was this terrific feeling (I think it was probably common of other people of my age) of desperately catching up with the lost years. The years 24 to 30 for a man are good years very often and they were lost.

In planning their house they allowed for the possibility of having children, but as Mr Jarret put it, they were of a 'mixed mind'. On the one hand they were tremendously involved in their careers and in their own experiences as a couple; on the other they felt that people who didn't have children were in a sense 'incomplete as people', having lacked this creative experience.

The Jarrets reached their actual decision to have a child during a holiday in France. They described vividly their idealized image of the child they would have:

Mr Jarret:

I always remember something rather sentimental – you were attracted by a neighbour's little French boy. I said how marvellous it was; he was a superbly elegant, well-controlled four-year-old who seemed to be quite happy and well organized at the same time. And we had a marvellous delusion that one would have a child like this, which was of course not what we had. But it was round about that time that one felt that this was the right thing to do.

Mrs Jarret:

I suppose at the back of one's mind one must have been beginning to think 'are we ever going to or is it going to be too late'. Up to then we had definitely thought that we didn't want to have children because we had so many other things we wanted to do, but then perhaps seeing this child and this couple who all seemed so happy made us start to talk about it.

Not being 'familistic' in orientation, and yet not wishing to forego the experience of giving birth, the idea of having one child was seen as a sort of compromise.

The actual arrival of their son was attended by a number of unfortunate occurrences that made the whole experience more disruptive than it might have been. Their son was born early and Mrs Jarret took three months maternity leave. A nanny was hired for his care, but he was a demanding baby and Mrs Jarret says that she only now appreciates how exhausting the nanny's job was.

He was born early which was very nice. They gave me three months off, so that was all fine, but he was so tiny and it was such a problem, he had to be fed eight times a day. When he came back from hospital we had a marvellous nanny but she nearly had a nervous breakdown, she got so exhausted.

Also at about this time, Mrs Jarret's father died and Mrs

Jarret herself became seriously ill with 'flu, adding to the general strain :

Then my father died and there was a certain amount of general chaos with that. . . . Then I was terribly ill. It was all ghastly, the baby screamed all night, every night. I don't know how we all lived through it but the thing about those kind of things is that you do because you have to, you don't have any choice. It was a tremendous relief when I went back to work. By then I think things began to calm down a bit.

Mr Jarret who does not have anything like the child-centred orientation of some contemporary fathers, found the whole period very difficult and unpleasant.

Although for two or three years afterwards Mrs Jarret worried about having an only child, the Jarrets did not try to have another. Mrs Jarret said :

He (Mr J) wasn't keen to have another and having had one I certainly did not want to have another, but I worried quite a lot about whether I ought to for the child's sake. In the end I gave up worrying about it because it was a bit late to do it by that time. I wouldn't have had them very far apart because the only point to have had another would have been to be a playmate and then this is a bit of a dicey throw too, I always thought, because brothers and sisters often hate each other.

The Jarrets' son has experienced a number of problems of his own as the result of being the only child of two very busy professional parents. Because his mother was neither constantly on hand, nor in and out of the house, responsible and high quality care was extremely important. The Jarrets were able to arrange an exceptionally good and steadfast daily domestic help who fortunately remained with them throughout his childhood. On the other hand, the nanny situation, so vital to him and to the peaceful running of the household, turned out less satisfactorily. When he was a few months old the 'perfect' nanny was found; a young woman of exceptional character and standards, who was equally appreciated by the whole family. It seemed as though continuity and stability, both factors by which Mrs Jarret set great store, were achieved. Indeed this was so, until the nanny's worth was appreciated by someone else, and she left to become a wife and mother herself. After this there were several changes of nannies, and later on au pairs, as each girl stayed her year or two. One returned for a second spell.

At eight the Jarrets' son went to boarding school, and there was no longer need for permanent resident help; it became a question of finding someone to come for each school holiday while Mrs Jarret was working. She felt very strongly that this person must be a cheerful and stimulating companion, as well as a responsible supervisor for her young son. After some not wholly satisfactory incumbents, the Jarrets felt themselves lucky to find the ideal young woman, who returned each holiday until the need for such supervision and companionship had passed.

It was inevitable that so many changes of mother-substitutes should have some repercussions on the Jarrets' son, but Mrs Jarret feels that it was these changes, and not the fact of her working, which created problems. She believes that if one nanny had been able to stay throughout the period (as in her own and her husband's childhood) no such problems would have arisen as a direct result of her going to work. On the contrary, she believes that it is very much better for a child not to be exclusively tended by its mother, and would not have wished, given the choice, to be such a mother even if she had not been a professional person. She thinks that any difficulties that her son has had to face were more probably the result of being an only child, and of the changes of nannies. It is apparent that these are problems which could have occurred in any kind of family, conventional or dual-career. The Jarrets, however, took the problems very seriously and a great deal of the family's energies has gone into working out ways of dealing with them. They feel that these problems are now resolving themselves; and that, as a family, they are able to communicate with each other much better than when their son was small. Indeed, it is interesting to contrast the Jarrets' attitude with that of parents who are happy and feel competent to manage small infants, but who fail to develop ways of communicating with their children when they reach pre-adolescence and adolescence. Whereas the latter type of parents may experience the later stages as providing new and unexpected intrusive elements, the Jarrets experience it as providing a more manageable form of family relationship. Mrs Jarret recalls that their conception of the place of a child in their family life was one that was not geared to the real demands of infants. Mr Jarret expresses this in terms of family stages, generalizing as follows:

I have never thought of the last twenty-one years in this way – but there have been three quite clear patches really: one up till (our son's birth); the whole young period of his life with all its tremendous strain; and the one which has only recently come which has sort of gone back to a calm on a different plane. This is a pattern which must occur in all families but I have only just appreciated it really.

Thus, the main points of strain within the family seem to have been over the tactics of child-rearing. The provision of nannies and au pairs, to provide stable care and to cover school holidays, has been an absolutely essential element given the commitment of each parent to career. Nevertheless, they feel that the toll on them as individuals is less than it would have been if Mrs Jarret had given up her career in favour of a more conventional form of domestic living.

While Mr Jarret sees himself as impatient in relation to his son's problems in infancy, he is on the whole a very patient man. Both in his work, and in relation to his wife, he is characterized as patient and kindly. In his work he has to think in terms of large amounts of money, materials and manpower over long periods of time. This calls for and receives very patient and meticulous planning and decision-making. In contrast, her work – on directing specific dramatic productions – proceeds at a great pace (as will be described below) and has a shorter cycle of intense involvement. He characterizes her as a person in these terms – as having a mind that 'goes much faster'. When she has problems, they tend to well up inside her and press for resolution. In these instances he listens patiently and gives support, but never tells her what to do. He feels that this helps to avoid recriminations.

Although Mrs Jarret functions effectively in the high-powered world of television, she considers that she has a separate domestic role which she must discharge as effectively as if she had no occupation. Her occupation role is seen to be quite separate from her domestic role, and both at the beginning of the day and at the end she functions as her husband's wife in a near-conventional manner.

In the morning, she arises and makes breakfast for both of them and their son when he is at home, and in the evening she usually arrives home in time to cook their supper. The breakfast is made along conventional lines – orange juice, eggs, coffee (tea for the son), etc. – but with great attention to efficiency of organization. All of the breakfast things are laid out on a single trolley so as to minimize extra effort in preparation. The whole preparation, including feeding their two dogs, is accomplished in under fifteen minutes, and then the cleaning up can be left to the dishwashing machine and the domestic who lives in the attached quarters.

As for dinner, the domestic helper prepares vegetables, but Mrs Jarret does the cooking. She experiences a transformation from her work role to her other role as 'my husband's wife' and goes rapidly to work, to prepare for the evening meal. This tends to be in the French manner, though with the less elaborate dishes. Mr Jarret buys their meat, fish, and wine and says about his wife:

... she specializes in producing extremely edible dinners – with the main part of the meal highly sophisticated – in the rapidest possible time. Whether it's breakfast or any other meal – I think that's her speciality ...

Mr Jarret leaves later in the morning to avoid traffic and arrives correspondingly late in the evening. They dine with candles and wine, at 8 p.m. Their son usually dines with them, but if he prefers to watch television, takes his on a tray to his room. Mrs Jarret says:

I have developed a fairly good sort of alarm clock in myself over the years that, whatever is happening, somehow or other I manage to get the dinner on at eight. We had a young friend staying with us for a while, and she said, 'I always admire you because whatever is happening – and it may seem a terrible hurly-burly – everything stops at eight o'clock and candles are lit,' and we sit down and have a slow quiet dinner and we drink wine and talk.

The non-conventional aspect is also imbedded in this 'we talk' aspect of their lives. They like to take time over breakfast to talk, and they talk in the evening, often until it is time to turn in, which tends to be early because of the demands of the day on both of them. The content of her conversation in such a situation is different from that of a conventional couple and given his strong interest in drama as a life-long hobby he is able to understand her problems. Conversely, with her interest in aesthetics and in the social significance of his work, she takes a strong interest in his work, making for a lively and persisting basis for dialogue.

The couple-fit in the Jarrets' relationship seems to be based on the long continuity of their acquaintance – providing a sense of security based on the past; on their temperamental complementarities – he rather more patient and supportive, providing stabilizing influences for her, she rather more volatile and impulsive, providing expressive stimulation for him; and in their shared valuation of social and creative endeavours. Mrs Jarret describes how their different temperaments complement one another as follows :

... he has learned ... to take things as they come and find a way of dealing with them, whereas I tend to be much more impulsive and volatile. I think this is quite a good combination because one balances the other. I certainly think we get on much better than one would get on with somebody who was awfully like one. Although we agree about all sorts of intellectual things, and like the same sorts of things, if I go off about something he won't, and if he loses his temper about something, then probably it's something that doesn't bother me.

The way in which Mrs Jarret reverts to her other job as 'my

husband's wife' each evening is reinforced by the pattern of
their social life as a couple. They both feel that they get a
tremendous amount of stimulation in their work, so that in their
private time they prefer to be relatively quiet and on their own.
They find that their work is emotionally absorbing and exhausting and leaves them little time or energy for social activities.
Mrs Jarret says:

Although we are not particularly unhealthy, we are not terribly
strong and we both find working as hard as we do takes quite a good
deal out of us. We do go to the theatre sometimes and things like
that because I have to. We do have people come to see us occasionally but we tend to see our friends once a year or something like
that. Although we know an awful lot of people, we tend not to see
them very much.

When their son was small they were aware of direct and implied criticisms of her pursuing a career. Mr Jarret says:

You always felt that you were frowned on by your contemporaries
who were not working, and they thought that you were wrecking
your child and so on.

Mrs Jarret says:

It was never anything that was said, but I used to feel that British
women were disapproving, but at the same time jealous because
some of them were people who had worked and had given it up.
Some couldn't and would have liked to. I think they felt that I was
too lucky. I was eating my cake and having it. I think there was
that sort of feeling among them, but less so with Americans.

Part of the cost of this pattern was, of course, that there were
fewer figures in their social circle on whom they could call for
help and support when difficulties arose in relation to their son.
They find that they have met very few couples like themselves.
She says:

We don't meet too many families who work in the way we do
as a professional family. We know lots of actors and actresses, but
it isn't quite the same at all . . .

When she is in social gatherings outside of those involving
her own associates or close friends, she finds that the assump-

tion is always that she is a housewife. Her reaction to this depends on the way she is handled, because she can relate to people in her wife-role without going into the whole career role side at all. If she is dealt with condescendingly, 'well, of course you wouldn't know because you stay at home all day . . .', she disenchants them rather quickly. If, on the other hand, she is treated as an intelligent person and the other person has some kind of an interest to discuss, she continues at the level of a person with many interests and a good deal of knowledge, without necessarily making her status explicit.

WORK WORLDS

As for all of the dual-career families described in this book, the meaning of work for each partner can be seen in individual terms and also in terms of the meaning that each one's work has for the other. This is quite striking in the Jarret family – not only as between Mr and Mrs Jarret, but also in the way their son seems to be integrating the talents and interests of both his parents into his own unfolding career aspirations.

Mrs Jarret

Mrs Jarret is a television drama director of established standing in her field. At the present point in her career, she is concerned with high quality dramatic productions and is one of a number of senior directors available for such work. She was one of the vanguard group directing plays for colour television when it first came out and is experienced in a variety of types of dramatic production.

Television is essentially a cooperative medium; the television director works with a great number of people from the inception of a production until its completion.

The idea for a production may start with the author of the script, who may send a play to a director, who then offers it for an appropriate spot, or the play may be commissioned by the head of the department, or the producer of a series of plays. It will then be offered to a director. The director is very much concerned with working with the writer so that his ideas can be most effectively expressed in terms of television pictures. Mrs Jarret believes that the director's role is first of all to interpret the play that the author has written. Some directors like to use the text as a springboard for their own ideas, but she especially believes that all her ideas must grow from the author's original concept, and must enhance it, always in sympathy with it. She says:

Once the author and I have agreed on the approach to the play, I have an overall idea of how it should be interpreted by my production. There are many aspects to a production, of course, but a play is brought to life in the first instance by the actors. So it is important to choose each one carefully. I spend a great deal of time and thought on casting. If I cannot get the leading man or lady that we think ideal, I may choose, for example, a different second lead: the important thing is for a play to have a balanced cast. There are all sorts of factors to take into account as one relates one character to another; looks, colouring, voice quality, and so forth.

Just as Mrs Jarret believes in working with the playwright, so she believes in collaboration with the actors. She does not like to dictate moves or reasons for behaviour. She says:

A good actor always has a good reason for what he does. He may see things in a character or a situation that I have not, because he is concentrating on that one thing. We work it all out between us: when I get back from rehearsal every day I sit down to review what we have done, to make sure that no decision I have made during the day conflicts with my overall concept.

The actors are only one of the ingredients in the whole production: there is the visual side. Here again Mrs Jarret works by developing a complete visual concept of her production, and very early on, having made every effort to assemble the best possible team, she explains her ideas in great detail to her lighting director, set designer, costume designer, and make-up supervisor. These members of the team will have ideas of their own about the play, and all of these will be discussed and assimilated. A complete plan for the staging of the production will emerge from many meetings, rough drawings, colour charts, costume and make-up sketches and so forth. Rehearsals cannot start until this side of the work is virtually complete. Once the play is in rehearsal costume fittings must take place, furniture and props be chosen, and all the elements of the production brought together for the intensely concentrated hours in the studio when the play is camera rehearsed and taped.

There will often be location filming or outside broadcast recording of exterior scenes. This usually takes place just before or even during rehearsals. A similar procedure to the main production procedure takes place in miniature for each location sequence.

During the actors' rehearsals Mrs Jarret has to relate the actors' moves to the shots she has envisaged. Of this too she has a general concept before rehearsals start, but it is modified as the actors' moves are consolidated and the play develops. The shots consist of the relation of the cameras, lights, scenery, and actors. After rehearsal each day, Mrs Jarret goes home, and before she has to become 'cook' she makes notes for her camera script and unites the ideas and work of the day to the visual results she wishes to achieve. Before the production can reach the studio, the camera script, and cards for the cameramen, must be typed by the production secretary. Mrs Jarret either dictates this script or marks up a rehearsal script for her secretary to copy. At the same time a fair copy of the scale plan of the studio and scenery will be issued showing all the camera positions as Mrs Jarret indicates. On another copy the lighting director will set out his lighting plot.

Finally the production reaches the studio. Mrs Jarret's day will then start about 9.30 a.m. checking that all the component parts of the production on which so much time and care have been spent have arrived and are as intended. There are often many problems, and decisions for compromises or changes must be made quickly so that camera rehearsals can start on time. As soon as the rehearsal starts, Mrs Jarret explains to all the operators what the play is about and how the rehearsals will be organized. Then, shot by shot, the actors go through the play, while every ingredient, from lights and camera moves to make-up details and the colour and placing of tiny props is determined and marked. As each scene is finished the director returns to the control gallery and runs the scene in sequence so that each person can check his own part in it. And so on each day. Finally the whole play has been rehearsed (or that section of it which is to be first recorded), and the videotaping starts. Absolute precision during recording characterizes a well-rehearsed play, but inevitably the unforeseen hitch or accident may occur; then retakes are quickly set up and recorded.

Once the studio session is over, Mrs Jarret goes over the script to determine the edit points. Then she will spend a couple of days on the videotape editing (which closely resembles film editing). Then she will dub on the music. Long before she will have worked with the composer in a similar way to her work with the others concerned in the play, and he will have prepared everything except the exact length, to the half second, of each piece of music required. A music recording session will then be held, and then the music track will be mixed onto the master sound track. Sometimes the music is written in advance and played in the studio, but this is a less accurate method.

All of Mrs Jarret's work is related to the production of a play, but there are many other aspects to it. There is much organization and general planning, including financial planning, and many other people are involved: heads of departments, programme controllers, producers, script editors, organizers, members of various servicing departments, engineers, publicity department, and so on.

The actual rhythms of Mrs Jarret's work have fallen into a pattern so that she can expect to do four to six major plays a year. One production may follow rapidly on the heels of its predecessor, or Mrs Jarret may have a relaxed period in between in which she can catch up on things at home or pursue any interest she likes – which may be future play possibilities or hobbies. She tries to fit in a family holiday with her rehearsal and production schedules. When she is assigned a play, she may also work a good deal at home in the initial planning and briefing stages. Rehearsals go on all over London in all sorts of halls, and she works within the framework of Equity rules – two three-hour sessions a day. She has her own car, and insofar as choice of rehearsal rooms is possible, she tries to choose those easily accessible to her home, and hours that suit her double-role pattern. When the rehearsal room is in a good shopping area she will do her food shopping en route to rehearsals, or in the lunch hour. If she is exceptionally busy, perhaps editing filmed sequences after rehearsal, or making an evening pre-recording, she will order all supplies by telephone. They will then be delivered and organized by the domestic help. If the rehearsal hall is close enough to home, during school vacations she will pop in at home for lunch with her son.

Mrs Jarret feels that her present work represents a satisfactory synthesis of a number of aspirations and needs in her life situation. While she does not feel that her work is as creative as some other kinds of work she might have done, or even as her husband's, she feels that it is creative in its own genre. She says: 'Directing is an end in itself.'

While they were not pressed financially, her salary has been important:

The fact that one has got a regular income coming in all the time is a very stable factor in life. I think this has been an important thing for me because it has made me feel fine. I know that the house can be run and I know that I can look forward to sending my son to school and I know that I can afford to hire people to look after him, if I can get them.

Mrs Jarret rationalizes her own pattern of carrying a responsible job and at the same time of switching to her second job as her husband's wife in terms of intrinsic capacities of women.

I think that women are extremely good at doing a lot of different things at once, because they have to be. I can switch my mind from one thing to the other quite quickly, whereas a man I don't think can.

She finds that when she employs women who are of the highly committed type, they tend to be more reliable than men precisely because of this need to 'try harder'. Many of the stereotypes, she feels, about women being less reliable – dropping out for family crises and so on – apply to women who have low commitment to their careers and characterize the lower status of women's jobs:

Women who do men's jobs have to be tougher and more determined and better at their job; otherwise a man will get ahead of them.

In general, she feels that a woman in a man's job has to work harder and:

One has to be nicer to people and much more efficient as well, because where a man can be perfectly foul and everybody shrugs their shoulders, they take it much harder from a woman ... will say, 'What do you expect from a woman.' '

She considers that there is a fundamental difference between women who work at roles that only women can fill, as do actresses, and women who work at roles that could be filled by men and are therefore in competition with men.

For herself personally she feels that the crucial problem is how to be tough enough to succeed in this way, but at the same time to 'remain human and ... try not to lose gentleness and humanity'.

Mr Jarret

Mr Jarret became interested in architecture when very young, and drew plans at the age of four. From his school days a secondary interest was the theatre, as has already been mentioned. This focused on both stage design and the design of the theatre itself as a building, and he now feels that this interest has always influenced his architecture as a whole. Another influence has been the social one, due both to the depressing time before the war when he was a student, and the more optimistic period immediately after the war when he was starting an active professional life.

Mr Jarret is now an architect in private practice together with a group of partners with whom he has worked since they were students together. The group has been concerned mainly with work in the public sector, for example in housing and in education. At the time of the interviews Mr Jarret was involved in a major educational project, which had the sort of combination of creative and socially significant elements towards which he has been oriented all his life:

I've been very lucky in the past few years working on perhaps the most interesting job that I'm ever likely to have. It's very much a thing of our time – to design for a new generation.

Mr Jarret is also involved in work for the profession outside his practice, which represents part of his conception of the full professional role he should be playing. In the past he has taught architecture as well, but found after a period that the difficulties of combining this with a full practice were very great and that perhaps neither was done full justice.

Mr Jarret's firm, although larger than some, has experienced a history during its twenty-five years' development similar to that of many of its contemporaries. The problems have been constantly changing and the prospect for the future is one of even greater change. Mr Jarret comments on this:

This situation has come about owing to the rapid technological and social advances since the war and their inevitable effect on one of man's most traditionally based preoccupations and skills: the provision of shelter. This preoccupation is the same whether it concerns a primitive hut or a part of the concrete jungle of a modern town. But the design and administrative techniques demanded today are vastly different from even a relatively short time ago.

In the early days Mr Jarret's firm was organized in a fairly orthodox manner. Each partner, having similar interests of a generalist nature, designed his own projects with the help of his particular team who saw the work through at all stages until the end of the construction period. The partners met once a week to discuss and criticize the various projects on hand, and also to coordinate the general activities of the firm.

As the office grew in size during the latter part of the fifties which was a period of considerable expansion in social architecture in Britain, the organization of the jobs, which not only tended to grow in number but in size as well, became more complex. Mr Jarret and his partners found that it was becoming increasingly difficult for them to work in great detail on each job, and so they had to work through others. At the same time the organizational problems of running both the jobs and the firm as a whole demanded the creation of new senior posts to provide deputies for the partners on all organizational aspects of their work.

A large firm needs large contracts and continuity of work in order to keep staff properly deployed, but while the role of the architect continues to change, ever-developing technology, coupled with the need to reduce the cost of building in a period of tremendous activity, continues to add to his burden. All these factors have led to a total reconsideration of the organizational structure of Mr Jarret's firm and a reassessment of the role of the trained architect as a member of the total team responsible for the design and construction of the man-made world.

The result of this re-think is inevitably towards specialization. Basically this means that instead of the individual architect maintaining his traditional role as the master designer, processor and supervisor of all matters concerning building (this process still goes on in some Scandinavian countries in a manner not seen in Britain since the end of the nineteenth century) the project, be it of whatever size and complexity, is processed through a series of groups, from the analytical pre-design stage to the final financial settlement of the builder's contract. These groups include as well as architects members of a number of associated disciplines, with their own expertise. These include not only the normal specialist groups of quantity surveyors and engineers, both structural and mechanical, who may still be based in their individual organizations outside the architect's office, but new specialist groups within direct control of the architects for such

work as planning analysis, technical research, production drawings for the builder, and a specially trained contract group to
supervise the construction on the building site.

However there is still a role for the generalist and design-
oriented architect, and the partners in Mr Jarret's firm for the
most part retain their overall position of general responsibility.
They are the 'conductors of the band', and enjoy a greater
variety of interest than the specialist, and a greater responsibility for the final architecture produced. But with this also
goes a heavier moral and financial responsibility which grows
at a considerable rate year by year, affecting the pressures experienced by the senior partners, including Mr Jarret.

INTEGRATION OF PERSONAL, FAMILY
AND WORK WORLDS

The Jarrets represent a dual-career family in which each of the
partners has a paramount, though diverse, commitment to
career. Family life as such has been of much less importance
to them as a source of personal gratification, and it is only since
their son has been able to participate as another individual with
his own quasi-professional interests that the fundamental basis
for their harmony is being restored. The relationship between
the marital pair, and later with their son, is on the basis of
each having a great involvement that the other(s) respect. Each
is expected to provide supports, to make the minimal demands
other than those for emotional support, and to participate as an
individual with something interesting to contribute to the
family's life. Where the Jarrets themselves were the only members, the contributions were clear – Mr Jarret provided a sense of
high moral and aesthetic purpose, and Mrs Jarret contributed an
enlivening set of interests and general intellectual verve. They
felt, after some experimental attempts, that they could not
actually work together on professional products, their modes of
thought and production being so different. However, each respects the other's work, and the other's hobbies which have

considerable overlap. Their son has found a niche in this family by providing a new integration of their interests.

The Jarrets' son is now interested in electrical engineering. Ostensibly this is not the field of either parent, and in it he is developing his own professional identity and competence. However, the specific ways in which he has applied this interest has been of relevance to the work of both parents, and in this he is making some kind of a creative integration of the influences of both. He applies his interest in electricity to the stage lighting for his school's dramatic productions and helps at home with the electrical aspects of domestic projects such as a new room extension. He also organizes some youth group activities; though neither parent considers themselves primarily as administrators, the work of each has strong components of direction–administration.

The Jarrets, then, are less 'joint' in their activities than the Bensons, and less interdependent than the Harrises (who not only respect one another's line of work, but actively seek out one another's help). Mr Jarret, like Mr Neal, is interested in his wife having a career, so as to enhance her own individual fulfilment. The Jarrets differ from all the others in this set in their lack of emphasis on familism. All of the dual-career couples described in this volume value families in some way, though this is not universally true for dual-career families in general. However, the Jarrets place relatively less emphasis on having a close family life and children, and are really only comfortable with their son now he is older. Other families, notably the Neals, believe in large families and are very fond of children. The size of the Neal family reflects this. Some of the others have felt that as the infants develop into adolescents their demands on the family's time and emotional resources increase rather than decrease, but this is partly a function of whether or not the child is at boarding school.

The Neals: Civil Servants

BACKGROUND — DEVELOPMENT OF THEIR FAMILY STRUCTURE

Catalogue of Events

Met: 1952 when they were both working in the Civil Service.

Going together: They were engaged in January 1953.

Married: 1953.

Children: Mr Neal had two sons by his first marriage, aged six and four when Mr and Mrs Neal had their first child, a girl born 1954. Subsequently they had three more children, born 1956, 1961 and 1963, all girls.

Establishment of home and residential history: Lived in Mr Neal's house in a suburb of London when they were first married. In October 1953 they moved to a larger house where they stayed until September 1967 when they moved to another house in the same vicinity.

Domestic help: From 1953 to 1958 they had a succession of au pairs and temporary household help. In 1955 they employed a trained nanny who came in daily; this nanny left in 1958. The last nanny stayed until there was 'no nannying to be done' in 1967. During 1958–69 they also had an au pair living in and working half day.

Major events in child-rearing: The boys went to nursery school, prep. school and a top public school. The girls attended a more progressive nursery school and prep. school and the two older girls have also gone to a top public school.

Major illnesses: In January 1967 Mr Neal was seriously ill after a haemorrhage; he returned to work in August 1967.

Major family separations: In 1958–9 there was a temporary family separation when Mr Neal received a fellowship for travel and research in the United States.

THE NEALS

The heart of the Establishment is perhaps an unlikely place to find people involved in an innovative pattern such as the 'dual-career' family. Public bureaucracies are usually conventional in orientation, yet the unorthodox situation of both husband and wife pursuing high level careers is found in the British Civil Service. This would seem to relate to the idealistic rather than the conventional aspect of the Public Service.

The Neals are an extremely hard-working couple and, like many dual-career families, their work and family worlds are both highly important to them. They have nevertheless managed to integrate the demands of traditional senior Civil Service roles with a family which includes not only themselves but also six active children.

There are four principal themes which seem to characterize the Neal family. Firstly they have a very high commitment to work and career. Secondly there is a high degree of participation in family activities. Thirdly an emphasis is placed on intellectual accomplishments, and fourthly the Neals have a very strong 'social service' feeling in the family which motivates them to make considerable personal sacrifice in relation to the demands of reconciling work and family life. None of these themes could be considered to take priority over any of the others for the family as a whole, although they have differing degrees of importance in the lives of each individual.

At the outset of the interviews the Neals' family, work, and home situations were different than at the conclusion of the interviews. This is principally due to a reduction in Mr Neal's work level as a result of a severe illness, which has forced him to alter his previous fifteen-hour work day to a more typical eight-hour day. In addition, various changes have been made in the domestic help situation, and the youngest child is now at school all day. However, as the intensive interviewing was conducted before many of these changes occurred most of the discussion that follows is based on the earlier period. Where changes have occurred they seem to show the degree of flexibility that this family has been able to demonstrate in dealing with changed circumstances.

PERSONAL WORLDS

Mrs Neal

Mrs Neal is a slightly built woman in her early forties who impresses one immediately as being extremely alert and with an active analytical kind of intelligence. She seems much more involved in the ideas with which she is working than with conventional 'feminine' modes of interpersonal relations. While her attire is casual, her conversation and the way she organizes her professional activities are anything but casual, and she gives the impression of being very intensely involved.

Mrs Neal is articulate and speaks persuasively. She approached the interviews with interest and concern for responding to the task set by the interview as well as she could. She compressed a great deal of information in direct and detailed answers to the questions. One feels that she manages to absorb all· the pressures which are directed at her, but that this leaves little energy for emotional involvement with non-essentials.

Mrs Neal's parents married shortly after the First World War. Their first child, Mrs Neal's elder sister, was born in 1921. In 1923 a son followed and in 1926 another son. Mrs Neal was born in 1928 when her father was fifty-five and her mother thirty-five. At the time of Mrs Neal's birth her father was retired, and for the first five years of her life the family lived in a small village in the Home Counties.. However, before this he was a marine colonel.

My father went straight into the marines. He was the sixth son in his family and had no idea at all what he wanted to do when he was nineteen, and his father said go into the marines. My father had no comment to offer so he went into the marines and spent twenty-five years there. The marines are a crack corps and I cannot really imagine my philosophically-minded slowly-thinking father in the marines. But he was quite successful.

After his retirement he wrote on philosophic questions and he encouraged a liberal, questioning attitude towards religion. Although he had a strong religious background (his own father and brother were parsons), he was at variance with them and wrote a paper on the subject 'Why I do not go to Church'.

Mrs Neal's mother was primarily a housewife. For a brief time after the war she also did part-time work which she seemed to enjoy.

She worked in a factory at one time, doing some sort of assembly work. She said she enjoyed it, meeting people and so on. Then she changed to another job, more the sort of job you would expect a middle-aged woman to be doing.

Mainly, however, she was active in various community service and charitable organizations, while supervising a large household.

Of very different temperaments, Mrs Neal's parents seem to have complemented one another:

My mother was dynamic. My father was placid. They got on extremely well. I certainly grew up with a favourable view of marriage. My father used to say how good their marriage must have been to survive the strain of both of them being at home – which I think is really true.

Mrs Neal's mother was married previously, her first husband having been killed in the First World War. Although there was a twenty-year age difference between Mrs Neal's parents, it does not seem to have affected their relationship because her father had always been youthful in spirit and manner. However, she remembers that the fact that her father was at home during the day distinguished her from all her friends whose fathers worked.

Mrs Neal admired both her parents, though she feels she resembles her mother more. She described her father as more stable and cautious and her mother as warmer, more emotional and energetic. She also spoke of some of the ways in which she hopes she has been educated out of her mother's weaknesses:

My father is a very solid type, cautious on the whole. I don't think we're very alike really. I'm probably more like my mother. I would hope to be like my mother but educated out of some of her inconsistencies. I suppose it is a matter of education and having been to university and taught to think around a question, and of working here where you can't take anything for granted and you realize how deceptive appearances often are. She is very warm-hearted, full of ideas, full of affection and tends to go off on tangents. She believes in being governed by her principles. She is the sort of person who would never dream of underpaying on the railway by a couple of pence, or taking advantage of anybody. I admire her in a way. I always took it for granted that people, the sort of person I wanted to be, would behave like that.

Mrs Neal's brothers and sister all went to boarding schools for part of their education and in this sense she was more continuously under her mother's care than were her siblings. Although her brothers and sister were all away from home after Mrs Neal was twelve years old, she said that she was never lonely because she saw a great deal of her school friends and for a period one of them boarded with her family. Mrs Neal's sister did not go on to university as did she and her brothers. Otherwise they were all 'fairly alike, untidy, forgetful and that sort of thing'.

At the age of five Mrs Neal started school in a tiny class in the village where her family lived. When she was about six the family moved to Cambridgeshire where they lived until she was twelve years old. Then the war broke out and the family moved into Cambridge to be closer to the children's schools, because of the shortage of petrol. After the family moved to Cambridgeshire, Mrs Neal was taught by her mother until she entered a kindergarten at seven. She went on to a girls' high school at the age of nine.

Although Mrs Neal's family was better off than most other families in their village, their only income was her father's pension and economy had to be practised so that all the children could be sent to good schools.

Well, we were much less well off than a lot of people at our school. We had an old car and it was expected that if you went to the cinema you would go in the cheaper seats. We had an old house which had not been modernized much and we had a large garden. I used to hear some worried conversations about how they could economize ...

Some alterations had to be made in the domestic help arrangements in the family as well. From a full complement of helpers, gardeners, etc., they reached the point where Mrs Neal's mother decided to learn to cook and a village girl replaced the live-in help.

Though occasionally Mrs Neal's father exerted his authority, in general family decisions seem to have been made by both parents jointly. She recalls her mother as having a major say in many decisions by a kind of unspoken agreement, but her father participated very actively in decisions about the children's education. Although the father tended not to advise or counsel his children on their aims and ambitions he was very interested in them and particularly in their education. Mrs Neal says that he found his satisfactions in his own work and life, and though he was pleased and proud of his children, he seemed to accept them as other adults in the world.

Mrs Neal's description of herself as a child conveys an image of a rather intense child, who set her own standards rather high :

Well, I remember my mother saying I was very determined. By the time I remember myself as a child : 'determined' is a fair description I think. I had my own ideas, I think I was very egotistic rather than selfish. I set myself goals a lot. From the earliest time I can remember, my self-esteem was very important to me.

Her sister did not get along with the mother as well as Mrs Neal did, especially when the sister was in her teens. The older brother around the age of seventeen also went through a stage in which there was friction between him and his parents. However, she feels that her father was generally on good terms with all the children.

It seems that Mrs Neal's parents did not have precise ambitions for their children, and she commented upon their philosophy of child-rearing as follows:

... looking back they seem to have had the most splendid detachment. They had the advantage of not having read any books on child psychology. I do very much admire them really. They never seemed interested in our battles at school for example but of course they were interested and sympathetic when something went wrong.

It was always taken for granted in Mrs Neal's family that she would have a job and it was accepted that a woman should go on to university if she were able. If, however, she had expressed a desire to go into nursing rather than to university, as her sister had done, her parents would have approved equally of this choice. Her mother once said that her hopes for her children were that they should grow up happily. In speaking of the value that she places on a stable, warm and emotionally secure family life, Mrs Neal said that she has modelled her ideas to some extent on the life of her own family when she was a child.

Both I and my mother had fairly large and active families. I think they're in the same sort of tradition.... In a way one models oneself on one's own family life if one's enjoyed it.

By the time that Mrs Neal was in secondary school and thinking about a career in social work, her mother was more overtly encouraging and went to some trouble to find out what academic preparation would be most suitable for such a career. After she learned of the P.P.E. degree programme at Oxford, Mrs Neal's studies in secondary school were designed to prepare her for this programme. The school headmistress also advised and guided her at this stage. When the time actually came she chose to go to the Oxford college that her father's sisters had attended. She received her degree in 1949.

Mrs Neal's university years were important in her development. When she first went to Oxford she felt 'shy and lonely for quite a time', but by the time she graduated and joined the Civil Service, she was more confident and felt less 'lonely and awkward' than many of her colleagues. Her academic career at university was one in which she worked hard at her studies and participated in several clubs. She made long-lasting friends there, but this period was not one of romantic involvement. At university she developed her interest in the general field of social studies and social work, but her career aspirations were still vague. The following gives some insight into what she sought in a career:

I wanted it to be interesting, I wanted it to be useful too. The thing I mainly toyed with was social work and if I hadn't got into the Civil Service I would have done house property management or become an almoner, both of which are in the general field of social work. It is very difficult at that age to know what one wants to do. I talked to various people about it and they said, 'Do you want to work with people?' I'm not sure what I used to answer. I didn't know whether I wanted to work with people or not, but I certainly didn't want to be shut in a room by myself all the time.

Mrs Neal thinks that many of the aspects of social work which she now sees as unattractive to her would not have impressed her as such when she was at university.

Shortly before she left Oxford she applied for a research position with the Royal Institute of International Affairs, a job she learned of through her tutor. The job did not materialize and she decided to sit for the Civil Service examinations (1949).

Though Mrs Neal says she would find satisfaction in running her household and organizing her family without a career, she is in fact combining a career and a family, each of which could absorb the energies of most people. This has put her into a position of functioning at the limit of her resources. She describes herself as follows:

Some people see me as very energetic, not necessarily in physical energy, but in the Civil Service one has to be ready to grapple with things. I tend to try and alter things rather than allow any slight error to go past. I've become increasingly bad-tempered. I don't think I was particularly good-tempered but one's patience steadily wears thinner, although I suppose I'm pretty patient in many ways. This of course is necessary both at the office and in dealing with small children. My mother regards me as having great patience. I'm very interested in our children's upbringing and in social fabric generally.

Her husband describes her as being very generous, patient and accepting. He also speaks of his respect for her intelligence, her honesty and her sincerity, and says that she 'will tackle anything and do it. She never admits defeat at anything.'

The theme of family life and responsibility to children is central in Mrs Neal's life. Not only has her husband encouraged her career, but without his strong feelings that she *should* maintain a career, she might have given it up for family life and the pursuit of many interests for which she simply does not have the time or energy now. She is very aware of the potential distance between herself and her children which may result from the demands of her career. She repeatedly stresses the fact that there have been

at least a couple of dozen times when difficulty arose which if it had gone on a little bit longer, I've no doubt I would have resigned and I think it's very likely if I had resigned that I would never have gone back. I suspect that the chief thing that has kept me working is simply inertia, the fact that there's never been a week when it didn't seem a little harder to resign that week or that day than to stay on other week. It's a very powerful force; it never seems easy to go back, and it never seems easy to stop when you're working.

Mr Neal

Mr Neal is in his mid fifties and of medium height and build. He has a robust but to some extent subdued look about him. At the time the interviews began, he was recovering from a severe illness and was on light duties; however since then, under doctor's orders, he has had his work load permanently reduced.

Mr Neal is highly articulate and speaks with a slight northern accent. Like his wife, he seemed to enjoy talking about himself and his family, and responds to questions in great detail.

Mr Neal's parents were of northern origin and lived in the

industrial north of England. They were not highly educated, having been forced to go to work from about the age of twelve. He remembers their relationship as very close and one of great mutual affection, but one which lacked an intellectual dimension. His father was originally a craftsman working for the railways, but because of unavailability of work for his particular skill he was forced to became a general labourer, working in the shipyards.

Mr Neal was the third son, born in 1915. Throughout much of his childhood in the 1930s, his father was unemployed, and the family lived in dire poverty. His father maintained his wife and three sons on a subsistence of 23s. 6d. a week; the mother did not work after their marriage.

Mr Neal's father was very interested in music, and when his first son was born he bought an American organ and learned to play hymns on it. This organ was to become important in Mr Neal's life, not only because of his own interest in music, but because to some extent it symbolized a rift between himself and his two brothers.

Simply by having this organ in the house and having had a year's tuition on the fiddle my eldest brother taught himself to play the organ and he taught the second brother to play the violin. I was always in those days the rejected one among the three and I had no such help at all.... It just was that they were both bigger than I. I was the little one and they used to go off with their big friends and play round the neighbourhood and the little boy was left out a bit.

While this feeling of exclusion by his brothers has been important to Mr Neal it was not the predominant theme of their relationship as children, nor is it in adulthood. Though there was rivalry, the brothers also shared various interests. They had what Mr Neal calls a 'community of interests'.

Mr Neal and his brothers had all learned at school how to solve simple substitution codes, and used to pass time making up codes for one another to try to solve. From this Mr Neal went on to teach himself to read music and to play the organ and piano. His description of this gives some indication of the level of intelligence and initiative with which he attacks any new area of interest.

It is a very interesting little pursuit, especially at that age when you are just getting a good grasp of language. We got to the point that even if there was a long unpunctuated succession of syllables, we could guarantee to solve it, just by simply thinking and by logic. We used to set problems to each other which was rather fun, it was one of our little pastimes. Just about this time I got interested in looking at music.... I said to myself one day, dash it all, it is just another code, clearly this stands for music and it must be notes and people can look at that and play something on this organ here and I set to work systematically to crack that code. I cracked it and at the age of thirteen I was in fact playing for church services. I have on and off ever since.... After I was married I inherited from my grandmother a piano, and I have now become a reasonably competent pianist. That is to say I get a great deal of pleasure out of it and my family don't even object to the pleasure I get from struggling my way through Beethoven sonatas, Chopin nocturnes and waltzes and so on.

Despite the feelings of rejection by his older brothers, Mr Neal's family seems to have been a fairly cohesive unit with a considerable religious orientation and a very strong apprecia- tion of hard work and achievement in school. There was value placed on cultural attainments, limited though they were by financial considerations. The poverty conditions of the family influenced the pattern of routine division of labour within the home. Mr Neal's father was the sole provider for the family, but when he was out of work he helped his wife around the house. His memory of his father was that 'he could do every- thing around the house to help – and did'. He says, furthermore :

My father never over-ruled my mother in any respect at all. Every decision that ever was made was made jointly.

The most important external relationship of Mr Neal's family was their connection with the local church. The whole family participated in church activities until the three boys were in their teens and rebelled against regular attendance.

Mr Neal went to a local primary school from the age of five

The Neals

to eleven. At twelve he entered the grammar school in his town on a scholarship. Very early in grammar school he began to do well and he was encouraged to try for a university scholarship. He remembers his grammar-school days as being happy. He is emphatic that the main source of his encouragement as a grammar-school boy came from his parents. His parents' ambition for him and his two brothers was to escape from poverty by education.

It was drilled into us, absolutely drummed into us non-stop, that we were in a terrible plight and in the most dire poverty and if we wanted to lift ourselves up out of that kind of rut, the only way that it could be done was by education. They were absolutely fanatical in their belief in education, as were many people in the north of England in those days. . . . When we began to do well. we were encouraged to do still better and told that was worth aiming at.

Apparently Mr Neal's parents were criticized by their relatives for keeping their sons in school rather than making them go to work as soon as they could get jobs. However, his parents' belief in the value of a good education was so strong that even when there was no food or money they would not take the boys out of school.

They never contemplated for a moment taking us away from the grammar school because they wanted us to get on and better our own prospects and they were convinced that education was the only way of doing it. . . . We were never encouraged or expected to do any remunerative work during the holidays. I think my parents would have been ashamed of themselves if they had sent their youngsters out in their holidays to make a bit of money. They would have thought they were exploiting us unreasonably.

Some of the school masters were quite important to him and after he left grammar school they became life-long friends. These men influenced many of his attitudes and embodied for him many of the attributes which he has grown up to admire. They were men whom he would call 'enlightened' and seem to underscore the feeling of welfare and doing 'good' for others which Mr Neal has felt all his life and shares with his wife.

Mr Neal was at grammar school on scholarship and did not have much money for extra activities. At this time he joined a Christian service organization that he was to stay with through his university career, and which was to become quite important to him.

From about fifteen I belonged to an organization known as Toc H. . . . Toc H is a movement which exists to get people of all classes and all backgrounds to come together regularly and to get to know each other and become friendly and have discussions and talks. And also to undertake certain jobs of social service as well, so that they were in a sense serving the community. At Cambridge I was one of the leading figures in the university Toc H group.

Following in the footsteps of his elder brother, he won a scholarship to Cambridge. He worked very hard and received in 1937 a first class honours degree in modern languages. After he received his degree he decided to stay on at university for an additional year in order to prepare for the Civil Service examinations. In that year he also sat for Part II of the European History Tripos. He passed the Civil Service exams with a high mark and took an upper second in History.

Early in his university career Mr Neal went through a period of deep depression. At this time he was active in Toc H and used to visit an older friend's flat where several of the Toc H members were accustomed to meet. One evening when he was particularly depressed he went over to the flat to listen to some music. His friend put on some Bach and as Mr Neal listened he had some kind of an illumination experience :

I had an experience which really hit me powerfully and the reality of it was enormous. I sat back at that moment, and with cold calculation and reason I tried to figure out the significance of the experience and I strenuously applied my mind to try to remember every aspect of the content of the experience; on the basis of it I worked out laboriously, step by step, what I regarded as my own philosophy, my own dogma, my own belief.

After this Mr Neal found he could devote himself to academic work at university. He worked long hours, studied hard and achieved considerable success. At this time he seems to have established many work patterns which have predominated through most of his life.

The themes which are central to Mr Neal's life and which he principally transmits to his family are those of the virtue of hard work, and a sense of concern for the welfare of fellow men. This has had a tremendous effect upon his life and perhaps is partly responsible for his having advanced so high with the Civil Service and being regarded with respect by others. However, as a result of his illness and the cut-back in his work load, the emphasis which he places on hard work has returned to a level more like that of others around him.

Mr Neal used the words 'hard working' and 'generous' to describe himself. His wife says that :

He is very energetic, very interested in everything. He rapidly becomes concerned with whatever he takes up. He is like the saying, 'Whatsoever comes to your hand to do, do with all your might.' He puts great energy into solving every sort of problem. He is very human, very unselfconscious. I'd say he is generous, warmhearted, very concerned with other people's problems, very intelligent.

Mr and Mrs Neal were raised in very different situations, but there are similarities as well as differences. Both were raised in families in which the father was at home throughout their childhood. However, Mrs Neal's father was retired and Mr Neal's father was unemployed. Both parents encouraged education and made sacrifices so that their children would not have to leave school but could go as far as they wanted. For Mr Neal the motivation was to better his situation in the world; the sacrifices were very extreme and meant the difference between having food and not having food, whereas for Mrs Neal the emphasis on education was because of her family's interest in it and the sacrifices were less extreme.

FAMILY WORLDS

Current Structures of Activities

The Neals' household consists of Mr and Mrs Neal, his two sons by a previous marriage (now aged twenty-three and twenty-one) and their four daughters (now aged sixteen, fourteen, nine, and seven years). His younger son is at university and returns to his home during his holidays and for occasional weekends. The older son is working in the film industry in London, and makes his headquarters at the parental house. At the time interviewing was begun the Neals had for a short time a resident housekeeper who lived in a flat on the ground floor of their home, with her baby and her brother; since that time this woman has left and Mrs Neal's parents now live there. They also employ a daily helper who comes in to do the cleaning.

Mrs Neal commented that each day was punctuated with minor crises. The description of a typical crisis is included to convey the flavour of the Neals' busy household and the complicated arrangements they make to fit all their activities into the day.

Last Monday the next to youngest (then seven) was down with a cold. She had a cough throughout the night. I didn't want to keep her at home because we had already taken advantage of the fact that the youngest was going out for lunch (normally she comes home for lunch every day) so that day our help had arranged a hospital appointment for herself. The car had been causing endless trouble and we had to take it into the garage that morning so I arranged for someone else to take the children to school. I had to decide about the third daughter going to school. I prepared breakfast and by that time I decided she really mustn't go to school. Our help was quite willing to forego the hospital appointment and this at once produced a crisis with the youngest, that she didn't want to go to school without her sister and with somebody else's mother. We were all booked. I had some work at the office and I thought I should be in by ten. However, our help said she would go in the car with her little boy and the third daughter because she couldn't be left. This is the sort of thing.

The Neals

A typical day at the Neal house starts at about 7.00 when Mrs Neal rises. (This was at the time of the early interviews. The routine changed with the departure of the live-in domestic help and the entry of the younger child to regular school; in general outline the picture has remained similar.) She calls the two older girls at 7.15 and then the younger girls and sees that they get dressed. She also calls the oldest boy. Mrs Neal then puts on the tea and, with the help of the older girls, prepares the eggs, etc. The family breakfasts at 7.45 and at 8.10 the older girls leave for school by bus. At about 8.30 the help arrives with her child and helps the younger girls to put on their coats and collects their things for school while Mrs Neal gets ready to go to work and Mr Neal gets the car out of the garage. Mrs Neal then drives the helper and her child to a day nursery, goes on to pick up some more children and takes them to school, leaving the five year old at the nursery school. Mrs Neal returns home to pick up her husband and the Neals drive to work where they arrive somewhere around 9.45 a.m. Before his illness Mr Neal was the first up in the morning, between 5.30 and 6.00. Since his illness he rises later, and spends a more relaxed morning before leaving for work with his wife.

The domestic help returns to the Neals' home after leaving her child at day nursery. She prepares lunch for the youngest daughter to have when she returns from nursery school, and tea for all the children at about 4.30. The little children are brought home by the mother of one of the children Mrs Neal drives to school, although initially they had some difficulty in arranging for their youngest daughter to be picked up from nursery school.

Since Mr Neal's illness they usually return home together sometime after 6.00, usually about 6.30 p.m. Prior to his illness he had often returned much later – at about 9.00 p.m. At about 6.00 p.m. the domestic help goes to her own flat and the Neals' two youngest daughters usually go with her to help bathe her baby. Mrs Neal collects the younger children from the house-keeper and helps them with their baths. The youngest child and the oldest girl usually bath together first. This allows Mrs Neal to leave the room to attend to some other demand for her attention. Next the other two girls would bath, normally without assistance. She also tries to find a bit of time to play with the children, especially the youngest. Sometimes she takes them out to climb a tree or play a game with them before they bath. After baths the two little girls eat and are put to bed. Then Mrs Neal prepares a meal for the oldest girl and for herself and her husband. The second daughter prepares her own supper and takes it up to her room. The Neals and their oldest daughter dine at about 8.30 p.m. The boys also dine with the Neals when they are home. After dinner Mrs Neal clears up the kitchen, washes any dishes necessary for breakfast and sets the table for breakfast. The Neals try to finish their evening meal in time to watch the 10.00 p.m. news.

If they have brought work home from the office this usually waits until 10.30 p.m. Since his illness Mr Neal has not brought home much work, but formerly he did and his day sometimes lasted twenty hours, often till 2.00 in the morning. Mrs Neal now brings work home more than Mr Neal, a mixture of reading and writing: she occasionally writes an entire report at home in several evenings. They retire sometime after 12.00, earlier than before Mr Neal's illness.

The Neals' weekend usually includes an activity for the whole family together, such as a picnic or birthday party. On Saturday morning Mrs Neal takes the children out to do the shopping for the week. Saturday or Sunday evening they may have guests. Their weekends seem to be as busy as their weekdays, and the demands of their work leave little opportunity for leisure at the weekends.

Since the early interviews there have been several changes in the family's domestic situation and daily routines. This is most noticeable in the fact that they no longer employ a resident housekeeper, but must rely upon the resources of the family members and daily help. However all the children are now older and can accept more responsibility and they make fewer demands on Mrs Neal's time. Also, having their grandparents around is a stabilizing influence for the children. Mr Neal says :

With girls of sixteen and fourteen ... the youngsters are very well looked after ... in a way, if my wife's mother is able to do it, she's the most stable form of having someone in the house that there is.

Another important change in the family which affects their domestic situation is that, at present, it is Mrs Neal who takes work home every evening. Mrs Neal said that she is more heavily pressed than her husband right now, and more so than when the interviews began. This situation is eased a bit by the fact that both the Neals are not bringing great quantities of work home at night, so at least one of them can be with the children.

Mrs Neal generally supervises the cleaning done by a daily help. She says:

I'm not very fussy about the cleaning anyway, but I certainly do feel that I've got less help now.

If there is something particularly tactful she wants to say to the help, she sometimes asks Mr Neal for assistance.

Although the Neals have four daughters living at home, they do not like to overburden them with household chores. But this is a family in which each member must join in the work to keep things running smoothly and Mrs Neal commented that she explains to the children 'that however sure they may be that their friends don't do any washing up, in this family they've got to'. There is an organized routine by which the children help with household chores, which Mrs Neal explains as follows:

The children do have jobs. The younger girls are supposed to help lay the tea on Saturdays and Sundays. They all help with the washing up one meal a week. The older girls make their beds in the holidays, not in the term, and they are all supposed to help clear the tables. The big ones also help with the little ones.

Mr Neal also expressed his views of the children helping to keep the household running in an emergency:

Our two big girls have always been extraordinarily competent. There was a day when the eldest girl was eight, when we were all stricken down with 'flu, and the children's nurse went down at the same time. The only healthy person in the house was this daughter of eight and she ran the whole shoot. She made the meals and looked after us, did the shopping and everything. So you can imagine, now that the older two are in their teens, they are very, very competent and generally very helpful. Competent children can make a big difference, and the two younger ones seem to be coming along well too.

The Neals perhaps felt that their lives were a bit freer to depart from a strict daily pattern when they had a resident housekeeper. Part of the restrictions they now feel are because Mrs Neal's parents, although on hand and available to help in an emergency, are quite elderly. Also, Mrs Neal does not want to put undue pressures on her children just to assure that she can continue with her career. She says:

I'm becoming more dependent on the older girls which I don't like doing really.... They're very good about it, but I don't want them to feel that they have to be good to enable me to do my job. In some ways I wish we'd left letting the help go till later, but actually the older children didn't get on very well with the help. They were very sure at the time that they'd rather my mother was here. I said. 'You'll have to help more if I don't have anybody on Saturday morning, and so on,' but it's worked out very well really. It's nicer to have my mother there. We like her. We've benefited in a number of indirect ways.

Like most of the dual-career families, the Neals have had a variety of domestic helpers. From 1953 to 1958 they had a daily nanny plus a succession of au pairs who worked in the mornings only and did the housework. She says:

When we were first married the au pair girls would baby-sit if they were in, once the children were asleep, but never put the little ones to bed. Whenever we wanted to go out and leave them in the early evening, I used to get the nanny to stay, but I hardly ever did this until we had been married about six years. She did stay from time to time. I didn't pay her for baby-sitting but she put the children to bed and if the au pair girl was in then the nanny would go home when the children went to sleep. I did this pretty infrequently, really, all through my married life, until I became an Assistant Secretary, when we gave the nanny a good deal more and asked her to stay more regularly because I found I had more office engagements, more things I'd need to stay two or three hours for, and for a time she used to bath the little ones once a week.

The second nanny, who did not live in, was hired in 1958 and stayed with the Neals until about 1967. During this time they also had an au pair living in and working half days. Because this woman was herself a very satisfactory person, and the Neals liked her very much, they seem to have been happiest with this arrangement. Mr Neal says about her :

The children's nurse that we had recruited from the day nursery was really superb; she was utterly reliable, she was really very fine.

Mrs Neal says that she structured the relationship with this one in such a way that the nanny was regarded as her deputy, standing in for her in most domestic matters when she was not there. This nanny stayed with the Neals until the youngest daughter entered nursery school, and there was 'no more nannying to be done'. At the same time the family moved into their present house and hired a resident housekeeper.

Mrs Neal does the routine food shopping on Saturday mornings. She prepares the everyday meals :

I would say from the point of view of any housewife, and certainly for the working housewife, things get better year by year. I don't know that I spend less time cooking now, but I give a far more varied meal. I reckon in half an hour now to be able to provide a very good evening meal with frozen foods, and so on . . .

Mrs Neal also prepares the special meals. They prefer to have a few guests to a dinner which she can prepare fairly easily. Her daughters often help with the preparations for family celebrations such as birthdays and Christmas.

When they employed a resident housekeeper she was responsible for washing and ironing the clothes, and some of the mending. Mrs Neal would do the rest of the mending in the evening while watching television. Since the housekeeper is no longer employed and Mrs Neal's 'take-home' work load has increased, she is thankful that modern aids have improved and help her a great deal :

Now the latest improvement in my life is that in the last two or three months in the local shops – instead of dry-cleaning being (a) rather expensive and (b) taking about five days – there's one of these places where you put it in – first of all you had to work it yourself, now there's a woman there who will take any load – they charge a shilling a pound and you can collect it next morning, and I can do that before I go to work. This has made a small but visible difference to the ease of keeping my house.

Formerly Mr Neal did most of the household maintenance, the remainder being done by a contractor. When the housekeeper's brother lived in the flat on the ground floor of their house, he took care of most of the maintenance as he was a carpenter.

Both Mr and Mrs Neal enjoy gardening and they do this themselves. Their sons sometimes mow the lawn. While Mr Neal was recovering from his illness he was not able to do much in the garden. Occasionally one of the Neals and the children will wash the car.

The Neals take their holiday together, three or four weeks in the summer, and usually a week or so at Christmas and Easter during the children's school holidays. During the summer they all go away, usually to a rented house, but sometimes on a camping trip. Plans for family vacations are made jointly; the children also participate in the discussion.

They have a joint bank account. Mr Neal has occasionally consulted his bank on investments. The Neals do not make a detailed budget, but let their income accumulate in their account and then either invest it or put it in the savings bank. Weekly one of the Neals cashes a cheque for household expenses.

They use a G.P. as their family doctor. They also have a lawyer and Mr Neal plans to take on an accountant. In the past he has taken care of tax returns with occasional assistance from his wife.

It is evident that the concept of a stable family life is central to the Neals' domestic arrangements and has always been a primary concern, particularly for Mrs Neal. The family has enjoyed very good health, with the exception of Mr Neal's illness last year, and everyone undertakes a full schedule of activities. Though the children have rarely been ill, it is reassuring to have Mrs Neal's mother around in case this should occur. Also, the Neals can, in an emergency, turn to his sister-in-law or their friends in the neighbourhood, as they did when he was ill. They both have abundant energy, but in the course of time the overtaxing of this asset might again have serious repercussions on their health. Referring to his work load and illness, she says:

Everybody said that my husband must not tax himself. He had high blood pressure. I think from hindsight his blood pressure had been mounting for the previous two months.

Referring to her work load and health, he says:

I don't think our work has taken a toll in health except perhaps a little on my wife. You see she has only been able to do this by dint of being terribly strong all her life. What she has been able to do would knock out any ordinary woman in no time.

This also gives a feeling for the tremendous pressures under which this family functions.

Personal experience of family development and current husband–wife relationship

Mr Neal had been married before to a woman he had met while he was in his post in the Civil Service during which time he did some social work in a youth club run by a Church of England curate. Shortly after they met the Blitz began and he sent the girl to live with his parents in the north, where she went to nursing school. Just before he was released from the army they were married, but she died in 1951 leaving him with two sons.

Mr Neal met his present wife in 1952 when she was his Assistant Principal. At the time Mrs Neal had been in the Civil Service for about three years. Before meeting Mr Neal, Mrs Neal had dated other Civil Servants, but does not seem to have been serious about any of them. She was not 'hell bent for marriage' and found excitement in her work. However, she felt that life without marriage would not be so full. She remembered talking with her girl friends at university and deciding that she would have liked to continue with her career after marriage and children; but if she had married someone who did not approve of her working or whose career did not allow her to work, she believes that she would have given up her job. Mr and Mrs Neal were engaged in January 1953 and married in May, when Mr Neal was thirty-eight and Mrs Neal was twenty-five.

'Integrity' was one of the chief words Mrs Neal chose to describe Mr Neal's qualities that attracted her:

He's a very much more worthwhile person than many other men I'd probably met.

He seemed initially attracted to her because of her abilities and her sense of adventure, which he feels they both share:

She came as Assistant Principal to me; I didn't approve of female Civil Servants very much – but by George, she was the cat's whiskers, so staggeringly first class that it just knocked me back. I also quickly discovered that she was very full of life and adventure, you know, everything. I had always been like that myself and she was so similar; we quickly began to get on like a house on fire and in a very short time we were engaged. Not very long after that we married and we have never looked back since; we have really had great fun.

Mrs Neal was very sensitive about being a step-mother to his sons and went to great lengths to become friends with the boys and to be accepted by them before they married.

My wife was absolutely wonderful with the boys, she really has been terrific. Before we were married she insisted on getting to know them and them getting to know her.

Civil Service practice does not allow married couples to work together in the same department (although Mr Neal said that they had made an outstanding work team before they married). One of the reasons is that they would want to take their holidays together which would disrupt the office. Shortly after they were married and before she was posted to another department, they faced this problem and solved it in a novel way, illustrating how their spirit of adventure and adaptability co-exists with a mutual devotion to their work at the Ministry :

There was an interesting time when we were just married and I was a Principal and she was my Assistant Principal. The office immediately wanted to separate us. It was very difficult for holidays, the Principal and the Assistant Principal wanting to go away at the same time, but they just couldn't manage to get around to moving her. I had my two boys when I married her and we solved it by having a little camping holiday down in Surrey within easy reach of London. We took turns coming to the office every other day. It was rather fun too.

When they were first married they lived for a time in Mr Neal's house in a suburb, but shortly decided to move to a larger house, nearer to their office. At this time Mrs Neal was expecting their first child. Mrs Neal explains why she and her husband decided to have a baby right away :

We didn't want a break in the family. You see we had two little boys aged six and four, and we didn't want the family any more split than need be.

They did not have in mind an ideal number of children when they were married. She says :

We talked of having two and when we had our second daughter we didn't particularly think of having any more. We had two boys and two girls. But we were both fond of children and one likes to have something small in the pram. So we changed our minds after a while and had two more.

He adds :

We never decided that our target figure was six or anything like that. The trouble was that every time she saw a baby in a pram she said, 'Oh what a lovely baby.'

The Neals' four daughters were born in 1954, 1956, 1961 and 1963.

The Neals lived in the house that they had bought before the birth of their eldest daughter for nearly fourteen years. When the fifth child was expected Mrs Neal felt they needed a larger house. However, Mr Neal presented some opposition to the idea as he thought the house they were living in at the time was big enough. But he was won over to the idea of moving.

I argued that the family was about to start falling off at the top and going off to live their own lives so that the house we were already in was big enough, if we could just tide it over the next couple of years or so. And there I was, one against many. I kept my end up as best I could until the eldest daughter, who is really a politician, had a brain wave and came forth with the stunning proposition that if we were to have this house then I could have a study of my own, which of course I had always wanted. 'Wouldn't that be nice...?' I discovered at that stage that I wasn't above a bit of bribery, so I succumbed. And they let me have my study too.

As the boys are growing up and beginning to lead their own lives, the new house is most used by Mr and Mrs Neal and their daughters, but is big enough for the boys to use as a head-quarters. The larger house also allowed for a resident house-keeper in the separate flat. 'It is a very good way of getting domestic staff.'

Both Mr and Mrs Neal emphasize shared ideas, interests, activities and a rich family life as being central to their conception of marriage. In separate interviews both express very similar views of their marriage. Mrs Neal says:

Family life is what I value most about marriage, I suppose. When I think about my daughters getting married, I naturally hope that they will produce families and have an ordinary sort of family life and I think that's what one gains mainly out of marriage.

Mr Neal says:

I would say both of us look upon it as an absolutely fifty-fifty part-nership. Right from the word go – we have always, for example, had a joint bank account. Everything is done jointly, almost every-thing as far as possible, as a family.

Mr Neal sees their partnership as one with some division of responsibility along conventional lines but with flexibility to interchange activities if the situation requires it. He describes the situation as follows:

It is true that there are certain jobs that are a man's job, which I would always undertake, except when I was too ill to do so. But if I have been out of action, my wife – this is her nature – will tackle anything and do it.... She is not supposed to know that kind of thing (rawl-plugging and plastering, mending fuses or pipes, etc.) but all these jobs she would jolly well tackle and nothing would ever beat her, if she has to. But these are always accepted as being my responsibility. In the same way, mending clothes, etc. is hers.

Mrs Neal has a more conventional conception of the primary importance of the husband's career. Her attitude also is one that emphasizes the wife's responsibility to the children, whether or not she works:

I'll say two things: one that I think the wife must put her husband's career first. If you marry a husband who is a geographer or an archaeologist, you've just got to adjust yourself to the fact of living abroad if necessary and giving up one's own job. The other thing is that I think people talk much too readily about shelving the responsibility of children – this is not something one can push off onto someone else. Being so well paid myself, I can always have somebody looking after the children and I certainly wouldn't work on any other terms. But both with pre-school children and school children there are a lot of things you cannot properly delegate to anybody else: this is why I think women should be able to work shorter hours.... My husband takes a great interest in the children, and I should be very sorry for anybody whose husband didn't. Obviously it is much harder to bring up children without a husband's support. In a way it is more his interest in the children I value than his actual expenditure of time, his co-operation in disciplining them and making decisions about them and going to school functions and that sort of thing. Like most parents with children, a lot of our lives are built round them.

In both Mr and Mrs Neals' own backgrounds strong family life had been important. Each contrasts their own marriage with that of their parents, pointing out that when they were young neither of their fathers worked at stable occupations and were home most of the time. This made for one kind of closeness between the partners. In their case it is their overlapping careers that have brought them closer together through the shared intellectual stimulation of work.

Mrs Neal says :

I do see my husband at work; we have lunch together most days. This is another part of our marriage and I do very much enjoy having this in common. Very few of my friends at home and very few other people here (except the other married couples) have somebody with whom they can turn over ideas about what one might do in one's own job and so on.

In thinking about their marriage as compared with the marriages of friends and acquaintances, Mrs Neal expresses in another way the view that the combination of career and marriage offer special fulfilment to a woman :

I don't very often discuss their marriages with them. They must be different on the whole; they are not working and there probably tends to be an emptiness in that they feel they're not doing so much as they were before they were married, while my problem is being too busy and trying to find time for things. I sort of console myself with that reflection when I feel that I'm hard done by.

The Neals did not mention any area of major difficulty in their relationship. Disagreements have tended to be minor and differences in background and personality are resolved by tolerant discussion. This pertains not only to disagreements between husband and wife, but also when the children are concerned and/or involved. Mrs Neal says :

We very rarely disagree about any important decision; perhaps it is our Civil Service training. In this job one inevitably learns to give and take which stands us in good stead. We've never really quarrelled over anything serious because we both realize that it's a matter of deciding jointly and we're prepared to compromise if necessary on everything except an absolute minimum of matters. On the whole I don't think there are any matters on which our essential minima have clashed, so we don't spend a lot of time quarrelling. When we do quarrel it's never about anything serious except each other's conduct at that moment really.

Mr and Mrs Neal receive considerable support and encouragement from each other. When domestic arrangements seem to become more than she can cope with he lends a hand in trying to find a solution, and his encouragement and support of his wife's career has been particularly important. She says:

He's always been in favour of my working. If I say I really don't think I can keep on with this any longer, his reaction is to show me that I can. I am sure I would never have gone on working if I had not had help from him or if he or any of the children had been ill; except that he was ill this last year and I am glad I did not stop working, I was very much better off working.... As I say, we're both quite energetic and prepared to turn our hand to things. I'm prepared to turn my hand to helping him with his problems and he with mine, so that we do manage pretty well.

They also turn to each other for advice and discussion when faced with a particularly difficult and challenging problem in their work. He says:

One of the outstanding features of this situation is that we have a tremendous interest in common. It's not like the chap that goes off to his business and never speaks a word about it to his wife because she's not interested in it anyway. Being at the level we are in the office we know what goes on and we are interested in the whole field and each of us is always interested in what the other is doing. I have always found it most invaluable to be able to have a little chat with her about any problems bothering me on the way home in the car, or on the way up in the morning.

Parent–Child Relationships

There seems to be a very strong family feeling among all members of the Neal family and Mr and Mrs Neal are concerned that their children receive both maternal and paternal attention. Mrs Neal is especially conscious of the effects of her working on her children. The children and their friends enjoy playing at the Neals' home. Mrs Neal says:

Our house has always been full of children, all of the neighbourhood children come over to play. I say to them, 'Why don't you go over and play with A' and they say, 'We don't like to go to A's house.' This applies whether I am here or not.

The children have been raised within a fairly rigorous framework of acceptable behaviour. However, the rules are flexible and the Neals are very conscious of the special needs of a child and to a large extent they tend to treat each situation as it arises. In the following Mrs Neal conveys an impression of their philosophy of child rearing:

It's a big subject, something I have been thinking about lately. Psychologists tremendously underrate the importance of habit. They think of all these very subtle causes but a tremendous lot can happen by chance. It is important in managing a child just to be clever and make things turn out the right way. If you are going to get your child to wear his cap it is important to be in the right position, not calling him back from behind to come and fetch it but being between him and the door at the time he leaves. You don't let him just walk out and say 'No, I won't bother today.' In the adolescent situation where your powers are very limited, it is important to make them feel that you have some authority and you have to choose the right moment to assert that authority.... It is important for them to get the feeling that they cannot be successfully naughty.... You've got to let them know somehow that they are part of the world and that they are chugging along and doing all right; this is easier for girls than boys because they can make cakes in the kitchen and they can see that they are doing something useful and getting praise for it and the cakes are handed round while the boys are out playing noisy games in the garden and get told to make less noise. The fundamental thing one is really trying to teach them is that there is some justice and that they can play without being naughty and they don't have to be rebels ... life isn't really as unfair as all that and they don't need to drop out of it.

Discipline of the children is, for the most part, a shared responsibility, although Mrs Neal tends to deal with the girls and Mr Neal the boys. They tend to punish the children differently, in that the boys might be physically reprimanded while the girls would tend to be denied a privilege.

In the Neal family all members participate in discussions and friendly arguments, and a general give and take is encouraged. Consequently when problems arise or decisions are to be made everyone talks about the pros and cons of the situation and tries to find the best solution. This is true as well for the children's difficulties in handling the world outside the family and Mr and Mrs Neal try to talk with them about their problems and to help each child to find the best solution for himself.

The Neals are proud of their children and make no distinction between the sons of Mr Neal's first marriage and their daughters. They are sensitive to the problems of each child and they speak of each with a feeling for his or her own individuality.

Mrs Neal would have preferred their eldest son to be more firmly inside their family life, even though now grown up, but she is certainly not hostile to his outside activities on this account. She says:

One might have had a boy who had the same amount of outside activities and even less interest in the home, or someone who had a good many less outside activities and still didn't really take an interest in the home – just regarded it as somewhere where he got his meals. However, our older boy is really conscious of what is going on at home; if he is there he joins quite happily with anything that is going on. He is not a boy that shuts himself off from the family at all. But once he is away he tends to forget that it still exists.

The Neals' aspirations for their eldest son are that he succeed in the field he has chosen for himself. Mr Neal says:

The older boy didn't want to go to university and I think that is why he didn't succeed in getting there. But he does very much want to make a career in the film industry on the production side. Now he is trying job after job, to worm his way into that industry.... We are rather sure he has many of the requisite talents and abilities to do this ... it would suit him fine.

As with their elder son, the Neals' hopes for their second son are that he be successful and happy in the profession he chooses:

The only thing he ever talked about wanting to do was teach; we told him that the best thing to do was to get a good university degree at a good university. So he tried to get to university and he did. Whether he will still want to teach, I don't know. I should be quite happy to see him go into the teaching profession. He'd make a very good teacher.

Throughout most of their lives the Neals' sons have been close and friendly. At times there have been difficult patches in their relationship but there is no repetition of the strong feelings of rivalry which Mr Neal experienced with his older brother. Although Mrs Neal does not see them as particularly close friends now, she explains their relationship:

They get along very well. As little boys they were good friends though they were constantly bickering. When the older boy began to draw away, he didn't take the younger one into his confidence any more than anybody else. I don't really feel that they are terribly close now. They do share a room although they could have separate rooms. . . . It used to beat me how they could both be in the same room changing to go out and then one would come down and ask us where the other was going this evening: they won't ask each other. I think they share clothes and records but that is natural. They do get on better now than they have in the past. When our older son had his 21st birthday party his brother came and it was the sort of relationship one likes to see.

The Neal's eldest daughter is a talented pianist, and at fourteen will be confronting the decision as to whether to pursue a musical career or a more general higher education. Mr Neal says:

I don't know whether the music will fade out, but she could make a career in music easily. She has tremendous musical ability. Unfortunately, in some senses, she also has pretty tremendous all-round ability. . . . I think she is thinking more in terms of going to Oxford now, following Mrs Neal, and fine if she does.

In talking about her eldest daughter later, at the time of the final interview, Mrs Neal indicated her daughter's thoughts about women working and what kind of career she might like to follow in the future, as well as some of the effect that Mrs Neal's own career has had on this daughter.

Actually she is in a rather gloomy phase of adolescence at the moment and she bears the brunt of the fact that my mother doesn't look after the little girls for long: they come running home to our side of the house. One might hit the other and then they cry, and either nobody comforts them or one of the big girls stops her prep and comforts them unless Mr Neal or I are there. So, although she's not against married women working she has said: 'I'd like to have some work I can do at home', which is, of course, a very satisfactory arrangement.

On the other hand, in comparing herself with her friends, she had described herself as lucky not to have her parents always at home and suggested that for this reason she gets on better with her parents than most of her friends do. Their daughter's requirements are possibly at present influenced by her music teacher who has two children and combines her piano teaching with her family.

The two oldest daughters went through a period of rivalry but recently they have come closer together. The manner in which the Neals have handled this situation is indicative of the understanding with which they handle problems of sibling relations. Mrs Neal described the second daughter's problems and the rivalry between the oldest two girls.

At five and three the older was a very kind little thing, and the younger was only too happy to trot around after her, following her wonderful ideas; then at seven and five, the younger found she had a will of her own and on occasions simply went on strike. For a time they really had quite bad relations. All children quarrel – it is more sort of a biting back between the girls – but if one is in trouble the other will stick up for her. Everybody had always taken the second daughter's part in order not to allow her to be swamped by the first, and our first daughter used to feel this. They seem to have grown out of it now. The third one is different: she is a shy, dreamy little thing, much more gentle than the others. She used to be laughed at in school and unhappy there – the others saw her cry and called her a baby. But she has settled down now. She only needs to get to seventeen because she is very cuddlable. She'll find a niche in life.

The Neals do not think that she has really missed her mother greatly because she is a very affectionate person and she had a very good relationship with the nanny. This daughter also seemed to make a better adjustment to the resident housekeeper than her older sisters did.

The third daughter seems to have had the most difficult time in adjusting to nursery school. Mrs Neal attributes this difficult adjustment principally to a set of unfortunate experiences in the particular school:

When I would drop her at school, the only person in the classroom would be the nursery assistant and she didn't want to go. The proper teacher always came later. If she'd had the proper teacher there·she would have been very ready to be handed over to her. I was constantly wondering whether I should complain to the headmistress, but one doesn't like doing that: you·feel this will set the teacher against the child and it didn't seem so big a problem then, in her first term at school, and that teacher was only there for one term. The next two terms she had two little friends in this class, one of whom unfortunately left after she had been there for two terms and the other one left the term after. She used to say to me about the second little boy 'It's quite all right, Jonathan's a friend now' and when Jonathan was away she was less happy to go and then when he was leaving altogether she was very unhappy.... This is one of these nursery schools where it seemed at the time that the children were free to behave as they liked. My opinion of four-year-old children left to themselves is not very good. Our daughter used to be teased by some of the horrid little things, you know, in carefully-raised voice: 'I don't like ... do you?', 'she's a baby'. I used to hear this when I went into the school with her.

Mrs Neal tried to help her daughter by talking with her about her problems and the situation was eased when the daughter went into a class with a more competent and very nice teacher. Although she became dependent upon this teacher, the Neals did not discourage it because it helped in their daughter's adjustment and in overcoming the pressures put on her by the other children.

About their youngest daughter, Mrs Neal says:

She is rather Napoleonic. ... She's a very able little girl. She has got a very strong will and would make a wonderful permanent secretary in the department in fifty years time; but when one is very small and has a strong will the more one comes up against difficulties in life, like having to go to bed at seven o'clock. However, she is learning to control herself very well and behaves well at school – I don't worry about her much at all.

After Mr Neal's operation he was somewhat disturbed by his youngest child's loud voice, especially early in the morning in concert with the voices of her sisters. Mrs Neal explained how she has handled this situation and her solution indicates the way in which she manages tactfully the difficulties of child rearing.

Our youngest child is naturally a very noisy child. Mr Neal has a loud voice himself but since his operation he can't stand noise. This is normal in relation to his specific illness. A sudden loud voice is actually painful to him but it's very difficult to sit at breakfast and to be quiet. One way I can get round it is to call my husband ten minutes late which is quite successful.

The Neals' two youngest daughters have not yet reached a stage of open competition and Mrs Neal tries to help each little girl to feel secure in her own right.

They are not terribly competitive fortunately. It hasn't occurred to either of them at the moment to be rivals. Our youngest daughter is still content to admire our third daughter. Our third daughter is ready to give in to our fourth when the occasion arises.

On the whole the two older girls' relationship with their younger sisters is very good. They generally enjoy helping with the little ones when Mrs Neal is delayed or busy in the evening.

The girls also look to their brothers with respect and special affection.

... the girls have always been very reluctant to criticize the boys or say anything to us. On the whole the boys have been very fond of the girls; they told them stories in bed and all this sort of thing and have always been very nice to them.

Mrs Neal has given a great deal of thought to the effect of her career on the upbringing of her children :

... the children whom it hits the hardest are my stepsons whom one would think it would matter least to, but I am really pretty satisfied in the way my daughters' upbringing has gone. With the boys there were more problems.... When their mother died, they took authority much less seriously altogether.... Although the nanny seemed to deal with them quite satisfactorily, I think they would have regained this sense of authority better if I had been there instead of just miscellaneous people. We didn't have a lot of changes but they certainly didn't respect the nannies as much as they did me. With the girls, they just did their prep and I didn't interfere. The boys didn't trouble about anything and they only achieved the results (consonant) with their intellectual ability if one did stand over them and say 'Now look carefully' and that sort of thing.

Mr and Mrs Neal have given much thought to the values which they feel are important in family life. They expressed similar feelings in individual interviews which can be summarized by what Mrs Neal said:

I think that an active family life is very important. We set a lot of store by (up to a certain age anyway) going on holiday with the children and making sure there are things we all do together. Obviously one doesn't want to stop them doing things that they want to do but there doesn't really seem to be any conflict of interest. They can have all the activities they want and still come home to a real family life.

Mrs Neal's parents are very important to the family and all of the children have been close to them. This relationship has been strengthened since the grandparents have come to live in the flat in the Neals' home because the children see much more of them. Mr Neal's parents are both dead.

Mrs Neal does not see her brother or sister very often because they all have such busy schedules.

I'm very fond of my sister and I'd like to exchange notes about her family life and so on much more than I do. In fact two months often go by without our seeing each other. We do have family expeditions over to each other's house occasionally.

Before Mrs Neal's parents moved into the Neals' house, she would occasionally see her brother when he drove her parents over to visit the Neals. Now he is a more frequent visitor.

Mr Neal's next older brother lives in Mr Neal's home town near the Lake District. About once a year Mr Neal takes a house in the Lake District for a holiday of fell walking with his family, and invites his brother's family. He also visits his brother occasionally when business trips take him into the area. Between Mr Neal and the oldest of the brothers, who is a physicist and teaches mathematics, there has in the past been some coolness, partly because they differed radically on religious questions, and Mr Neal characterized him as a 'terribly hard-boiled scientist'. However, since his brother got married some of his rough edges have been worn down, and Mr Neal and he get on better as time goes on. Each has visited the other occasionally when business trips have provided an opportunity.

The Neals' friends tend to fall into three groups: friends from before the Neals were married, friends they have made through their children, and friends they have made at work.

Examples of friends from before the Neals were married are friends and relatives of Mr Neal's first wife and Mr and Mrs Neals' school and university friends. The family feels quite close to Mr Neal's first wife's sister and her husband, who cared for the boys after their mother died. This couple are the godparents of the Neals' second daughter.

Mr Neal formed many friendships with staff at his grammar school and these have been important to him. He has also maintained a close contact with one of his fellow students from the grammar school. This man is the godfather of one of the Neals' children and he visits the Neals at least once a year although he lives in Canada.

At university Mr Neal made one or two friendships which have lasted since they graduated:

One, the best of all, will last all my life. My best friend at university was a student at my college who later went into the Church of England and is now a Minister in the Church of England. I always had great admiration for him. He's a great chap and the most adventurous soul imaginable, and we had the most fantastic adventures together.

Mrs Neal has kept in touch with many of her school and university friends as well.

There are quite a few school friends with whom I'm vaguely in touch who live in different parts of the country and some of them are the children's godparents. There are school and college friends who we send Christmas cards to and occasionally if it's convenient (e.g. on our way up north on holiday) we go and see them. I've got one college friend actually who lives within a mile of us and I see her fairly often: she brings her children round to tea and vice versa.

The friends that the Neals have made through their children are regarded as family friends; social exchanges with them mostly involve family get-togethers. Most of the Neals' weekend social life involves this group of friends. In this way the children can be included.

Mr and Mrs Neal have felt these relationships outside the family to be of great importance to their children and each of the children has been given godparents. Whenever possible the Neals have encouraged a special relationship between each child and his godparents. This has been especially important for the oldest son as his godfather 'is somebody outside the family who he can turn to'.

The third main group of friends are work colleagues: the Neals' work friendships overlap.

We make the same friends, the same people appeal to both of us. ... Any man I find myself becoming friendly with, my wife seems to take to instinctively and all her friends I like very much indeed.

Some colleagues have become family friends although the Neals do not see them frequently. Mrs Neal does not seem to see a great deal of her colleagues outside the office:

I've never had my boss out here, for example, or any of the people under me. There is no atmosphere of compulsory entertaining. Of the senior staff of this department, I suppose something like fifteen have been to our house one time or another. I'm very unenterprising myself about any sort of entertaining; sometimes we write down a list of people we ought to have over and we gradually get through this list about once every two months.

The Neals received a great deal of emotional support and many offers of help from their friends at the time of Mr Neal's illness. They feel that in any emergency they could rely on their friends and they also try to help others in any situations they can. The Neals feel they have many friends and contrasted their wide circle with the idea of a small circle of friends whom one sees a great deal of. Most of their friends do not know each other.

WORK WORLDS

The Neals are both civil servants in a ministry located in London. The ministry for which they work originates and implements policies and programmes dealing with an important aspect of the welfare of the nation; it is associated with ancillary organizations.

Mr Neal

Mr Neal has been unwaveringly committed to his work in the Civil Service and to the work of his ministry. He has given unstintingly very long hours and devoted his intellect to the problems facing the departments he has worked with.

In choosing a career in the Civil Service following university one of Mr Neal's prime motives was to be able to help his parents.

I took my degree in 1937 at Cambridge and then I had a choice to make. I was pressed very strongly by my tutor to apply for a research fellowship at my college and although I hankered after it, I decided against it. This was because of my parents. I was quite determined to get into a pretty remunerative job as quickly as possible so I could help them. So I decided to go to the Admin Civil Service. I also knew that the examination was the most highly competitive in the world and so I decided that I needed another year at Cambridge to prepare myself for the Civil Service.

Mr Neal did very well in the Civil Service exams but there were so many candidates and so few places that he received an appointment to the ministry of his third choice. This presented some problems for him.

They wrote and said they were going to put me into the War Office. This put me on the spot: all my life I had been an ardent pacifist. These were the days of Dick Shepherd's movements and all that and I didn't like the idea of going to work in the War Office. It became a conflict of conscience. This was all annoying me because I wanted to get a lucrative job and so I thought, 'O.K., I'll take the job.'

The usual practice was for the Civil Service to call up an appointee about six months after he had passed the examinations. Mr Neal was counting on this time for a rest because he had been working terribly hard at university and had just sat through several weeks of gruelling examinations. Unfortunately he was posted almost immediately.

By the time I had finished that examination it was physically impossible for me to lift a cup of tea to my mouth and drink it without spilling it; I was in this highly nervous state and realized that I needed a rest. I was put into this department that I had no desire to get interested in and the result was that I just didn't do any work. . . . The job I had was Assistant Principal, a good job which allegedly enabled one to get to know how the office ran and brought you into contact with a lot of different divisions.

When the Second World War began and young men became eligible for conscription, Mr Neal registered as a conscientious objector and his dilemma was resolved by agreeing to accept non-combatant duties. He served in the armed forces from 1940 to 1945 and his experience in the Army improved his health after the pressures of working so hard in school and university. He was stationed on the edge of Dartmoor and although his job involved physical labour it was a complete change from what he had been through at university.

It really restored me physically like nothing on earth could possibly have done. There was plenty to do, a lot of it was sheer physical work, but this didn't worry me – scrubbing floors, polishing floors. It was so simple to do, no brain work at all, complete absence of responsibility, this was the great thing.

Mr Neal's time in the Army also extricated him from the position in the Civil Service which he did not enjoy and when he was discharged in 1945 he accepted a post as an Assistant Principal in his present ministry on the basis that he wanted to do socially constructive work and really could not envisage returning to the War Office.

I immediately made good. I was put on the local government side to begin with, chiefly in local government law. . . . I worked like a devil and got back to old habits, taking cases of work home. My superior was very pleased with everything I did and before I knew where I was, almost within a year, I was promoted to Principal.

Mr Neal stayed in the department to which he was posted after the war until his recent illness. At the time he became ill he was an Under Secretary. Each Under Secretary is in charge of a division of the ministry and is responsible for organizing the execution of the Minister's policies in his division. The horizontal relationships between Under Secretaries seem relatively less important than the vertical relationships between Under Secretary and his superiors (the Deputy Secretary, the Permanent Secretary, and the Minister) and between Under Secretary and his subordinates (the Assistant Secretaries in his division).

Before his illness Mr Neal had charge of a division with a staff of about 120 with a very heavy work load.

I had five Assistant Secretaries, which was an excessive number in spite of the enormous amount of work. I once looked through the little book in the office which showed the lay-out of many Government departments, division by division. I looked to see if any other Under Secretary had as many Assistant Secretaries as I. I did not find anyone else with more than four and the usual number then was two or three. So you can see the enormous work load we had.

Mr Neal had very friendly relations with his subordinates which helped him to get good work done quickly. The following conversation, which Mr Neal had with his Director of Establishments, indicates how Mr Neal was thought of by his superiors and his relations with them when he was Under Secretary.

I once complained to the Director of Establishments that a certain friend of mine wasn't getting promoted to Assistant Secretary. The Director said to me, 'Look, if he had half your drive he would have been there long ago.'

Until recently Mr Neal worked an almost superhuman amount, often up to fifteen hours a day, spending perhaps ten hours in his office and then coming home with two or three briefcases of work and working until one in the morning.

After his illness Mr Neal's position in the ministry was changed slightly and he was in charge of two smaller divisions with a combined staff of 120. The two divisions are unrelated and only placed together under one administrator for convenience. Mr Neal pointed out that the level of responsibility was the same but that the work load was much less because one division is really an autonomous organization outside London, and the Assistant Secretary is very competent : 'He knows more about the job than most Assistant Secretaries ever do.' Mr Neal's chief responsibility for this division seems to have been to sustain good relations between this outlying unit and the ministry, and 'to make them feel that they are not left out and forgotten'.

Although the doctors hoped that he would be able to resume his former post, Mr Neal was a bit uneasy about his ability to handle the very heavy work load of his Under Secretary position. When the interviews began a final decision on his future in the ministry was pending and Mr Neal explained later how the situation was resolved.

They asked me to revert from the rank of Under Secretary to that of Assistant Secretary. I resisted this – it was a little difficult to take a substantial cut in pay and it would have spoilt my superannuation. My pension when I retired would have been assessed on the overall figure. I resisted it until the office discovered that the Civil Service had arrangements which enabled me to retire on medical grounds and to be re-employed the following day in a lower grade, and make up the balance of my pay to what I was earning before out of my pension. I'm in fact, therefore, now on a mixture of pension and full pay of an Assistant Secretary supplemented from a pension to the level of an Under Secretary.... At the same time, as an Assistant Secretary, they gave me a very comfortable post indeed. In fact, I've never had it so good; it's delightful ... compared with what I was doing, there's no strain involved at all.

Mr Neal's illness and the subsequent change in his work situation have not affected the satisfaction in his work. He says about it :

I've had to accept it philosophically. I am not one that likes to moulder away; I am not quite mouldering away. I have quite enough work to do.

Mr Neal's commitment and dedication to his work springs from a profound religious and-human sense of generosity and concern for human welfare. In addition, Mr Neal's own childhood was an experience of penury from which he escaped by extremely hard work.

Mrs Neal

Mrs Neal entered the Civil Service as an Assistant Principal in 1949 at the age of twenty-one. The Civil Service has offered her meaningful work with the opportunity for advancement to positions of greater challenge and responsibility. The advice of her college principal was influential in the choice and Mrs Neal felt she would 'get a fair deal as a woman' in the Civil Service.

I was more inclined to do something like the Civil Service where you just go in and the wheels go round and you either go on up or you don't, rather than a job where you had to keep thinking for yourself, 'Ought I to go after a new job now?' Some people no doubt like worrying about that sort of thing but I am only too glad not to. I have other things to worry about, I have my career taken care of.

Mrs Neal was not assigned to either of her first two choices of ministries in the Civil Service but she soon found satisfactions in the work at the ministry where she was placed and still works.

Mrs Neal is an Assistant Secretary at present in charge of organizing and executing a staff training programme and of negotiating for payments to people with whom the ministry has dealings. She has two direct subordinates, one who assists her with the training programme and one dealing with payments.

Mrs Neal deals with questions of policy and communicates with her two assistants on payment primarily by telephone and by discussions, memoranda and folders of papers. This relationship appears to be straightforward administratively from Mrs Neal's point of view.

All the work is ad hoc. This is the characteristic; anything that becomes routine is no longer for me to do. If it is no longer a matter of settling a policy and is a matter of executing a policy, it is for people lower down.

Mrs Neal is in charge of a new training effort which is being fashioned for the most part in committee meetings. These committee meetings are group discussions of many problems that cut across categories of knowledge and responsibility.

There is one way in which the training programme is qualitatively different from Mrs Neal's payments work. In her work on payments there is an accepted framework in which decisions can be made, responsibility taken and policy executed. But the training work is an innovation and Mrs Neal is proceeding cautiously and thoughtfully into new territory.

We haven't expanded nearly as quickly as some people thought we would partly because of my temperament: I think it is possible to waste a great deal of money in this field. I've never had experience of building up a new organization and my natural tendency has been to 'wait and see'.

Mrs Neal works from 9.45 a.m. to about 6.00 p.m. five days a week. She takes home work from the office more now than she has in the past. Her work load tends to be heavier in the winter than the summer. She has six weeks holiday a year.

Mrs Neal's conception of herself in her occupation was evident in her comment on the position of women in the ministry.

Mrs Neal is alert to the potential difficulties for a woman in a high position but seems to turn them into advantages.

I don't think I've come up against any prejudice in this department. In some ways it's an advantage to be a woman, you're in a minority and people do at least remember you being there because you've probably been the only woman in a room. When one is young, one talks more equally with people older than oneself than the male staff do.

At one time Mrs Neal did feel that her colleagues in the Civil Service did not sympathize with her trying to fulfil her obligations as wife and mother while carrying on with her work. She did not talk about her children at work because she thought people would be thinking, 'Why don't you go home and look after them?' But she has since discovered that her colleagues were more sympathetic than she had imagined to the problems of a working wife.

Mrs Neal strives to do any job that she is given with zeal and devotion. Indeed the challenges of her job and the satisfaction from it stem from solving difficult and meaningful problems as well as she can.

One is dealing with things which raise both intellectual and moral issues. It is important what one is doing – that one is not wasting one's time. Certainly one is putting to good use one's intellectual ability and one's ability to write English and all those sort of things.

She feels a sense of accomplishment in conveying a point of view or arriving at a compromise solution to a problem and presenting it to her colleagues persuasively. But there are difficulties in this:

I only get things when there is a problem, when there is no right answer and it is a question of deciding between two awkward alternatives both of which are bound to be criticized and have a lot of unsatisfactory features.

At Mrs Neal's level in the Civil Service any further promotion depends on the existence of vacancies further up.

There aren't such a lot of grades as there are in some ways of life. In the Civil Service there is quite a gap between each of the grades. One doesn't expect to get many promotions in one's life.

Mrs Neal evaluated the likelihood that she would be promoted to the next rank of Under Secretary in the following way:

There is nothing automatic about it but I'd be in the running for an Under Secretary promotion say ten years from when I became Assistant Secretary: but it depends on supply and demand. In this particular department mine should be quite good. . . . When I came in, we had some very young Under Secretaries and now these people are mostly quite senior and about the time I'm ready to be promoted a good many of the top staff will leave.

Mr and Mrs Neal are not overtly ambitious people. Rather than working primarily with thoughts of advancement in mind, they both seem to enjoy their work and tackle it with enthusiasm. This dedication is in turn rewarded by promotions and interesting assignments. They are fortunate to be in a position in which they can both actively sympathize, understand and participate in the other's career. Now that Mr Neal is ineligible for further promotions he said that he would be very happy to have his wife made an Under Secretary, even though this would put her above him in rank.

I would relish her becoming Under Secretary now because I'm no longer moving in those circles . . . I'd certainly be interested to know just what goes on.

However, it is an open question as to whether Mrs Neal would be prepared to handle the added strain and pressure of this level. Her comments above, though, indicate that she does not completely reject the idea. Much will depend on the family situation when such promotion is offered.

The Neals work at such an involved level that they do not have much time for leisure activities. Mrs Neal tries to keep her free time outside the job for family activities.

. . . there just hasn't been any leisure. What I like doing is gardening . . . whenever I do have any spare time I do some gardening but I don't have any regular leisure activities outside the house. I sit and watch television like other people in the evening and do sewing; I like doing that and I read a lot of periodicals and a fair number of books. We take the children out quite a lot ... for picnics at Richmond Park and that sort of thing and sometimes go out into the country.

Mrs Neal can arrange her schedule at work to adapt to her family requirements if necessary.

Most of one's time if one isn't in a meeting is pretty free and this is a great advantage of Civil Service work. If the children have a concert say on June 15th then I can keep June 15th free: I put school engagements into my diary to keep them free and I take half a day's leave.

About the 'costs' and 'benefits' of both husband and wife working, Mr Neal mentioned the possible effect on the children:

In these circumstances life can become pretty hard at times because there is a lot for everyone to do. We all have to cooperate at home to help keep things going. I suppose there is always the danger, when we both have been working flat out on office work for a week or two at a stretch, that temporarily the children have not had quite as much attention as they could have done. But right from the start my wife has made a very, very careful point of ensuring that they do get maternal attention and indeed she turns to me to make sure they get paternal attention as well. We have managed to do it by terribly hard work.

Mrs Neal, especially, regrets the shortage of leisure for any other activities and wishes that she could spend more time with the children. With reference to the 'costs' which her career has had on her family she said:

One of the costs is the shortage of time. When you get there the children are in a hurry to get out their points and complaints. . . . If one sets out to create a family home and the sort of environment that young children should come back to, sometimes one isn't there and one feels that one isn't as much in control of the whole situation or able to represent their home to them as one wished. . . . I think that one's home tends to be untidy and worse kept but that's not very important.

The benefit that Mrs Neal emphasized most strongly was that her career brought her closer to her husband, and Mr Neal mentioned the benefit to their children of the intellectually stimulating atmosphere provided by both parents in the home.

We have both felt that it has been an important factor in relation to the upbringing of the children, that we have had this level of intellectual life between us.... Each of them has reached the stage, one by one, at which they start to participate and find this of value.

With regard to the children's attitudes towards both their parents working, Mr Neal feels that when the children went off to school they accepted the idea that their mother also worked during the day without particular difficulty. However, Mrs Neal has for some years felt herself on the margin of accepting the strains of the dual-career pattern as worth while. She says:

Though the need to 'mind' pre-school children is the most obvious of a mother's responsibility, there are many others which to be done properly take many hours every week right through school and which cannot be imparted to anyone else, if one is to give the children the sense of family cohesion they need. This is why I feel that married women should be able to work shorter hours. To do a full-time job, occupying say 40 hours a week plus travelling time, and also give the children all the care they need, means a continuous strain over 20 years or so on one's time and energy which seem to me in retrospect very doubtfully worth while.

The keynote of the Neals' relationship is sharing in a partnership of interests and commitment to their work and to their family. As intelligent people and all the more so as individuals trained in the Civil Service, they talk out problems and differences and arrive at compromises when necessary. Rather than opposites complementing one another, the Neals fit together as a couple composed of two likes reinforcing one another.

INTEGRATION OF PERSONAL, FAMILY AND WORK WORLDS

Each of the dual-career families presents variation within the structural framework joining two careers with a shared family life. In the Neal family there are two striking aspects to their integration of work, family and personal worlds: the central value in family life of a stable, secure home environment for their children, and at work of the value of social service.

In many ways Mrs Neal is an ambivalent career woman – requiring the intellectual satisfactions provided by her career and at the same time begrudging her work world the time it demands that she take away from her family. Although she says that at times she would have liked to give up or reduce her commitment to her job, she has not done so. When she presses for an ideal career which is reduced in its demands, she still means something that many people would call a full-time job.

I think it is terribly important that the whole of women's employment should be organized so that, whatever happens to a man's hours, women shouldn't work more than say thirty hours; not a terribly short time, but it's extremely hard otherwise to provide a real home for children. This applies equally to women who are in a position to have help at home as those who are not.

Mrs Neal also was asked about other ways in which employers can make it possible for women to enter top jobs and make it easier for them to function at the level of their ability in their careers. She feels that if employers allow greater flexibility in working hours, as in the Civil Service, then this alleviates some of the strain. She also feels that it helps if circumstances allow workers to take unpaid leave more easily, in the event of domestic crises. The personal experience of a friend in the Civil Service illustrates the necessity of this sort of provision:

I know a colleague of mine who left the Service because she couldn't get any domestic help at a particular time. She asked for more leave and just wasn't given it and so she went. I think if someone was told that this would be sympathetically considered in the light of one's working commitments when one needed it, so that it wouldn't be regarded as impossible to take unpaid leave for specified domestic needs – that would be much better. The difficulty is the demands of the work itself. Not that I think that one needs very often to take unpaid leave, particularly if the hours were a bit easier or if one was able to work part-time.

What is actually possible in any given instance depends on the attitude of the immediate superior. This is illustrated in Mr Neal's attitude towards members of *his* staff.

I always make it perfectly clear to my staff – they can take any time off that they want to take off, provided they tell me, so that I know they are not around if I should need them, and provided the work is going to be all right and nothing is going to be held up that should be done. So if one of my staff says, 'I'm taking tomorrow afternoon off, I say 'The work's all right?' and he says, 'Oh, yes . . .' then that's O.K. by me – it's up to them, it's their responsibility. If the work doesn't suffer, why should I worry? Then secondly, I have an overriding principle: that where matters which are more important than the office are concerned, they can take time off whenever they want. If it is a matter of domestic commitments, illness in the family, or the welfare in any shape or form of the family, this to me – I don't know if it is to anyone else in this office – is an overriding consideration, and they must take time off, the rule is they must take time off and the people that are left on the job must carry the responsibility for the work themselves.

The second aspect of importance in the pattern of integration between their various responsibilities which the Neals have worked out is the feeling of social service. Throughout their discussions of their work or family or personal backgrounds, both Mr and Mrs Neal have continually shown an important altruistic aspect of their personalities. This is even more striking when considered in terms of the amount of stress and the high level of energy which normal day to day living within the core family demands of these people and yet there is something extra which they give to others. Not only does Mrs Neal have six children of her own to deal with on a weekend but she has often gone to collect more children from a local authority residential nursery to bring them home to play and for tea. And Mr Neal often will make a special effort, while on a business trip, to do such things as going to see friends of his first wife whom he knows are having financial difficulties and lending them some money. This all seems to fit in with what Mrs Neal termed 'being concerned with the fabric of society'.

The Neals

The actual structure of their work–family integration, then, seems to be bi-focal, with a family centre which is given high priority as an important shared area of interest, to which they apply similar administrative practices of negotiation and rational management as at work; and a work centre, at which they work on different but similar tasks and feel a sense of unity in their orientation to the humanitarian values described.

The Harrises: A Designer and an Executive

BACKGROUND — DEVELOPMENT OF THEIR FAMILY STRUCTURE

Catalogue of Events

Met: 1952 at the Edinburgh Festival.

Going together: For four years before they were married. During this time Mrs Harris re-located from the north to the London area where she worked for a large London-based firm.

Married: 1957.

Children: Two children born 1959 – girl; 1964 – boy.

Establishment of a home and residential history: By the time their first child was born they had moved into a flat in a luxury block. It was a small flat and they moved into their present five-room flat at about the time of their second child.

Domestic help: Both children were cared for in their early years with the aid of domestic helpers, primarily au pairs who lived in the building, but not in the flat. Both children went to nursery school from age 3½.

There have been no major changes in household composition: Mrs Harris's mother still lives in the north, and apart from visits they have not had anyone else living with them.

Major illnesses: The only major illness was that of their son's when he suffered from pneumonia followed by a gastric disturbance from the antibiotics. This is apparently over now with no persisting effects.

Major family separations: None. Work trips are generally just overnight and holidays away from the children have been rare and well covered by Mrs Harris's mother and domestic helpers.

THE HARRISES

The Harrises were interviewed in 1967–8. At that time Mrs Harris was a fashion designer with her own entrepreneurial business. During the course of our contact with her, her business was taken over by a very large company though she continued to function relatively autonomously within it. Mr Harris, at the beginning of the interviews, was marketing director of a company in the food industry. He later became managing director.

Mr and Mrs Harris live in a large luxury block of flats in a London suburb with their two children, a girl and a boy who were eight and three years old at the time we first met them. Mrs Harris was born in Germany and came to England with her family when she was about ten. Mr Harris was born in London's East End.

PERSONAL WORLDS

Mrs Harris is a poised, attractive, dark-haired woman in her early forties. She is an intense person who expresses herself well and with great feeling. She appears to be a warm person who, however, is selective in her likes and dislikes, and has rather great mood swings. Once she has decided to do something, e.g. going through with the research interviews, she enters into it very fully and communicates very directly without subterfuge.

She sees herself as a very conscientious person, who does not take a job unless she thinks she can see it through to the end. She has high and uncompromising standards in the work she does; is creative and somewhat temperamental along with it and is also a wife and mother who cares about maintaining standards in her home as well as in her work and in providing what her children want and need as they develop.

She sees herself as a good employer, particularly of women workers, and makes allowances for her helpers to deal with family schedules and crises; along with her high standards goes a feeling of warmth and tolerance for the shortcomings of her staff – a secretary's spelling deficiencies, an assistant's lack of initiative, and so on.

Mrs Harris describes her own mood swings, associated with the mounting of stress, in terms of her 'best self' and 'worst self'. At her best, she is efficient, decisive, warm and charming – able to put things in perspective. At her worst, she feels indecisive, exaggerates difficulties and problems in a situation, is difficult to get along with, and sees things out of their proper perspective.

She also has a conception of different levels of her personality, and indicates that certain elements both of her work and of the family situation do not fit the deepest levels of her personality, though she performs them as required in the situation. She says:

I have not ever been a housewife in the sense that I have found domestic duties thrilling or that I haven't given myself a chance to have other outlets. But during all this period I have felt that a great deal and a great part of the work was alien to my inner personality . . .

The part that is alien to her involves some of the administrative aspects rather than the creative design elements.

Mr Harris sees his wife as a person who has a tremendous wish to be a known designer and who also has very high expectations for an economically secure life because of her early deprivation experiences. He sees her as a very volatile and expressive person and one who is subject to great mood swings, like other very creative people.

Several times, Mr Harris described his wife as a person of tremendous dedication and integrity. She over-performs (e.g. does many more designs than are actually required) and cannot do anything in a slipshod way, or half-hearted way. Her high standards are not always comfortable for him, because she has sometimes directed these expectations towards him, and this may give him a feeling of inadequacy. He feels that she drives herself too hard and ought to be able to relax more and enjoy herself and the benefits of their life together.

Mr Harris is a tall, thin, balding, bespectacled man who communicates a feeling of restless energy. He is in his early forties and is also rather intense and moody, though on the occasions we saw him his prevailing mood was ebullience. At the same time he, like his wife, is a very introspective person and expresses himself particularly well and articulately. He speaks with verve and puts a case well; before we knew that he was a sales executive, we guessed that he might be a lawyer (he actually read law and performed as a barrister in television plays).

Mr Harris sees himself as a person who has a dramatic flair, who could have been a success in a career in entertainment or politics – each of which calls for the capacity to grip an audience and to express oneself well. Instead he has followed a business career which made use of his talents in another field – that of salesmanship – to provide a solid economic base for his family.

His business flair, which has been successfully demonstrated in helping his wife as well as in his own business, comes as something of a surprise to him. He is surprised, indeed, that all of his brothers have become quite successful businessmen, even though their earlier interests were in the arts and professions.

When Mrs Harris describes her husband, she remembers that when she first met him, she was impressed with his cheerfulness – 'there he was, with a big smile'.

In discussing his part in helping her to build up her business, she describes him as 'generous'. Aside from his generosity in putting forward his role in her business as a minimal one ('I have taken a friendly interest in this . . .') he has played an active part in developing strategy for the business, making high-level contacts and negotiating arrangements and contracts at various points. She describes his personality as effective in each of these areas :

He is the negotiator behind this – because I quite frankly can't visualize such a big thing, it is a huge million-pound enterprise. . . . He is able to put his finger on things.

The Harrises collaborated in a series of interviews which took place both in their house and their respective places of work. They are very busy people and though the research interviews were lengthy and time-consuming, once having committed themselves, they continued to be fully involved. During this time, their oldest child was in primary school and the youngest in nursery school; the latter is now in primary school while the eldest is on the verge of making the transition to secondary school.

A few focal themes or concerns underlay the material discussed in the interviews. Some of these are enduring concerns for the Harrises, some were more related to the specific phases they were in of their work life cycles and of the family life cycle.

One of the focal themes indicated the Harrises' wish to optimize their participation in and satisfactions derived from both career and family life. Unlike women who choose to develop careers while sacrificing or disregarding family life, Mrs Harris wished to maintain a strong involvement in both and this was accepted by both Mr and Mrs Harris. Even when Mr Harris argues that Mrs Harris ought to withdraw temporarily to participate more in family concerns that have fallen behind or especially need attention – e.g., to spend more time teaching their daughter to cook etc., to buy and fix up a house – it was in the context of a much needed rest, a sort of sabbatical from which one would proceed invigorated onto a new line of career development. Furthermore, Mr Harris saw himself as actively involved in this, having made sacrifices and given up career lines that would have been geared more exclusively to his interests. They refer to the resolution as a team effort.

Another theme implied an alertness to the fact that the course they have marked out for themselves is one that involves a great deal of strain. This is partly intrinsic to a dual-career situation together with a highly-valued family life, and partly a function of the Harrises' temperaments. They recognize that they are an expressive couple, given to experiencing deeply and sensitively reacting to events in their life course; for example Mrs Harris's mood swings.

Related to the theme of strain, is the concern with the heightening of feelings and increase in complexity around major decisions which they confront. As with other couples who are attempting to maximize a double career and family situation, major life decisions are not only perhaps more frequent than in other families (partly because there *are* two careers) but the resolution of these issues is more complex. Sometimes a tenuous balance is worked out which may be maintained only at considerable cost. As there is a high degree of involvement between different members of the family, the repercussions are great and affect everyone; there is little room for each person to make adjustments that will affect that person as an individual but not the others.

In the Harrises' case this leads to a decision-making process in which there is a considerable trying-out of possible new solutions, rehearsing the dangers and pitfalls imaginatively between the two of them (and others involved with them), until the full implications of a possible decision can be experienced in their feelings (without carrying it through to action). This often involves changing positions in a given discussion or controversy, with a certain confusion resulting as to who really wants which solution and for what reason. There seems to be about a three-year cycle in these major decisions in their lives. The first was getting married at all; the second, his decision to give up some of his career aspirations to work out a 'team' solution that would be better for them in terms of the first theme mentioned above. This coincided with setting Mrs Harris up in business. Another major decision occurred at the time of the birth of their second child, about whether Mrs Harris should continue to work. The major decision that was in process at the time we interviewed them had to do with the issue of whether or not to merge her business with a large public company.

A further theme had to do with financial security. Both Mr and Mrs Harris wish to earn relatively high incomes and to live at a comfortable standard and ensure this for their children.

In neither case is this wish associated with the desire to accumulate as much wealth as possible for its own sake or for the power that wealth can bring but rather for a complex of other reasons. Comfortable living is important to both of them. For Mrs Harris this is partly related to the shock of sudden deprivation which occurred in her childhood when her parents fled the Nazi regime. For Mr Harris comfortable living represents a sign of steady advance in the world, but he sees in it also an element of fun and excitement arising from the life of the tycoon. For both, recognition is perhaps more important than the income itself. Both also enjoy, with slight differences in emphasis, the aesthetic objects and activities that can become part of a comfortable standard of living.

Mrs Harris

Mrs Harris was an only child, born in Germany in 1927, to a middle-class Jewish family who were interested in cultural activities. Her father was a manufacturer of knitted fabric and she showed an early interest in his work.

My father knitted rayon jersey fabrics, better known then as Bemberg. As a little girl I remember my delight in surrounding myself with cutting waste in the factory and making clothes for my little dolls.

From the time that Mrs Harris was six years old her family was subject to Nazi persecution. Her mother's family were well-to-do and her 'maternal grandfather's family lived in palatial grounds – they were bankers'. Her maternal grandparents were put to death in a gas chamber. Her paternal grandfather died when she was six and her paternal grandmother was no longer alive when she was born. Mrs Harris has fond memories of her grandparents.

Before her family fled to England, Mrs Harris's mother did not work for money outside the home. However Mrs Harris describes her mother as having:

... tremendous energy and ability which has never been challenged ... she loved singing ... it was just something to do. My

mother grew up in the First World War and did a lot of wonderful
voluntary work. She was in charge of *Kinderhalte* so that women
could be free to work; she took the children and looked after them;
they were dreadful slum kids – she washed them, scrubbed them ...
this was all voluntary work done by nice ladies.

The division of labour in their home in Germany was the
conventional one, with father doing nothing in the household
and mother being helped by domestic servants. One figure from
Mrs Harris's early life that has remained important to her is a
family housekeeper who was a quasi-family member; Mrs Harris
still retains contact with her.

Mrs Harris feels that she had, in general, a happy background
in her early years. However she feels she only got to know her
father as a person much later in England, because he was at
work all day and she was in bed when he got home. She feels
that the main thing she got from her father was an artistic bent.
She perceived her father as a 'truly artistic type' who was mis-
placed as a businessman. Mrs Harris always remembers her
father as :

a bright and wonderful man and very gentle ... very sweet and
kind. On Sunday mornings he used to take me for walks. There used
to be a post delivery in Germany on Sunday mornings, and he used
to go to the factory to look at the post. He often took me with him
and I enjoyed playing with buttons and things. There was a pleasant atmosphere in the factory and I remember it as a pleasant place.

After five years of persecution, the family finally left Germany and came to England in 1939. This was a traumatic relocation and had tremendous effects on Mrs Harris as well as
her mother and father. Her father had to endure a great drop
in occupational status as he had no work permit. Their departure
from Germany had been delayed and when they finally did
emigrate it was no longer possible to take anything out with
them and they were penniless. This sudden change in their life
circumstances and the psychological effects on her father have
played an important part in Mrs Harris's own development. She
describes the impact as follows :

... I was brought up with a strong sense of duty and one of the things that I was faced with was a complete disruption of a home, a family, a place to live and everything that any child or any person holds dear. It was my greatest ambition from the age of ten onwards to reassemble a home, to reconstitute a home; I think it was that rather than talent, flair or anything else which made me forge on because my parents came with ten shillings in their pockets which even in those days didn't go very far. They had no permit to work here so they had to enter domestic service and do very menial work which bore little comparison to the sort of home they had had. It broke my heart so I really felt, come what may, I must make a success of things. You know, do something to build a home.

This all affected Mrs Harris's relationship with her mother. While in the early years this had been very warm, a difficult period arose when her father tried to persuade her mother to emigrate. Her mother so identified with the life in Germany that she wanted to stay in spite of everything. However, in recognition of their obligation to their daughter, the parents arranged for her to be evacuated to England before they themselves were. Both Mrs Harris and her parents were sponsored by English Jewish families who guaranteed their care. When Mrs Harris first arrived in this country she stayed with a family in which the man was a representative for one of the oldest English silver firms. However, when the war broke out he ran into financial difficulties and could not keep her any longer. During this time, just prior to the official declaration of war, Mrs Harris was very preoccupied with getting her parents out of Germany, which she was finally able to do.

My parents came to England. How, I shall never know. But I worked – eleven years old as I was – like mad. I wrote letters to the Home Office ... felt that I'd got to do everything. By some miracle my parents arrived in England four days before war broke out ... (after that) all the barriers were down.

Once the parents arrived, her mother became a housemaid and her father a handyman. Officially they could not earn, so they had to work for pocket money of about ten shillings weekly.

This was around 1940 and at the time Mrs Harris became ill. She had a history of pyelitis and developed a very high temperature. When the school finally called a doctor she had to go to hospital. At the time, her father was interned in the Isle of Man and her mother was working for a dentist. The dentist was also a refugee who had arrived earlier and established himself; he became a great friend of the family. When Mrs Harris fell ill, he arranged for her to be taken away from school and to come to live with her mother in his flat in Birmingham:

By that time I was twelve. It was a tiny room and I slept on the mattress on the floor but it was absolutely marvellous. . . . I had my mother and my father was interned – that wasn't nice but at least he was safe.

Mrs Harris's father was eventually released from internment camp and her mother took a job as a 'sort of matron or whatever one calls these people of a girls' hostel of refugee children . . .' The job was a difficult one – the girls were between sixteen and twenty and many had great problems. This hostel was housed in an old derelict vicarage. It was cold, the air raid shelter was under water and 'it was terrible but we survived that as well'.

During this time, Mrs Harris's father took a job as a shop assistant but this was short-lived as it was illegal. From then on 'began economic problems such as I had never known in my life, and never want to know'. All their belongings had been lost, confiscated, or stolen and never reached them in England. From then on she could 'only remember my father not having a job, doing goodness knows what (all sorts of odd jobs). This business of being an enemy alien was so against one. It was years of horror . . .'

A second major point of tension between Mrs Harris and her mother occurred during this period in which her mother had to carry the role of financial supporter for the family for a very long time and was in a very stressful job (involving long hours, weekend work, and certain indignities). At this time her mother was very irritable and critical of Mrs Harris and the latter felt that she had to get away. She later expressed considerably more sympathy for what her mother must have been experiencing, saying:

.. at home it was very sad. My mother went through a very critical time; she was very nervous and much of it was let out on me. I can look back on it now and understand that it was a dreadful hardship for her – my father had no work – it was the coldest winter ... it was appalling.

She indicates that her mother always kept up standards and aspirations even though they were living in such dreadful conditions.

During this period she became highly motivated to create a home for her parents through her studies and career. When her father died, aged fifty-four, she says she experienced something like a 'dynamo dying inside' – as the purpose for her working had been so tied up with her wish to re-establish her parents and to make a financial success of her work so as to build up a bulwark against necessity.

Mrs Harris's schooling experiences are relevant in understanding her later career decisions. Her earliest memories of primary school in Germany were dominated by the fact of being Jewish and being told to behave better than anyone else. This was no idle threat. She was in fact not permitted to go to the top-level grammar school because she was Jewish. The primary school that she went to in England was better in this regard but feeling different had become quite firmly established by then. She attended :

... a school for nice young English ladies in an old higgledy-piggledy Tudor house, with no learning and the stress on dancing and riding and speaking nicely. It had its advantages. I learned to speak good English, and I think it was probably a way of learning the English way of life, but it was hard ...

However, she discovered in this period that she liked drawing. When she first arrived she could not speak English or follow the lessons, so she was sent to do 'botany and draw rabbits and plants and things. And I copied them and I really loved this and that kept me going.'

After her illness in 1940 she was sent to a good grammar school. At the time she was doing her matriculation examinations she was getting up early in the mornings because she was very worried about them and this coincided with the bad time her parents were having. She felt that the examination was vital for her. She also sat an exam for the art college, and passed both of them and got a grant to go to art school. She was also awarded a city scholarship to university. During her last years in grammar school, particularly in the sixth form, she was very happy. She experienced great kindness from teachers and help with awakening her to new subjects. They recognized that she had talent, and she was urged by teachers and advisers to pursue various careers – languages, the BBC and so on. She herself felt that she had to take advantage of the opportunity of doing well in her exams and her artistic talent opened for her the world of design, but at the same time she was only beginning to be awakened to the more scholarly bent that she had, and to appreciate English literature. In retrospect, she would have loved to have paused then and just delved into literature.

Her father was instrumental in her making the decision to go to art school rather than university. While he himself appreciated literary and scholarly pursuits, he said that :

I should learn something more practical because he felt that even when all the letters and titles are behind your name (it was too risky, particularly as) I wasn't a born teacher and he was right ... also, I was influenced by my cousin who had done a course in dress designing in Paris ... she became a buyer ... so I accepted. I was sixteen then. I went to a college of art.

While Mrs Harris found the college a 'peculiar' place, the students there 'made a deep impression' on her 'with ideas, ideologies, and so forth, and for the first time I began to feel that people respected me for the sort of funny, peculiar person that my circumstances had made me. I began to lose a bit of my inhibitions.'

This was a very fertile ground for friendships for her and she has kept some of them up to the present time. Throughout her college days her parents took an interest in her educational development, and her father actually came with her to see the college authorities to make an arrangement for a more suitable curriculum for her.

At the point where Mrs Harris was ready to leave the art college, the head of her department introduced her to a well-known designer who wanted 'young designing talent' to join her in a new enterprise with a big London firm designing 'young fashion for young people'.

This was in 1946 and the idea had been inspired by a trip to America that the known designer had made. Mrs Harris came to London and stayed at a hostel provided by the firm. She shared a room with another girl who became a 'wonderful friend'. She refers to those years as 'the happiest years of my life . . . when I sort of spread my wings all on my own'. While she frequently went home for weekends, she enjoyed her independence and loved exploring and discovering London. She lived well on a pound a week, and sent her remaining four pounds home. She says :

I could not be better looked after and all my friendships and relationships were at their best; everything was wonderful . . .

Mrs Harris stayed with this firm for two years; she also attended more advanced courses at the Royal College of Art and did some lecturing at the College. The designer, who was also professor of fashion at the College, urged her to go to America after two years :

She called me in and said 'I think you have learned enough here. Go elsewhere.' I asked where she suggested and she said 'America' and I did.

When she went to America she was not only successful in her work but was courted by a wealthy American businessman. She wished to bring her parents over to America to give them conditions of comfort which they had lacked over the recent years, but her father's doctor indicated that the move would not be good for him as he had developed a heart condition. With her income from her earlier work, she had been able to set her parents up in a flat in Birmingham by the time she was twenty-one, and they lived there during her London and American period.

She returned to England to be near her parents. Though this was a difficult decision, she felt that it was right:

... Afterwards I had a great feeling that I had made the right decision. I could have made a decision to stay in the United States and do far better personally for myself and also have the advantage of bringing my parents over to America.... But I came back and the doctor said he couldn't guarantee whether (my father would take) another up-rooting.

After returning to England she went to work for a company owned by a distant relative, who was an older bachelor, who before long proposed marriage. She became engaged to him but was not happy with the situation. Two things happened at around this time that led to her breaking off the engagement. First, her father died. Second, a couple of years later she met her husband-to-be at the Edinburgh Festival. He described the meeting very vividly:

She had lost her father; I had lost my father. I felt very protective towards her.

She moved to London primarily to escape the undesirable engagement. When she was there she began to go around to musical entertainments with Mr Harris while re-establishing herself professionally having been away in America and in the provinces for so long. She describes how some of her earlier experiences and attitudes now fed into her work:

I had this feeling: unless I am at the top and doing the very best, I wouldn't like to do it at all. (Having been) to America and learned American methods I was more valuable when I came back here.

Her interest in bringing in American-type styles and in improving quality, fed into her work with some of the top fashion manufacturers during this period.

Mr Harris's Personal Background

Mr Harris was born in London in 1924. His family were East European Jewish immigrants who became naturalized British citizens. He was especially close to his mother and somewhat distant from his father. There were three boys, of whom Mr Harris was the second. In a previous marriage his father had had two sons who were left with him when his first wife died in childbirth. His mother tried, as far as possible, to treat the boys as a single set. The parents, however, were not harmonious. Mr Harris was aware of the tension between his parents when he was quite young and of his father's withdrawal from family life. He subsequently discovered that his father was frequently ill during his childhood and speculates that this may have been a factor. In spite of these tensions, however, Mr Harris recalls that there were many times when he felt that it was a happy family all together :

My memories ... are on the whole happy. There was a great deal of warmth in our home and it was a strong force. My mother's (Jewish) Orthodoxy is something I remember very firmly, and we had a pretty happy childhood on the whole.

In addition, Mr Harris considered himself closer to his mother than were the other boys. His interest in drama and music could be traced to his mother's early support :

... she certainly encouraged me with anything I wanted to do. For example, I wanted to play the violin and she went out and bought a violin; where she got the money from I don't know.

He did not know until later that his mother was also interested in drama. He said that while nobody in his family was directly involved with the stage, his mother 'had the kind of theatricality or theatrical instincts about her ...' which, he discovered recently, were actually channelled into an active hobby which she pursued.

... only recently visiting the Yiddish theatre in the East End of London ... I watched part of a Yiddish play and I met old friends of my family who used to live there ... one of them said to me, you know, your mother was forever here when she was a young woman, she loved this place, she knew all the songs by heart. I said that this is probably where she got them because she was always singing little songs ... very often sad ones, very sad ones ...

His father was a factory worker – tailor's machinist – and is recalled as a 'very keen unionist'. His mother did not work out-side the home during his childhood. The family was orthodox in their observation of Jewish rituals and traditions. Their accommodation was poor, but there was an emphasis on pro-viding good food and on sheltering them from some of the hardships that the family experienced externally.

Though they lived among people like themselves, Mr Harris recollects the family's attempt to better itself :

We were favoured in a way because we lived in one of the latest estates which had been put up by the County Council ... and I am really astonished at the forward thinking.... They had shops be-neath them and there was a sort of central point where the streets met; there was a circus and in this circus was a bandstand and you could sit, stroll and play there. There were parks for these blocks of flats.

He belonged to a boys' club in his neighbourhood when he was young, but due to an endocrine disorder he was not par-ticularly good at sports :

We joined a club called the Bethnal Green Boys' Club; this was very good for us. It was led by young men who were models of social responsibility, very often public-school boys, mostly Jewish, but by no means all, and we went camping and developed a wide range of hobbies ... there I went to dramatic classes, appeared in plays and so forth. It was a very good outlet for us and we learned sportsman-ship.

All of the brothers did well academically and all won scholar-ships to secondary school. One of his early ambitions was to go on to the stage :

It was something very strong – I wasn't sure what else I wanted to be. I thought I also had a leaning towards politics but it was very much in the background. I certainly liked the idea of the stage, theatre, show business; I also began to think in terms of law, prac-tising at the bar. I then finally went into that very deeply and had there not been a war possibly I would have gone into this if the family budget would have stood it.

In relation to choice of secondary schools, there was a line of development that was followed by the brighter boys in the district; Mr Harris went along with this when his time came :

The trail started with my older brother who got his scholarship first (as a school that was) in the tradition of the public schools ... but it came within the orbit of the County Council at the time that I joined. A year later it was on the verge of becoming an L.C.C. grammar school ... a splendid school, with the most beautiful grounds ...

During his secondary schooling and subsequently when they were evacuated, the boys boarded out. After two unhappy experiences with families that he felt were rather mercenary in their orientation to the boys they took in as boarders, Mr Harris moved in with a family with whom he stayed for several years.

I finally wound up in a house where there was another boy whom I met the other day for the first time in twenty-five years – a reunion – and this family was the most wonderful one I could ever wish to meet in a lifetime. They have remained friends of mine and I am still very much attached to them.

In secondary school Mr Harris's performance was good but 'nothing dramatic'. He describes himself in those days as 'reasonably good material, ambitious':

I think it was taken for granted that I would go on to University if I had the chance and got through the examinations. The only problem was what was I going to do. This is a problem that most people have though few are prepared to admit it.

During his school holidays he worked on a farm and taught physically handicapped children. Then came the war and in 1939 his family was split up – his father going to the north where the factory at which he worked was evacuated and his mother staying at home. When Mr Harris left his secondary school he went to one of the London University colleges, which was relocated in Cambridge for the war period, and he was called up for service in 1943:

... I went into the Army and had a really unspectacular career until 1945 when I was posted as private soldier to a combined Anglo-American mission which was to follow in the wake of the armies and discover prisoners of war and collect them together and repatriate them. When the war finished, I was sent back to Germany (as I had learned German) and worked as interpreter for the allied group that was set up to control the coal mining industry. I actually found myself filling in on various other jobs and finally became involved in a very interesting one with responsibility for the employment of 19,000 men in a particular area. I sat on the various boards with all high ranking military and civilian officers though I was only twenty-one and my rank at that time was Staff Sergeant. I was rewarded with a small medal for this particular mission.... I then came back and got a job because my father was very ill. I didn't think it was fair or right of me to just go on studying without bringing in an income so I studied at night reading economics and law, and worked during the day with an organization ostensibly training one in executive management.

The job was in a large family business, where Mr Harris was supposed to learn the business and at the same time consider developing a career in commerce. He continued to cultivate his musical talents and read law – both earlier interests – partly because he felt that his work situation was not satisfactory, and partly because these interests had been fostered in some of his Service experience.

Just as he was finding his feet again after the war – developing his musical and dramatic talents, reading law and having some preliminary experiences in the business world – he met his future wife and the course of their courtship and marriage affected his ultimate occupational choice of a business career so as to secure his family's future.

FAMILY WORLDS

Mr and Mrs Harris both value family life highly; they want relationships within the family to be warm and close. What they do and the decisions they make in their work worlds are closely related to what they wish to achieve in their family. They are concerned with getting the right balance between work and family involvement and getting gratifications from both spheres. They feel that their work and family lives should be so arranged that Mrs Harris gets 'controlled excitement' from her work, and

at the same time when she wants to, she should be able to
'walk on Hampstead Heath with the children and enjoy to the
full the life of a mother as well'. Thus, in making a major work
decision, Mrs Harris is concerned with its impact on the close
relationship she presently enjoys with her daughter. These are
not easily compatible goals and in describing the actual structure
of the Harris family activities and relationships the dilemma
areas will be highlighted.

The idea of a happy family, with the children having fun, is
something about which they talk a good deal. One issue that
this gives rise to is whether they should have a house rather
than a flat. Mrs Harris says:

... You could say this flat is very delightful, charming, it is very
convenient, it is near the studio; we have a lovely garden, we have
tennis courts, a swimming pool, everything; what do we need a
house for with its extra work and all the rest of it? But at the bottom of my heart I know it would be right to have the house to give
the children the extra space to play in and the extra nooks and
crannies and for my own personal pleasure as well. I have nowhere
to put a piano here. ... One compromises on all sorts of things all
along the line and I just feel if you are a responsible mother it is
an alien thing to do. You don't compromise, you do the best for the
children, that is the only thing that is good enough. This flat hasn't
got the conveniences for the super-helper who wants her own suite.
There is nothing wrong with it, but if a woman is working there
have to be substitute mothers, and you can't get a good substitute
mother without having good accommodation for her.

The Harrises never did want a large family and when asked
whether they intended to have more children she replied:

No, that's it. I certainly didn't want one child. I insisted on the
second one. From a woman's point of view the first is the most
difficult. It is easier afterwards. One is not so frightened, and everything falls into place, (but two are enough).

The concern is rather with the quality of the relationships in
their small family; they want it to be close-knit and happy.

Weekends tend to be kept for family activities and there are
a few special rituals that the family participate in. Either Mr

or Mrs Harris is always at hand to tuck the children into bed and hear them say their prayers. On Friday nights they celebrate the Jewish Sabbath with prayers and lighting of candles. As far as secular rituals are concerned, Saturday tea is made a high tea for the children, with salads, fruits, and so on. There is a nightly bedtime ritual of this kind, with Mrs Harris making a special cocoa recipe for the children if they want it.

Structure of Activities in the Family

The composition of the household is Mr and Mrs Harris, their daughter and their son. They have an au pair who lives in the block of flats in one of the rooms which are reserved for domestic helpers. They also have a daily who comes to clean the flat each weekday.

Typical weekdays in the Harris family start with Mrs Harris helping to get the children up before 7.30 a.m. The au pair comes in at 7.30. Mrs Harris says :

I see that we all have breakfast together. I lay the breakfast table the evening before if I am here. If there is a baby-sitter, it is her job to lay the table in the evening for the next morning.

Mr Harris leaves for work at 8.15; their daughter leaves for school at 8.30, walking to school with a friend who also lives in the same block of flats. Their son leaves at 8.55 for his school, taken either by Mrs Harris, or

... if I have to go somewhere or if I'm not quite ready and have telephone calls to make and various things to do here, the au pair walks him over to the school – it's a short walk – and comes back here.

When the little boy was still at nursery school the au pair fetched him home for lunch. Mrs Harris would prepare his lunch in advance or he would be given something which may be warmed over from the previous night's dinner. Alternatively, the au pair would prepare a light lunch of 'pancakes or something'. In the early afternoon, after the little boy had his lunch, he played with one of his friends in the block or from nursery school. Sometimes the friend comes to the Harrises' flat, and sometimes the boy would go out to friends. As this was all in the neighbourhood the au pair picked him up or, alternatively, made tea for the children. Mrs Harris says:

... and sometimes I will pop back or do something quickly in the lunch time for them – a jelly or something so that there is something attractive for them and I find that this works very well. They don't really need me the way they needed me a year or two ago. He doesn't come rushing out the way he did every few minutes and say 'Mummy, what are you doing?' or 'Can you do this, that and the other?' They have intelligent games and their cars and tents and they play. This is all great fun for him. On the whole I would say I try to be available in the afternoon ...

The daughter returns from school later in the afternoon, and they play together until tea.

The children actually have their last meal at tea time. They have something on toast, the English sort of tea ...

Mr and Mrs Harris have dinner together later, when the children are in bed, at about 7.30. Normally, Mrs Harris cooks on Sundays, not only for that day but for several days in advance.

I'll probably do a chicken and some beef and some schnitzel and some goulash, and then I only need to worry about vegetables, and that's nothing.

She puts these pre-cooked meals into the freezing compartment of her refrigerator, and takes them out during the week as required. She says about their meals:

I don't make the sort of complicated meals I might make, coming from Continental parents. . . . I mean I don't have to have a gorgeous joint all the time. I can make do with mince – meat balls – and we don't mind eating spaghetti bolognaise one day and that sort of thing if the sauce is good ... I can't make puddings and things, but fresh fruit is good for you. I just think that one can become an awful slave to all this sort of thing ...

Given Mr Harris's value of family life and his concern with his wife's fulfilment at work, he participates by helping in various ways in the home and is relatively active with family and household activities at the weekends. In addition, he helps by not being too demanding, for example, he does not expect an elaborate dinner in the evening.

Mr Harris returns from work around 6.30 or 7.00 p.m. In the evenings they discuss issues in the lives of one or both of them. At the early stages of the study, this mainly concentrated on the issues surrounding the merger of her business, but it may be issues in his work as well. They also plan the children's activities and the au pair's in relation to their own programme for the following day.

Typically, at weekends Mr and Mrs Harris do family errands. Their daughter has a maths tutorial on Saturday mornings, and the parents and their son may drive to the local shopping centres. Mrs Harris describes a Saturday as follows:

While she (the daughter) was busy with him (the maths tutor) we took the little boy with us and got things from the ironmonger, the bakery. I had to go to the building society – all sorts of things I don't get around to doing all week – and my husband came with me. We rushed around and got everything done, got shoes from the shoemaker and all these sorts of things and arrived back in time to put the meat on.

They usually have Saturday lunch all together. From Saturday lunch to Monday morning, the au pair is off-duty and there is no other domestic help.

Saturday evenings are kept for leisure activities. The Harrises listen to music or do family things. The Saturday prior to the second interview, they listened to music, Mr Harris wrote a profile of his wife for a trade journal, and Mrs Harris made shoe bags for the children. Sometimes they have people in and sometimes they go out.

Sunday they ordinarily spend at home *en famille*. There are exceptions. On the Sunday prior to the second interview, Mrs Harris had an outing with an old friend to an art exhibition, following which the whole family went to the friend's home for lunch and stayed the afternoon. This was unusual. Ordinarily she is busy cooking the meals for the family for the week.

Departures from the pattern are handled either by prior

planning or on an emergency basis. If she has to make a trip, she organizes different hours for the au pair or baby-sitter and organizes the children's programmes in advance. A major illness of one of the children has been the only serious emergency. She describes what happened at this time as follows:

My son had pneumonia just before Christmas and then it was followed by something much more unpleasant, the ill effects of antibiotics and he was ill for at least six weeks. ... Suddenly on a Sunday he had a very high temperature and a terrible kind of spasm which contracted his whole little body. At one time I thought well, he had given up, he has given in, he just doesn't want to fight any more.... I was very worried. Finally the doctor suggested ... bringing a specialist. So naturally during this time I didn't really care about work, I just stayed here and conducted my business telephone calls the best I could. I got my secretary to come up here, got my assistant to come and I mean I didn't really go out at all. When the boy was asleep I would slip across (to her studio). There had been a lot of ear infection so really I cancelled everything at Christmas time, every engagement I had, it would have been impossible and as a result, in spite of the fact that the little boy was poorly, during the times he wasn't poorly we had the most lovely time. My mother was with us and it was relaxed and we did not have to worry about this and that and it was absolutely wonderful. I made pretend-stained-glass windows for the children, cutting cardboard boxes out and putting tissue paper behind them – we really had lots of fun so I really enjoyed it and the boy soon got better.

Mrs Harris's mother helped out during this crisis and her work colleagues helped by coming to see her so that she could keep things going at the studio while staying by the side of her child.

Short of actual emergencies, various contingencies crop up. Mrs Harris describes how she manages these, in this case a weekday dinner party.

On Wednesday my husband has some business associates he particularly wants to bring home. I shall cook on Tuesday evening and prepare for Wednesday and come home early on Wednesday in order to be adequately ready. ... I think one just has to be a leap ahead. ... I couldn't have the sort of man who rings up and says, 'Darling there are three of us tonight,' because I just couldn't cope with that, you know. My husband wouldn't dream of doing it to me because I am the sort of person who wouldn't want to slap on anything. I'd want to do it nicely.

To make concrete the rhythm of Mrs Harris's day and what goes on in the family at different times a brief but graphic diary covering one week is included.

SATURDAY 3 FEBRUARY 1968

8.00	Up at 8 a.m. All had breakfast in dressing gowns.
	Bath – lovely Boots pine essence.
	Laundry man.
	Arranged lunch.
10.15	Mr T (daughter's tutor) arrived 10.15 – husband and son left to go to studio.
	Daughter worked with Mr T.
	Mr S the carpenter and Miss H the cleaner were at work (at the studio).
	Cleaned out passage – moved furniture to the flat. Got a little room downstairs just for a few days to shelter wood and odd bits from the studio.
	Husband cut himself trying to put new keys on a key ring which is wickedly tough.
11.45	Returned to flat to pack daughter's bag for weekend visit with friend.

Husband takes daughter to friend and collected laundry from launderette.

I return to village for quick shopping.

1.30 Lunch.

Too late for poor little son. Halibut, creamed potatoes, peas and gooseberries with caramel pudding to follow.

Bought some pink and white coconut clusters which I loved when I was little.

Husband and son loved them too.

Au pair washed up for me.

Mrs L (neighbour) rang to ask son over to play with her little boy.

3.30 For the first time I am alone in years; today twenty-nine years ago I arrived in England. I noticed the date when I looked at my diary to make baby-sitting arrangements.

Called mother in

Birmingham. Long chat. She was just writing to me. Glad I called.

Mr M my landlord died last Monday, poor little man, so young, great pity. Called in at the people opposite my studio where Mrs C died recently; very nice and they will offer me the house when they are ready to leave.

Beautifully kept furniture and everything spotless.

Writing letters to Paris and preparing for my trip to Paris on Sunday 11th–14th; taking out addresses etc. to plan and prepare trip fully. Son had good afternoon with friend, watched me dress, he played car in my bedroom and didn't mind my going out. Rosenkrantz and Guildenstern tonight. Husband has gone to the office to catch up with lots of work. I shall meet him at the theatre. Reminds me of going out before one is married, rather nice.

It is cold – snowed in big flakes for a little while mid-morning but all gone now.

12.50 Very interesting and enjoyable play.

Met K and F (old friends and good friends) at theatre. Went to Swiss Restaurant, Leicester Square after.

K's car was stolen outside the theatre but we nevertheless enjoyed our meal and wine. Husband takes friends home.

1.00 To bed.

SUNDAY 4 FEBRUARY

7.30 Son snuggled in about 7.30 a.m. and we played about with him.

Breakfast prepared by husband in the kitchen – leisurely because daughter away and no rush to Hebrew classes.

10.00 Mr R (Tenants Association) calls, husband and he off visiting tenants. Tidy flat. Cooking lunch, chicken casserole, sprouts and potatoes, fruit to follow.

Mr F, Mr A-J, called, rushed to studio to catch carpenter still doing work there, missed him. B rang, wanted to settle to have hour rest, not possible.

Tea, husband to collect son, then on to collect friend from Hampstead for a 'little supper'. Children to bed quickly, 'did the bird' for daughter.

8.30 Supper – cheese, salads, coffee with friend. Later friends (couple) at 8.30 for coffee – very pleasant evening. Husband looked tired and others were rested and very happy to talk religion, theatre and Vietnam. Son woke – not well. temperature, into other bedroom. Administered Disprin. Both children unwell.

MONDAY 5 FEBRUARY

Husband up very early. Son not well at all – fever. Daughter dragging instead of dressing. Mr T called for husband at 8.15. Coffee together. Daughter looks poorly too but no temperature. Made her a packed lunch. Not well, she doesn't want breakfast – I undress her and return her back to bed. Friend of daughter

calls and I told her she is not well.

9.00 Call Doctor to children. Call studio and leave instructions. Au pair knows where to get me. Leave for the display rooms to discuss style for promotion, colours and new lines. Mr M re Czechoslovakian samples. Call L and C. Try to correct something the factory has done wrong. Mr N very happy with collections. Sandwich at Danish Centre, eat it in taxi to Manchester Square where my car is. Angry – caught with parking ticket by minutes.

1.30 Rush home. Doctor not there yet.
Go out with laundry to launderette. To studio to collect various costings etc.
Give assistant instructions, letters. Get daughter little get-well present, a compass and geometry set in a plastic bag and son a little 'wreck truck' which he has been itching to have and a Beatrix Potter book.

4.00 Doctor came. Son with upper respiratory

infection. Daughter trachitis, both have anti-biotics to take. My throat aches.

Au pair to chemist and to collect costings file for the night's 'home-work' from studio.

Daughter asleep when I had tray ready – son also asleep.

6.30 Both up. Re-made tea, both miserable. Not eating. Just poor little things.

TUESDAY 6 FEBRUARY

Up early.
Breakfast, husband and Mr T.
Children up but not well enough for school.

9.00 Cleaning lady here at 9 a.m. Her daughter also unwell.
Children quite happy, so off to studio.
Worked hard till 3 p.m. Then home with shopping for household and little presents. Biscuits and Rowntrees winegums for the children.

4.30 Daughter to bed at 4.30 again. She's not well and I am worried she is so poorly.
Worked hard at the desk with interruptions from son.

7.00 Husband home early. Phoned Mrs H, had snow in Birmingham, she was not out and apart from cold, fit and looking forward to coming here on Friday.
Little supper in kitchen. Phone calls.
More costings with husband and discussed personnel problems in his office.
Decided that unless major catastrophe prevents it (business-wise) we would be reckless and go for a week to the Swiss mountains end of February.
Too late for Harry Secombe on T.V.
Listened to News and switched off because everything so poor and morbid.

9.25 Going to read *Times* and work on introductory notes for programme for April fashion show. The notes sent to me are not good.

WEDNESDAY 7 FEBRUARY

It's 12.30 a.m. and really the 8th.

Up early, son asleep but daughter up and miserable.

7.30 Mr T here. Breakfast, dressed. Daughter has a little breakfast in bed, still 102 degrees, call doctor for a visit. Arrange son to visit friend. Daughter asks him for lunch. Very nice, he needs to see children. He is better. Call studio, make hair appointment and arrange to borrow the outfits for children. Domestic phone calls. Comfort daughter, promise to return for lunch.

Work hard at studio, don't feel good – take Dr Collis Brown's mixture to settle tummy. Return home with Milly-Molly-Mandy book for daughter. We listen to children's programme together and I have a little lunch on tray in her room. She looks poorly. Doctor still not here.

2.00 I leave for bank and display rooms. Run into Chairman, ends in long conference, very good and helpful to me. Pop into showrooms of designer friends for two pretty dresses for daughter and shoes for me, all settled in five minutes.

Home, doctor has been, daughter has influenza, new medicines prescribed. I rush to village. Chemist very nice, makes it up right away.

Pop into studio, take mail folder home.

Au pair off to classes. Phone calls. Mrs H also bad chill.

Invitation for Saturday lunch for us all from P. Husband likes the fashion magazine photograph of one of my styles.

Settled daughter, made supper just for two in kitchen. Neighbour phoned, thrilled with new item which he imports. We ask him over and we have coffee and cake and lots of interesting human stories are exchanged. He is a lawyer turned business-man – very nice!

We take up talking work, but it is not work, it is fun!

11.00 Clear up with husband. Daughter arrives in kitchen coughing, can't sleep. Make her a warm drink and settle her again. She is still coughing. Husband is asleep and I am very tired.

12.45 It must be 12.45 now.

THURSDAY 8 FEBRUARY

Up early, children asleep. Daughter still fever but happier. To work with husband and Mr T at display rooms before 9.00 a.m. Cleaners are still active. Interviewing young cousin of husband's recommended for Trainee Salesman.

9.30 Meeting on fabrics colours with A. Interesting developments ahead, lots of thinking and planning, very exciting. Magazine write-up and picture out with New York background and lots of inquiries New car advised for next Friday. Lunch sandwiches and coffee and delicious Danish pastry at Danish Centre. Model comes, I like her. Assistant's draft activities quite wonderful.

4.30 Work till 4.30. Rush off, raining, run to get sample, place shuts at 5 p.m. Call on designer friend and make contact with husband from there who is at board lunch. He fetches me and we go home together . . . friend stepped into partnership we left in Manchester – they are very unhappy. I understand them well. Nice, hardworking pair. Daughter up, son asleep. Daughter has a little food with us in her dressing gown, I don't like it, she is not well.

11.15 In bed. Very tired but full of pleasant feelings for the future. We plan lots and look forward to the winter break, expensive yes, good for us certainly! Daughter up in the night, she has a little cystitis and feels horrible, poor little thing. Mrs H had cold, can't come Friday, much too poorly.

FRIDAY 9 FEBRUARY

Up early, Mr D calls for husband, breakfast with son in dressing gown, daughter in bed unwell. Bath leisurely and settle children, to studio, work hard, plan all work during my three days away, brief assistant and . . . Phone rings constantly. Very unpleasant letter from customer. Not receiving adequate old series by factory right on top of similar criticism by another major customer yesterday. Husband calls to see that my currency etc. are ready. I mention this worrying letter and he gives me brief on how to act. I agree with him.

12.30 Launderette, cleaners, bread, off to 12.30 appointment at showrooms. I booked a facial. A break, have never had time or money, costs 2 gns., for cleanse and proper make up. I like some of it but don't like a mask and all in a little room with an air extractor rushing above, not very relaxing. I cannot make lines on my eyes and am interested to see myself – quite good but make up too yellow and too heavy, not me at all.

2.00 Sandwich lunch, appointment with Mrs B; finished at 4.45 p.m. Called husband. Bought sweaters for children at Jaeger and a suit for myself, very simple, not wonderful cloth but most pleasing. Collect husband – take colleague to his relative en route. Daughter playing games with au pair. Son asleep. Make supper, candles. Daughter goodnight with prayers. Mrs H still very thick with cold. Friend calls. L and B over. Brandy for all, very jolly evening. Tired! Husband does not like make up, does like the suit. Planned Saturday morning. Shopping list etc!

From the above it can be seen that Mrs Harris leads a hectic life. She also does most of the conventionally 'feminine' activities in the house with the help of an au pair, a daily, her work colleagues in emergencies, and her husband. She decides on and prepares everyday and special meals. The routine food shopping is planned by Mrs Harris and carried out with the help of her husband. The regular cleaning is done by the au pair and daily help with Mrs Harris deciding on whom to hire and doing the supervision. Mr Harris, however, will fill in gaps when required and gives his opinion about potential domestic helpers.

Clothes washing is done at the launderette, usually by Mrs Harris. Living in a block of flats means there are few maintenance problems and a minimum of the extras involved in running a house, such as looking after a garden.

As far as the care of the children goes, Mrs Harris usually gets them ready for school. About disciplining them, she says: 'Mother does the chastising, father does the spoiling.' Mr Harris says: 'I find she can be very tough by her tone of voice – it puts the fear of god into the children.'

Mrs Harris says:

I like discipline. I don't like things scattered around on the floor. I give them a chance. I tell them that tea will be in half an hour's time, but if there is no movement, I put on the pressure. If I find I am wrong about something, for example, who made the marks on the wall, I apologize because I feel that they should feel that one could climb down. Our daughter sulks quite a lot. The boy has tears in his eyes and says 'It's not a very nice thing you're saying to me.'

Planning and organizing holidays are jointly discussed. They have not taken long holidays but plan to take more in the future.

Mrs Harris is very alert to the children's health needs and decides when the doctor is needed, though Mr Harris may telephone for him.

As Mr Harris maintains more ties with traditional religion than his wife, he takes their daughter to Hebrew school on Sundays. Mrs Harris maintains sufficiently traditional practices, e.g., in relation to food, to keep her husband comfortable, though neither is orthodox in religious practices.

The Harrises handle their finances by joint discussion and

together decide how much income to draw, how much to put back into their business and how much to spend on major items.

In general, the family division of labour and decision-making is characterized by a marked flexibility – sometimes in spirit, sometimes in practice. Mr Harris is able to cope with most emergencies, either familial or in relation to his wife's business interests, because of the flexibility he has in arranging his work times, within the limits of the pressures in his business. His flexibility in relation to domestic chores is more in spirit than in action. She says that he does not mind pulling the Hoover over the carpet, or helping with the beds on Sundays when the au pair is off, which certainly does help. However in relation to cooking, his good intentions are not always so welcome. She describes his attempts to help as follows:

He makes the most unholy mess and is not to be tolerated in the kitchen. Actually he tried once making chips because I was away and he wanted to make egg and chips and I found the most horrible sight of fat everywhere and I forbade him ever to set foot there again.

However, Mr Harris makes tea, as he did for us all on the nights of the interviews.

At different phases of the development of the family, the arrangements described above have altered. After the first child was born, the help they had was particularly good and the strain on Mrs Harris was not so great as it later became. The addition of a second child increased the strains.

Personal Experience of Family Development and the Current Husband–Wife Relationship

Mr and Mrs Harris first met at the Edinburgh Festival in 1952 at the Jewish Social Centre where people could meet participating Jewish artists. Each experienced a 'very happy sensation' about the other. His feelings crystallized rapidly about the part she might play in his life; with her, the situation was more complex. Mr Harris describes their meeeting as follows:

What struck me about her at the time when I met her was that she was just the sort of girl I would like to marry. She looked the right part, she had a very warm personality, she had a nice voice with a great deal about her, visible, that I just found most attractive... she laughed readily, she was a highly intelligent sort of girl and I think, if I have to analyse all the reasons, she seemed to meet all the requirements.

Mrs Harris's recollection of the same incident is as follows:

...it was a sort of cocktail thing, 'Hello, who are you' and so forth. They all seemed to be solicitors...oh yes, they all seemed to be tiny and I felt very self-conscious with people who were half my size. There was some speech being made and I remember a well-known beautiful actress was there...who was sort of holding court...and I was chatting to some people and suddenly he appeared and he had a great big smile on his face. We just sort of hit it off and decided we would go to the afternoon performance of a wonderful documentary film which had been made for UNO on Mexico and on another country; it was really quite marvellous. ...Then we went to the Festival Club and grabbed a sandwich and he took me to my train. That's how we met and then he called me up when he was in London.

While she found the acquaintance 'very jolly and very nice' he set his heart on marrying her. This was far from simple in the circumstances; she was deeply involved with another man and he was still living at home partly to attend to an aged and ailing mother (all his brothers having already left home). She was more established professionally and moved in more affluent circles than he at that point. Both describe this period as difficult. Mr Harris says:

I found her very, very difficult, much more difficult than I thought she was going to be.... I don't think she'd really decided on what sort of person she wanted to marry. She had various ideas and I think there were many psychological pressures on her that she couldn't sort out. Because of her experiences and her parents' experiences I think that she was looking for some tremendously successful man who was in the thick of a highly successful career. ...Possibly I didn't meet the book at that time because I was just finishing being a student. I had an interest in music and so on, but I was just working for an ordinary salary which was modest.

Mrs Harris does not, retrospectively, assign much importance to the fact that he was not yet financially established, but recalls difficulties raised by her impressions of his mother and her illness, and by her own psychological hesitancy about marriage in general.

It was rather a dragging affair and his mother was never well during all this period ... he was at home because of her and he was the last one of five boys to leave – all this wasn't too easy really.... Also I was always afraid of making the decision to marry.... I had baulked several times ... it was a decision I couldn't easily make.

In this period following her return to London her father had died, she broke off her engagement to her former boss, and she was working to re-establish herself professionally after an absence in America.

During this period Mr Harris was attempting to develop a career in television. Though he had taken her around to musical events and so on, he felt he could not compete with the affluent businessmen who were also interested in her. For a period, he gave up his pursuit. When she became engaged to a wealthy American businessman he considered his suit lost. However, she decided not to marry the American, and she realized that she really wanted to marry Mr Harris. He described this as follows :

... she suddenly got in touch with me and said that she was doing nothing. I never questioned her on this. I didn't want to go into it but I was very, very happy. She told me afterwards that she had no hesitation whatsoever, that she was absolutely certain that I was the person she wanted to marry ... whereas I had worried, I was afraid, I couldn't sleep for days and I wondered, 'Is this the right thing?'

The decision to marry illustrates a pattern that has characterized the decision-making process in their relationship. Whereas Mr Harris was certain before and she uncertain, when the decision was made and unmade, Mrs Harris became certain and he uncertain. His uncertainties had to do with the possible effects on his career of undertaking marital responsibilities.

In any case they married in 1957 and the process of developing their interlocking careers began. In outline, as it relates to the developing family situation, the picture was as follows.

His career in television had been promising but was subject to ups and downs and was not sufficiently secure to support a family with high standards and expectations befitting the experiences and stage of life that they as a couple were in. His mother was ill and his brothers were not in a position to accept responsibility for her, so this additional burden fell upon him.

She, at the same time, felt that her potentials for making a name for herself in the fashion field were high, as she had already demonstrated, and that the income that she derived from working for others as a design consultant or staff member was not as high as it could be with her own business. Together they worked out a plan for starting a business that set her up in her studio close to their home, designing fashions that would be manufactured by partners in the north and marketed through mail-order firms.

At the same time they both wished to have a family. Their first child was born about two years after they married, and Mrs Harris continued working all through this time as a fashion consultant. Following the birth of their first child, the Harrises began to think of ways and means to stabilize their income and to make her work both more manageable as well as more remunerative.

The launching of the mail-order business preceded the birth of their second child, and there was a major family decision crisis at the time. The business, started about five years before, 'rocketed' after two years; with its success and demands for expansion it presented problems. Mr Harris describes the difficulties of combining an expanding work situation with an expanding family situation at that time as follows:

The crucial time was almost three years ago. The business really rocketed for two or three years ... we were handling mail-order business and a chain-store business, *and* began to go into the retail trade; we began to employ agents, against my will – I hated the idea of it, I found them so thoroughly unreliable and untrustworthy; it seemed to me that one needed to have only partners in a small enterprise, people who identify themselves so thoroughly with the firm that they really work in the interests of the firm *only* because it is identical to their own interests, or people who were employed by the firm and not freelance agents, more difficult to control. We went through all those things and just about that time we had (our little boy); we consciously had him as our second child. But I think at that point it was clear to me that we were going to be in a cleft stick from then on because both needed an equal amount of attention – the baby that was the human one and the baby that was the firm. My wife was designing and writing memoranda and leaving instructions etc. on Saturday morning at her studio ... about what to do while she would be away in the nursing home; in the evening she had the baby. She came out of the nursing home and about two weeks later she was rushing around again seeing the mail-order customers. I don't think she has stopped for a breather once since.

After the business built up like this, they were made an offer to merge with a much larger concern. The decision to do so became very much an inter-related work–family concern. They finally decided to go ahead with the merger on condition that Mrs Harris could arrange to have more time at home with the children in the afternoons and that she could have greater flexibility about taking holidays. Accepting the merger was seen to benefit the family also by increasing their income which would allow them to buy a house and a chance for 'a momentous capital gain' after five years, which would secure the children's financial future.

The major issue in the family to date, has been how to keep in balance the commitments to both work and family life. When work commitments have become so pressing that family involvement was suffering, the Harrises rehearsed a solution that would allow Mrs Harris to drop work commitments in favour of family commitments entirely. Before making the step finally in this direction, however, they realized that this would be an undesirable situation for them both and they achieved a compromise – in which the balance between work and family commitments was restored, hoping to use the resources of a larger organization to decrease rather than increase the pressures on Mrs Harris.

Changes in family life style have not been radical from one phase to the next. As Mrs Harris always worked, there was no change related to the difference between working and not working at any point. The values and goals for the family have remained consistently defined in terms of creating a situation in which both Mr and Mrs Harris could work productively, profitably and enjoyably and at the same time that they could have a full family life. The material aspects of their life have consistently improved, and they are working towards a continued improvement that will include a style of life involving a home and garden, several holidays a year on the Continent, further cultivation of aesthetic interests and a mixed group of friends. They each emphasize that they wish to achieve a comfortable standard of living but not great wealth. It is a way of life rather than the sheer amount of money that they can accumulate that appeals to them.

Mr Harris sees a balance in the family and between family and work as being the highest goal rather than the 'pursuit of happiness pure and simple'; he feels that men more than women must work out this balance. He feels that women can pursue happiness more directly, as they need not bring in the element of economic responsibility so clearly. When asked if men can use the 'happiness' or 'avoidance of excessive anxiety' criteria as well as women in making career choices, he says:

No, I don't think so, I think it is different. I think I have considered different things at different times and I have thought about happiness but I have tended to put certain other things first. I have turned down a proposition because I have thought that I may not be happy in the end, but it has only been one factor . . .

We have seen that this couple has a very high degree of involvement in each other. Both are intensely involved in both work and family. Mr Harris's involvement in his wife's work takes a very complex form. Until recently her work has been his hobby and he has provided for her advice based on his business acumen and experience, and so a certain amount of actual participation in her business, e.g. in negotiating contracts, finance and so on. It is very difficult to separate their work and family lives in discussing their relationship.

Their interdependence works very well at times, while at other times it may create difficulties. In general, they give the impression of caring a lot for each other and what the other does. They are generally supportive of each other through conflicts of interest do arise and there are often difficulties in resolving them. The difficulties arise partly because of their intense involvement with one another, as each tends to use the other as a sort of 'alter-ego'; and in conflict situations, as indicated, each takes one side and then the other of a problematic issue.

There are strong elements, particularly on Mr Harris's side, of a traditional Jewish family conception. On the other hand, there are also clearly differences in their conception from the traditional one, in which Mr Harris is more helpful and less demanding on the domestic front than he might otherwise be. Neither thinks in highly stereotyped terms about men's and women's roles in the family despite Mr Harris's relatively traditional orientation to women and home-making tasks. This orientation is seen in his emphasis on how much their daughter needed her mother to teach her all the things that girls want to learn – cooking, sewing, etc. In choosing a line of work, however, women, he feels, can and should have personal happiness as the major criterion, while men cannot do so as they *must* work. Here we see his deviation from the traditional; he feels it is important that his wife should be able to obtain personal fulfilment from work if she wants to and they have shaped their lives as a combined effort to achieve this. She says 'behind every successful woman there is a man', and that she has in fact depended on his participation all along the way. Aside from the practical assistance there is a good deal of mutual involvement with what one another enjoys in the work situation. Because he had had a career in entertainment and quite frankly enjoyed

popularity and acclaim, he understood what it meant to her to
be a 'known designer'. Both of them like elements in the way
of life of the business tycoon and appreciate in one another
the positive aspects of this – the excitement, the thrill of getting
things done and so on, rather than merely mercenary aspects of
the businessman's aspirations.

Each of the Harrises have expressive and rather volatile temperaments. When they are doing well, they find one another
very stimulating. When they are in difficulties they may gener-
ate a high level of tension, but this is preferable, he says, to
indifference which she regards as the worst situation in a
marriage.

If someone throws a brick, at least you know they care. I find it
revolting if someone just says 'Good morning' and so on. The very
polite British row. I prefer a solid row, and then make up, and
everything is better for it. There are sad experiences, bad patches
in marriage, but if one can overcome the difficulties, it cements the
marriage. It is better and nicer once these things are overcome and
left behind, then you are on the next phase of things.

When difficulties and major issues arise the Harrises try to
solve the problems by discussing them together. If the resolution is not arrived at quickly the characteristic pattern of
interaction arises that has already been described. Each takes
the opposite side on an issue, and they go backwards and for-
wards, each accepting the position of the other and changing
positions. They then come to an impasse. In the most recent
major decision on the merger of her business this was clearly
manifested. In a joint interview with both he described the
process as follows :

Very much brinkmanshipping – we were pushing each other over
the brink and back again. This was a kind of puzzle . . . we do this
terrible thing to each other, we push each other from one extreme
to the other so often we are unable to decide on the fundamental
issues because we keep seeing the opposite situation. . . . Each wants
to please the other.

When first interviewed together, he was arguing in favour

of their rejecting the business offer and of her returning to a more domestic role. He says:

I felt that I was able to persuade my wife to accept this thing, and I considered doing that; it was very tormenting. I decided that I could not do that because the risk was too big to take. ... If she accepted this big responsibility with such pressures for immediate success at a time when she needed a break desperately her health might fail. ... I would never be able to rest because of that, and what's more if that happened we would have achieved disaster.

At that point his argument in favour of his wife retiring and concentrating on her home and children prevailed. Then, when they had (after weeks of torment involving themselves, their friends and colleagues) made the decision to reject the offer, Mr Harris decided that this was not right. He felt that he had swayed her into making a decision that was based on a romantic notion of the return to a familistic ideal that was unrealistic and not appropriate for her. At the same time they would be throwing away a business opportunity for which they had both worked for many years and which could be brought to fruition in such a way as to protect her and the family situation. He then changed sides and 'sold' her the idea of accepting the offer. She describes it as follows. After indicating that her husband had made the final decision, she says:

(He said, let's go and try it) and although I say that we both agreed on it, that very night I remember, and will never forget it, in his office, me stomping up and down like a wild lion. He put all the things before me and he swayed me rather like a good lawyer would sway the jury and I was swayed, and I knew myself to be swayed ... afterwards I said why did you do this to me, I was perfectly happy not signing.

This interactive process takes place in other areas of their life and in their history together. When Mrs Harris is at what she calls 'her best' she is able rapidly to make decisions – e.g. on the employment of domestic help or on work issues. However, when she becomes, in her terms, at her 'worst', she is very indecisive and exaggerates problems. Her husband under these circumstances tends to take a position and very persuasively to win her around to it. Sometimes after experiencing the first resolution he decides that it was not really the right solution and reverses his position.

The Harrises feel that it is best that they do not actually work together even though Mr Harris obtains a great deal of gratification from his wife's work. They think that if they did, they would recriminate when things went wrong. It would be difficult to establish who was responsible for a given line of thinking or decision. In addition the fact that all their eggs would be in one basket, so to speak, would mean that each would become very intensely involved and this might lead to difficulties. With each one semi-detached from the concerns of the other, they feel that they are in a position to help one another better. His own pleasure from identification with her is indicated when he says :

She is already somewhat of a public figure in this particular field. She is known and she is written about and her picture appears from time to time in the press, and I am delighted about it. In fact, I have propagated it, as it were, for her for a long time.

Parent–Child Relations

As already mentioned, the Harrises have two children. They tend to treat their children like little adults, drawing them into discussions about topics they are concerned with. Mrs Harris sometimes takes the children to her studio and to fashion shows, even using her daughter to model dresses, which is experienced as great fun. They are very proud of their children and took us to see them though they were asleep on our first interview. They told the children we were coming and the eldest child left messages for us each time. On one occasion she waited up to see us. The Harrises see their daughter as a happy child who has creative talent, who gets on well with other children, but is not a leader. They perceive their son as an active, busy child with great powers of concentration and drive.

The children's needs are highly salient to the Harrises. Hence the periodic conflict that Mrs Harris feels about the pulls of work conflicting with the pulls of her children. Similarly, Mr Harris experiences conflicts between his wish to have his wife fulfilled and engaged in a business in which they share excitement and both have a stake against his wish to have his home and children well looked after and his wife under less strain. Whenever a big issue comes up for the Harrises the effects and implications for the children are very much in focus in taking decisions. In the most recent dilemma on the merger, for example, although there was concern about accepting an enlarged work situation and the possibility that Mrs Harris would not in fact have more time at home, they felt that the ultimate financial gain would benefit the children. She graphically describes her conflicts and indicates how they are partly related to the particular stage of her children's development:

In making this decision I can sort of sit here and talk fairly coolly about it ... but I am not being cool about it I can assure you. I am an emotional sort of person, I don't think I am the tycoon type really, because of this I have often thought very strongly, 'Oh really this is dreadful,' I've got to go running to a work appointment and I can't go and take my children into the garden as I see other mothers do.... Then when I think about it logically, I imagine that the other mothers would probably love to be rushing to an important appointment instead of sitting in the deck chairs. At times I have felt that it's an awful price that I am paying.... I haven't been able to reason this thing out easily ... it is rather miserable to say to people, look – I have achieved something, I have been asked to hit the top but I am bowing out. Naturally it is nicer to bow out when you are asked to join the top and you are the one that is bowing out than to be kicked out. Nevertheless, it seems on the one hand a great material gain which one would say goodbye to, and also I would be saying goodbye to some of the glory that one deserves after putting in five years of hard work. On the other side of this ... and this is what my husband is terrified about of course, what would I do if at 12 o'clock everything was done, and my little girl came home from school and said 'I'm going out with Mary,' and I would feel awful ...

Mr Harris completes the line of thought:

... after planning to take our daughter to an art gallery or to someone for tea, or a stroll in the woods or whatnot, or some cooking, and she simply did not want to do it because her friend called and they wanted to go and play in the garden, and this would happen two or three times and then we would have recriminations ...

In this family, where there is such high salience of both work and family worlds, the care of the children has presented problems from the beginning. Originally the problems had to do primarily with finding appropriate domestic help, and managing the household with their assistance. The domestic helper situation has become less acute as the children entered school but a different sort of issue arose – that of providing enough constructive interaction with their children. He says:

We both felt that our little girl needed Mummy more, she needed her Mummy for guidance, she needed to come back and find her Mummy at home, and not to come home with the disappointment of not finding her Mummy there; and doing things with Mummy in the kitchen, learning a little bit about cooking and all this sort of thing – the little domestic things that a child must learn from its mother. I see my daughter at about half-past six, seven o'clock, sometimes even half-past seven in the evenings – sometimes she is in bed by the time I get home because I leave the office late – I feel it is bad enough if one parent does that but it is really atrocious if a mother has to go on and on in this situation, because ... the time flies ...

Mrs Harris tries to get home to spend time with her children in the late afternoon when they have returned from school though sometimes this is not possible. Mr Harris participates in the children's activities mainly at the weekends. Mrs Harris helps both children make things. When the children are ill she stays at home more with them making artistic playthings with them. In general if there are problems at home she arranges her work so that she can do some of it at home. Otherwise she only works at home when the children are in bed at night.

Mrs Harris recognizes that the children often wished she was at home more. She feels that both children have indicated their unhappiness about the total situation by various behavioural difficulties at different times. However, the crucial element seems to be tied up with whether they like the domestic helper at the time or not. If they are left with someone they like, the absence of the mother is not felt so acutely – and her return is experienced with pleasure rather than upset and anger. Mrs Harris notes that her daughter is proud of her mother's work, for example, when Mrs Harris designed the uniform for her school, and this makes up somewhat for the feelings about her being away so much. She also says her daughter expresses feelings of being proud to have a mother who is 'doing something'. Mrs Harris describes all this as follows :

I think I am much more prone to look for negative effects on the children because we are bogged with an awful lot of literature and an awful lot of things are said to provide more guilt feelings than are necessary. I have seen women who are at home from morning to night with problem children, where it obviously stems from within the child or from her (the mother's) own attitudes, inhibitions or whatever, but certainly not from the fact that the mother has another life so to speak. In my case I would say my girl has a lot of pride. . . . She said to me the other day, 'All the little new girls have come to me to show me their uniform and said "Isn't it your mummy who designed it," and I say "Yes." ' I could see the little bit of pride in her which obviously helps her; and it became a part of her life. . . . Last year about this time we had a show in which I asked my daughter and her friend to participate, to come in and wear the little children's things; the glowing enthusiasm – it was tremendous to have a mummy who was doing something; it was lovely and naturally this made up for an awful lot of 'Oh Mummy I wish you were home'.

The Harrises feel that it is important for the children to attain a sense of discipline. They explain, for instance, that their daughter is somewhat cocky at present and resents being told to toe the line in front of other people. However, they feel that this must not prevent them from disciplining her, because they feel that if a child is not disciplined this can really ruin its life later on. Mrs Harris recalls her mother saying 'You're not bringing them up for you but for life.'

The Harrises' concern with warmth in their family relationships has apparently got over to their children. She says:

... they are wonderful together, I don't know how this is, I sometimes don't trust it, it seems too good to be true. She (daughter) can
be made responsible, she is more of a little mother than an intellectual; she really enjoys being a *good* girl, and I think she enjoys
also – although obviously at times she gets thoroughly browned off
with (her brother) – she may be just drawing something and he
comes along and scrawls through it or something like that; but on
the whole they play awfully well together and they really do
manage when they have to be together not to be at daggers drawn.

Mr and Mrs Harris's aspirations for their children are still em-
bryonic. His views are more traditional and sex-linked than his
wife's. He feels that his son should be guided into a professional
career but she says:

I want them to have a chance for a year to kick up their heels
and find out how things work. I want them to have the time and
not to feel pressured by financial strains to go into something that
might not be right for them. I feel that they are small and I
wouldn't want to force anything yet. Whatever she does, I feel
that what my father told me, 'You must have something in your
hands and then you can use it in various ways,' may be the best
thing. The important thing is that they should be happy with it
even if it is only using it to decorate a house for one's husband.

He says:

I have been thinking about my son, that he ought to have an
opportunity to be able to select a career that will give him great
pleasure rather than necessarily be financially advantageous. He
should be helped to look at the professions rather than business
or commerce or industry. He should be given the right kind of
schooling that would help him with that. For our daughter, she
should be helped to develop her talents, to develop a career with
a small 'c'; if she has talent she might have her own ideas about
this.

Both of the Harrises have a great sense of providing a stable
future for their children, financially, and also of providing adequate funds to support themselves after they retire. They do

not wish to be dependent upon their children as their own parents were on them. Her emphasis is more on the shock to the parents, his on the conflicts for the children. He says :

I don't want any burden on our children so that they should be worried about whether or not we can be supported. They shouldn't be torn in their loyalties, we have been through that, I don't want them to.

As indicated above, the type of domestic help which the Harrises have is very important to the state of functioning of the household. The first girl they had when their daughter was born was a Swedish nurse who was experienced, lovable, and complementary to Mrs Harris. The family came to love her and she stayed for two years.

Their hope has been to find a person like the housekeeper Mrs Harris's family had when she was a child. This woman has remained a family friend, and recently visited them, underlining the way in which relationships with domestic care people may enrich a family's life. Mrs Harris describes her :

...she was a very old lady, who was my parents' and grand-parents' housekeeper. When I stayed with my grandparents in Berlin, she used to go away with us and so forth. She knew my mother from a young girl of seventeen or sixteen and was the sort of family retainer, a wonderful woman. She has got this inner tranquillity, this complete peace, her presence is reassuring. We love her and my husband loves her very much indeed and I asked her over when I got married and invited her when our daughter was born – not when our son was born because my mother-in-law was seriously ill and died and so it wasn't possible to arrange.

However this ideal is elusive in present-day London. The Harrises experienced the difficulties that are far more common in these arrangements.

Over a period of time we have had girls or women in here who have caused us untold anxiety one way and another. They have not been able to look after the children, they have not been able to tend to the home – it causes a great deal of worry.

Mrs Harris, after describing various bad experiences with

domestic helpers, indicates how work pressures can sometimes prevent this from being adequately dealt with :

(This past year) I went through a fearful year of holocaust sweeping through this place in the shape of one lady or another but part of this was because instead of saying 'I'm taking a month off in order to organize this' I was forced to battle on come what may which nobody should do. . . . I could write books on au-pairmanship, it was awful.

Recently the Harrises had a satisfactory arrangement with an au pair and daily.

They have noted, as mentioned above, that the problems that have arisen with their children have been related to the quality of the domestic help. They see the root of the problem as a sense of powerlessness of the child. Adults can move away or change an association if it is difficult. Children have people imposed on them much more. When their daughter was seven she went through a very difficult period – nail-biting, finding herself unable to concentrate, and so on. She was very unhappy at the time and her headmistress, who is a friend of the family, pressed Mrs Harris to spend more time with her daughter. Mrs Harris knew that the problem related to the domestic help they had. The daughter did not like the au pair but was unable to express it. With a change in the help situation, their daughter recovered her equilibrium.

The problems that have arisen with the little boy have seemed less closely linked with the domestic help situation. Viewing it retrospectively, now that he has entered school and is happy in it, Mrs Harris feels that the basic problem was one of channelling his activities :

Now he comes home from nursery school and he has grown up. I don't know how it has happened, at first I was very worried about (him), up to quite a little while ago because I thought that little boy is whining and I am obviously the reason why he is whining and that sort of thing, and that he just wants to kick me for being away from him. Now, I found that he needed school desperately; he's a very bright little boy . . . doesn't stand still for a minute, it's all busy, wound up. Beginning school last September was the most wonderful thing, he so enjoys it; he enjoys the companionship; this term he has just been moved up a class. The teacher has told me that he has a wonderful ability to concentrate on things which other children older than himself have difficulty at ... he apparently comes in, sits down and gets on with plasticine or whatever.

Relations with Others Outside the Home

With the exception of Mrs Harris's mother, most of the Harris's meaningful external relationships are with friends from both their work worlds rather than with relatives. Mr Harris's parents are dead. With regard to Mrs Harris's mother, she says her mother is happier living on her own in the Midlands where she has a circle of friends and activities rather than coming down to London to stay with them. They are in constant communication with one another and her mother is available to help with family emergencies, such as illness of the children or being on hand if the Harrises wish to take a holiday away from the children.

There is another family in the same block of flats who have a little boy the same age as the Harris's son, but Mrs Harris says:

... the set-up is so completely different and the personalities are not the same ... The parents (of children that used to live in the same block) were on the same wave-length intellectually and in every other way too, even economically ... with the other neighbours we aren't and this makes a difference ... the mother does not work but there are four staff there ... the expectations of what will be done for the children are different.

Mrs Harris also has made friends with the woman whose daughter plays with her son in nursery school:

She is a charming woman who works as a speech therapist and has a lovely little girl. She has tape-recorded a conversation the two children had together and they live in a wonderful sort of fairy world; they play wonderful games.

The Harrises expect to be able to share problems and difficulties as well as pleasure with their closest friends; they do not like to enter into relationships in which they cannot reciprocate.

The support that they have sought and received from friends recently centred on making major life decisions, particularly the recent one about the merger of Mrs Harris's business. However, crises of various kinds may arise, and friends are people who will tolerate and 'stick with one' when one is behaving badly under stress. Mrs Harris feels that the indecision and sense of despair which sometimes ensues during crisis-episodes taxes the tolerance of people who are not true friends.

Of her early friends from college, there is only one woman who has persisted in a full-time career but this woman is now in America in the field of market research. They keep in touch and retain a sense of deep friendship despite the distance. Mrs Harris indicates how she feels a sense of obligation and a wish to help her friends by describing a situation that has arisen with another college friend whom she feels she can help through her larger business connections :

I was very close with one particular boy who was the most wonderful silversmith. His wife, whom I didn't know at the time, is an interior decorator. They had three children, and with this largish family she maintained her own career as an interior decorator, though only on a part-time basis. It wasn't something that she did as a business on her own. Recently when I went to see her, we chatted and their ambition is to start what was also in my mind – a sort of design workshop. I am sure they will do it.

Mrs Harris planned to speak to her own financial backers to get help for this couple. She also takes an interest in other women who are attempting to combine careers with family life.

As far as contacts with professional service people go, the Harrises are very involved with solicitors because of the complexity of their business contracts; they tend to become friends too. There appears to be a similarly close relationship with their physician who has discussed with them the personal conflicts arising from work crises and decisions.

The Harrises

WORK WORLDS

Both the Harrises are in business. Mrs Harris was mentioned to us as an example of a successful 'entrepreneur', having started and developed in business in women's fashion. In the course of the interviews, it became clear that Mrs Harris was in a dynamic situation and during the study she became an executive in a larger firm (which absorbed her firm) as well as continuing as design director. Both Mr and Mrs Harris as a consequence are working at a high level of managerial responsibility, and both situations are changing.

Unlike the Bensons, the Harrises do not formally work together. Mr Harris helps his wife in some of her decisions and, to some extent, regards her enterprises as his hobby; she will discuss aspects of his work situation with him but their spheres of participation are separate. Consequently, 'work worlds' are discussed separately though there is a moderate degree of overlap.

Mr Harris's Work World

Mr Harris is the managing director of a company which imports, processes, packages and distributes a food product to a variety of retail outlets. The major interest in the firm is in the hands of a large British corporation with diverse interests, but a substantial secondary interest is held by an American company with specific involvement in the food product.

At the time the interviews began he was sales manager for the company and he has since become managing director. This has led to an increase in his responsibilities with an attendant lessening of the flexibility he formerly had to cover family events and participate in his wife's work.

Part of the additional load that he has recently experienced has been due to the general increase in demands on his time that comes from the movement from a functional specialism to the general management role. Additionally he has been involved in a number of new undertakings which, while also common for companies of this type today, are nevertheless highly specific in detail and require very close working through with one's associates. The company, to meet problems of rising costs, new competition and so on has invested in new plant and equipment. This has involved considerable negotiation on a variety of levels. In addition, the absorption of new equipment has coincided with the general movement in the company towards rationalization of many of its functions and modes of operating. Working together with management consultants, Mr Harris has initiated up-to-date systems of personnel management and career planning. This has taken a good deal of time, and has involved working out new relationships between plant and headquarters.

Being managing director involves making strategic plans on investment and pricing as well as the internal operation of the organization. This has included negotiation about equipment, supplies of the food products, and assessment of the economic and market situation generally, entailing considerable travel.

In his work, Mr Harris derives satisfaction from the style of life of a senior executive, and also from having risen within the company to be its chief executive. He enjoys the element of challenge that comes from assessing and responding to a very dynamic market situation, finding within the organization some expression for his entrepreneurial talents and interests (now no longer being expressed in his wife's business as it has become part of another large corporation).

While his present position still allows him some flexibility, for example, in timing his holidays to correspond with his family's, he is less free than formerly to spend time on smaller issues that require his immediate presence. The fact that Mrs Harris's business has been absorbed by a larger company has also coloured this, as will be indicated in the final section on integration of work and family life below. On the other hand, Mr Harris remains strongly family-oriented, and the integration of their activities is more around shared family interests than shared work interests at present.

The Working Situation of Mrs Harris

Many aspects of Mrs Harris's work world have come out in previous sections. When we first began the interviews she was a well-known dress designer with a small company half owned by her and her husband and half by the manufacturers in the north. A state of crisis arose during this time about a proposed merger of her business with a much larger international company and continued for some months. Eventually the decision was made and Mr and Mrs Harris now own one quarter of the company bearing her name; this company is part of a large conglomerate of companies. Mrs Harris's company designs and produces knitwear, ladies' and children's fashions. The design work is still done in her own studio near her home and the marketing from a showroom in the West End. The manufacturing is undertaken by one of the conglomerate's companies in a neighbouring London borough.

The philosophy, goals and values of her company seem to have several themes, some of which run through it from the beginning and some of which are new emphases developed in the course of the amalgamation.

One of the consistent goals of the company from the start has been the emphasis on producing good fashion designs with meticulous attention to quality and available at economic prices. Mrs Harris says about her early conception of the business :

I had no ambitions in respect to promoting my own name as long as I was building and I was producing the right thing and they were nicely made and they were value.

Another theme is that of appropriate remuneration. It was recognized from the beginning by both the Harrises that she had special design talents and that having her work for other companies was neither optimal financially for them nor for their wish to develop a happy family life.

Mrs Harris says :

. . . if you are an employee in this country you never stand a chance if you want a certain level of living; neither of us are status-symbol seekers but I think there is a level of living that we enjoy and as an employee it is jolly difficult to save . . .

Mr Harris says :

. . . it seemed nonsense for her to go tracking around the country in order to design; (we realized) that we ought to set up something in London built around her requirements as a mother not to travel far and all that sort of thing . . . which we did . . .

Mr Harris recognized that business talent as well as design talent is needed for success. Mr Harris's participation with early decisions on marketing strategies etc. has been crucial in this respect from the beginning. He recognized the financial potential in her work. For her, it was an important element in her motivation but *not* the whole of it. Because of the traumatic changes in her family's fortunes when she was a child, she has all her life been particularly concerned about financial security and the provision of a good standard of living for the family. She does not see this as only her husband's responsibility.

From the point of view of the large company which their company now belongs to, there are additional goals, stemming from the economics of the larger conglomerate. The chairman of the fashion group initiated the whole train of events when he rang Mrs Harris and said : 'I need some designing done immediately.' Mrs Harris replied that she was too busy with her own company, whereupon the chairman, with the resources of the large company behind him, said : 'Can we buy you?' As the discussion progressed, the conception emerged that she should be relieved of her concern with other functions – passing them over to other parts of the company – and concentrate on design, becoming ultimately what they refer to as a 'design fountain', having around her assistants and apprentices of various kinds and serving various interests of the fashion group, for which she would be 'design director'. Mrs Harris had found the business administration side of her work irksome so she responded positively to this but not without a period of intense soul-searching and conflict (personal and interpersonal) as described above.

In addition, she has had a long-standing wish to develop her work in the context of a 'vertically integrated' organization. She sees the new tie-in with the large group of firms as providing an environment within which she may be able to achieve this. She says :

... my personal deep ambition was always to have a vertically integrated firm where I can produce the fabric and design the fabric as opposed to just choosing it and being completely in the hands of those who knit and make and offer it all around the trade. ... In vertically integrated firms ... you don't just make the garments but you have to design the fabrics as well.... You have an end product in mind when you design the fabric ...

Mrs Harris concentrates her day to day work on designing in her studio. She considers that her strength as director lies in the fact that she is not only a creative designer but is meticulous and thorough in putting out the product – following through production, packaging and so on with great care and attention to detail. She mentioned a recent incident that shows how this is done even though her own design company is now separated from the production and marketing of the products. She says :

For example, I had some samples done of a design and they arrived at the factory earlier than scheduled. I got a telephone call from the man there who asked me whether he could get on with the cutting and grading of the patterns to the relevant sizes, even though it was ahead of the schedule. As it happens it is a complex garment, it involves zippers, buttons, a top and a bottom and just to pass out the skirt, for example, into the grading of different sizes without paying attention to the relationship between the skirt and the jacket might produce the wrong effect in other sizes. So, I said that it was necessary to see the people that were going to do this to check that the zipper sizes on the top would fit the proportions that the top had to change in relation to the bottom and so on. I enjoy doing this; apart from just the joy of seeing the design, I enjoy everything about it, the way it is packaged and put out and so on.

Mrs Harris's present studio staff consists of :

... one girl and a sample hand. The sample hand does the stitching of the first model, the other girl can interpret a sketch or under guidance do what I want her to do. I had her straight from art school, she has been with me for four and a half years nearly, so that she's quite trained in. But she's not a girl with flair; unless I say something she'll just stand and say 'Where's the next brief' ... however she is complementary and not trying to do the same thing. ... I believe very strongly in building a team.

She can now hire additional people and is quite excited about the possibilities that this opens up :

I will gather in young designers and experts in different fields, not make the whole thing only a fashion thing but really sort of a design unit that can pour out anything to do with design, advice on colour of labels, do all sorts of things so that I can see a kind of growth in the direction that I feel I like.

One new assistant that Mrs Harris decided to take on is much more the sort who could stand in for her rather than depending on her. This is a new form of complementarity that seems to be developing. She describes this girl as having 'a good basic education' and therefore being more at home with people; having poise; having the desire to work and having flair.

The advantages of now being part of the large group of companies include less administrative work :

I was doing a lot of paper work ... which I am not particularly gifted at – sorting out credit notes and so on ... because the accounts section was in the north I had to write out extremely explicit and detailed memoranda to send them. Now I can pop in the car and it takes me exactly ten minutes from here to the (manufacturing company's office) where an accountant has been seconded to me so that it is one thing off my mind ...

More space in her studio :

If I have difficulty machine-wise or if I need a job done, they have the personnel. I can draw on people. All this has eased my situation enormously. If, for example, my sample hand falls ill, that wouldn't be the end of my world ...

Less travel and tighter lines of communication :

Before, my tiny unit was the nerve centre for a factory, in the north ... and now all this travelling up and down to the north has been cut out. Also (for the mail-order business) the fact that the West End showroom has been put at my disposal means that I can have big customers come there, and they are delighted. (Thus) big journeys up to the north are at a minimum ...

Mrs Harris has also been able to employ an additional assistant.

The main disadvantages of the merger involve a series of ambiguities of Mrs Harris's relationship within the larger organization and the pressures that may be put on her through organizational commitments and personnel.

In general she tends to go to work at about 9 a.m. after getting the children off to school. Sometimes, prior to going to the studio, she does some telephoning from home. Sometimes she stays home a bit in the morning

to design or to do some things I might prefer (to do) without the phone continuously ringing, which it does when I am at the office and people will want me for silly things ...

But usually she goes to the office 'and organizes everything'. In the past she has not been able to get back in the afternoon until about six o'clock or later, to be with the children, but one of the things that was important to the Harrises in creating the conditions of her new contract was to be able to make it possible for her to be home more in the late afternoons. She hoped that this could be achieved by cutting down on travel to the factory, delegation of functions, and having more assistance. She would like to be home at about four o'clock. But though this is working to some extent, there are new demands due to the expanded scope of the business. Mrs Harris says:

Now there are people coming – someone in Austria wants this, the Russians want that, and there's export and all sort of things. I'm trying desperately hard to be home in order to be with my children for a couple of hours. At present times ... it's not really working out. Like tonight for instance (but anyway) I was home early enough to tuck the children in and still early enough to give my daughter a little time to talk to me about school and that sort of thing. And I think somehow I am more relaxed about the whole thing because first of all I have made a decision which is always better and secondly I am really trying to discipline myself not to worry about all aspects of the business. You know, rather let the others make the mistakes, after all I can't do it all.

In fact she finds it difficult to shrug off pressures from the organization and to disregard deficiencies of colleagues in the overall process from design to marketing.

Her high valuation of efficiency is illustrated in the following observation by Mrs Harris about the conditions under which she likes to work:

I must say I have always been used to a degree of high efficiency which I find much healthier because people find it safe; just like a mother who is firm with her children, they feel immediately confident, they feel that there's a certain discipline that is to be adhered to *and* this is all very comforting; I feel people are like that; they feel whether somebody is mumbling and bumbling along, you know, today this will do, tomorrow something else and ...

In addition to the qualities of hard work, efficiency, integrity, intensity and warmth in her relationships at work, Mrs Harris is subject to mood fluctuations which she and her husband see as part of the creative personality at work.

He says she has periods when she

wallows in misery, when she is at the depths of inability to fulfil herself – inability to create ...
... this happens to all designers – for a period of time they seem to lie fallow, they seem to be unable to create. They *feel* they are unable to create, they probably could – but then they would just produce things that were put together somehow but didn't have line, grace, didn't excite; but when they are in a happy frame of mind and have got a few ideas, they just absolutely sail away, they can do it at any time of the day or night, it doesn't matter where they are, the sketches come out. (This is the same for) a poet or a writer or what not.

Apart from the satisfaction gained from being creative, other components of satisfaction from her work come from public recognition and acclaim: she always did have the most great desire to be a 'known name' – to be *recognized* as a designer and to have a good income and standard of living. She has always wanted financial security and seeks through making a 'momentous capital gain' in her business to provide for her children's future. Mrs Harris accounts for this element of her motivations in terms of her history. She says :

The only thing I have never done is I have never had *no* actual earning capacity of my own; I've always had earning capacity ... having been a refugee you need that little bit of security.

INTEGRATION OF PERSONAL, FAMILY AND WORK WORLDS

It has been seen that participation in both family and work activities are of high importance to the Harrises. While they also enjoy various leisure and cultural pursuits, their primary satisfactions come from working and family life. Mr and Mrs Harris have overlapping but separate work involvements, both of which are necessary to them. While each of them has some feelings of ambivalence about her occupational participation – particularly the amount involved – both of them feel, in the final analysis, that this is necessary and desirable for their goals in life.

Apart from the fact that Mrs Harris's work is at a high level, the Harris family structure is relatively conventional. The 'unconventionality' comes from her actual degree of career commitment. Within the family, however, the Harrises expectations of their responsibilities and obligations – as well as their rewards and privileges – tend to go along conventional sex roles with only moderate overlap of activities. While Mr Harris helps at home, he does not have unusual responsibilities there. However, he has been quite active, though indirectly, in his wife's occupational world and expects less from her of the conventional wife's submissiveness to the demands of his occupation. In fact, much of his 'family' life has been taken up with working out his wife's problems – which have been a sort of hobby for him until recently. However, with Mrs Harris's absorption into a larger group of companies this congruence of interest has been harder to maintain. Their work is now less interconnected than previously, and less than the Bensons' or Neals'. On the other hand, they relate over work interests more than do the Kileys or Jarrets who feel they do not share work involvements nor do they wish work concerns to play too large a role in their domestic relationship. Again, the Kileys' domestic life shows a much greater degree of overlap in the accomplishment of household tasks than the Harrises'. Their children are also more involved in keeping the domestic sphere operating co-operatively.

How do the Harrises compare with the other families in the way they integrate their children into their work worlds? The Harrises, like some of the others, take their children to their place of work, bring home materials for them to play with, talk to them about their work, and so on. Mrs Harris is active in involving her children in her work where possible. Apart from playing with the materials she uses in her work, she uses her daughter as a model occasionally and has created a sense of pride in her daughter for what she does; this has been facilitated by designing the school uniform for her daughter's school, thereby bringing her professional life into a meaningful sphere of her daughter's life.

While Mr Harris does not participate very actively in the domestic sphere, it is crucial for the family that his work life is arranged so that there is a degree of flexibility which allows him to be available in emergencies and to be involved to some extent in the concerns of his wife. This, together with a family organization which is efficiently managed and kept to manageable proportions in a flat rather than a house, enables the relationship between family and work that they have developed to be maintained. With the increased responsibility of Mr Harris as he has taken on the managing director role in his company, and simultaneously his diminished involvement in his wife's work world, the Harrises face new challenges for mutual co-operation and support. They are aided in this by their holding relatively established positions, and by their children being older and more independent. The basis for their integration as a couple has devolved, for the time being, around their family rather than their work.

Analysis of Dual-Career Families

The dual-career family is a structural type emerging as an important option for a future in which both men and women will have increased education and training and in which family life is likely to remain a fundamental institution fulfilling essential social and psychological functions. The analysis of the life experience of the dual-career families presented indicates a number of elements in complex interplay. There seem to be many paradoxical elements, the resolution of which is essential in sustaining this pattern.

The dual-career pattern provides major sources of satisfaction while at the same time creating burdens. Each couple operates at a high level of strain but they have all chosen this as their style of life; and when contemplating other patterns they usually reject them as less satisfactory for themselves as individuals and as families.

The individuals in dual-career families are singularly determined and purposeful and yet they seem to have evolved their patterns through a series of almost accidental events and choices. They have ended up with patterns reflecting their flexibility and their general determination rather than a specific pre-conceived goal.

The individuals are in some ways self-absorbed in promoting the kind of life they want, and yet their orientations are often in terms of some higher altruistic value such as social service or aesthetics or some combination of the two.

In some ways, the individuals seem strong and, at the same time, often in some sense weak and dependent in their relationships. A successful career wife, like any other woman, can be quite feminine and ordinary, and in need of help as are other people at work and home.

While most of the people studied – men and women – say

that they relied on being healthy as families, they are not on the whole 'Amazon' types in terms of sheer physique but rely on organizational and decision-making abilities. Though all of the couples studied used highly efficient and rational management methods in their family affairs – not being able to afford as much of the luxury of 'muddling through' as many conventionally organized families – they did not necessarily end up with a cold, hard and calculating home environment. These families do not fall on the relaxed and placid end of the continuum of family atmospheres, but this does not mean that there was a loss of warmth or interest or value for them and their children.

In short, the paradoxical element is strong among these families, but it is partly in relation to social expectations about what kind of person might be able to operate such a pattern and what sort of person might have the drive to overcome various obstacles in the way of achieving it in the first place. Given the actual descriptions, which serve to some extent to dispel these stereotyped expectations and to show the couples as the people they are, it becomes important to sort out the similarities and differences among them so as to be able to understand better how they actually function as distinct from how one expects such families might function.

The more overt aspects of the common features of the dual-career families were described in the first chapter. It is now possible to present, against the background of the more detailed descriptions of five families, both some sense of variations and of common elements at a less overt level. This will be done in three sections – the first on variations, the second on motivational syndromes observed, and the third on 'strains and gains' that seem to be experienced by the couples in operating this pattern.

VARIATIONS

The families presented were selected to show the different occupational careers of the wives, so this source of variation is manifest in the materials. The more individual 'entrepreneurial' way of organizing one's occupation provides greater flexibility to the individual but also entails greater risk. The woman who is a salaried employee of a large organization, who is in a more 'bureaucratic' work setting, must conform to the norms of the organization (and these may be relatively rigid or relatively flexible) but she gains the security of a known income which has advantages in planning and domestic organization, children's schooling and so on. The husband may see either work context as advantageous, assuming that he supports the general idea of his wife having a career. If she has a career within an organizational structure, he may feel that he can take greater risks in his own work, or at least that his economic responsibilities towards her and his family are being shared. Alternatively, he may opt for the more secure occupational situation for himself, encouraging entrepreneurial activity by his wife as a way of engaging as a family in the excitement of risk taking, but covering the hazards at the same time.

The way the couples integrate their work situations is as important as the characteristics of their jobs *per se*. The husband and wife may have the same occupation or different occupations; they may work for the same or different employers (including themselves); and their work may be highly interdependent or independent of one another in either of the above situations. The Bensons have the same occupation, are self employed and work together as partners; they have the greatest degree of overlap at work and at home in the sense that each can perform many elements of the other's activities in both spheres. Next are the Neals who are both in the same occupation and work for the same ministry but they work separately in different departments. The Neals have considerable overlap in home activities but at work their overlap is moderate – sharing interests and knowledge but not interchanging tasks. Both the Harrises and Kileys work at separate occupations for different employers, yet in each case there is moderate overlap in their training and experience so that each member of these couples can participate to some extent in the work interests of the other.

The Kileys have more overlap in domestic activities than the Harrises, who show only moderate overlap in this sphere as well as in work. In the Jarrets there is a lower degree of overlap in this particular sphere, which is unusual in its characteristics, but there is nevertheless a sharing of interest in that Mr Jarret has had theatre as a hobby all his life and this is her work. Mrs Jarret has had a strong respect for aesthetic and socially significant activities, and this is his work. Their actual involvement in one another's work problems, however, is that of sympathetic listeners rather than active participants.

The Kileys have the greatest degree of shared division of labour at home with Mr Kiley doing more around the house, usually together with his wife, than any of the other husbands. The Bensons are perhaps a close second, partly because of the physical presence of the work activities in the household. The Neals also share a good deal while the Jarrets and Harrises maintain a more conventional division of labour between husband and wife. In all cases this issue is eased by the provision of domestic helpers, who take on many of the less desired aspects of domestic work, freeing the two heads of the family for the activities they choose – usually cooking (which remains primarily the wife's domain) and gardening (which may be either and is often joint).

Child care is an area where the variations are marked not only in terms of general philosophy of child-rearing but more particularly in relation to the conception held of the child's role in family life. In some of the families, the child has been protected from involvement in the chore aspects of family living. In the Jarret family, for example, the son's involvement in domestic chores came only when he became interested in electrical wiring as a hobby. In the Kileys and Neals by contrast, the children have had definite roles within the family and the expectation has been that they will help with what has to be done. In the Benson family it is assumed that the children will be relatively independent, and they are not assigned specific tasks.

It is probably true to say that in all of the families – whether the children actively participate and carry responsibility for family chores or not, there is an emphasis on enhancing the children's independence and competence. None of the dual-career families show the pattern sometimes found among families of their income level of having their children waited on, serviced and chauffeured around. Delight is expressed by the parents when the children show mastery and aspire to a high level of accomplishment, whether in one of the parents' fields of interest or not. The emphasis on high standards and excellence at what one does is very marked. It should be noted that this is not an emphasis on 'going higher' but on doing whatever one does as well as possible. This emphasis is independent of the sex of the child. In no case among the dual-career families was there a stereotyped conventional orientation to sex roles. Where a daughter may favour a more conventional role this has not been discouraged but tends to be regarded as a personal choice.

Other variations are in terms of the personalities of the individuals – the way they have fitted together and in the styles the couples have shown in their interpersonal relations, for example, in decision making and conflict resolution. In personality there seems to be a general tendency for the marital partners to see themselves as temperamentally complementary. The wives tend to be described as more expressive, volatile and moody and the men as calmer and steadier.

PERSONAL MOTIVATIONS

The contrast in dual-career families between the psychological climate and alignments in husbands' early family and that of their wives has already been mentioned in the first chapter. The detailed case descriptions now allow discussion of another element of their personal and interpersonal life, namely, the way in which the couples manage potential difficulties of competitiveness and envy in their relationship.

To review the points made in the first chapter; the dual-career wives tend to be 'only-lonely' children and they frequently come from tense family backgrounds in which there were elements of support as well as tension. Mrs Kiley had extreme tension in her relations with her father but support from her mother; Mrs Benson had a tense relationship with her mother coupled with the experience of evacuation and an important relationship with her maternal grandmother. She also had a relatively close relationship with her father who was home at a time when many fathers were away. This was all accompanied by a general sense of tension between her own family and the surrounding society; Mrs Jarret felt very removed from the values of her parents but had an elder brother as a supportive figure. Mrs Neal, like Mrs Jarret was a youngest child with older siblings some distance removed. Mrs Jarret, in particular, fits the description of being a quasi-only child. While Mrs Neal's family were relatively comfortable financially they went through a period of hardship which would have made Mrs Neal aware of the necessity to be economically independent. Mrs Harris had the shock of relocation and the subsequent difficulties of readjustment that her parents experienced in the Second World War. Her relationship with each parent went through major changes during this time but one or other was always very supportive of her.

The men seem to show a picture of greater familial harmony in their backgrounds, and in most cases more social mobility than their wives. Mr Neal's family experienced poverty and unemployment and he continually emphasized the need to put himself out of reach of such disaster; Mr Kiley's family wanted above all that he escape from the whole occupational system of the Welsh coal and steel industries; Mr Harris' family was poor but his mother was particularly ambitious for her children; and Mr Benson's family showed a similar syndrome in a different social setting. Mr Jarret's family was the only one of the husband's families described here who lived at the same general social level as do the current dual-career families themselves. In other instances the encouragement of the wife's employment may have had an element of insurance against economic difficulties as well as the wish for a high family standard of living. Many of the husbands had a particularly close and sympathetic relationship with their mothers, though this is not always true. Where it did occur, the man in question took greater responsibility, for example, for the care of the mother in her old age. Often the closeness is also in comparison with the man's feelings towards his father which, our data suggest, may have involved remoteness or hostility. Father frequently had a tense relationship with mother and children (as with Mr Harris) or simply was not very much involved in the family's early life (as with Mr Kiley).

Taking these background syndromes into account, it is possible to understand the way in which the other's activities are meaningful to each of the individuals in the dual-career families. This allows us to see how these couples have been able to deal with the problems of conflict and competition intrinsic in this kind of dual relationship, where both have career commitments as well as family involvement.

In each of the couples, it was important to the husbands themselves that their wives developed their work lives as they did. For the Bensons, the pair had evolved a creative partnership which continued to work productively and was seen by them to have advantages over other working relationships that each had known. In developing a successful working partnership while they were very young, they were able to tailor their working conditions to suit their personal needs to a greater degree than is usually possible for people at their career stage. Mrs Harris's entrepreneurial success was important to Mr Harris, expressing for him some of his own fantasies and wishes about risk-taking and public acclaim. For the Neals, Mrs Neal's career development was important to Mr Neal because he had experienced the tragic loss of his first wife whom he had seen as frustrated through not having had a career. Mrs Kiley's drive and determination were important in expressing a latent part of Mr Kiley's character which otherwise might have remained dormant under an easy-going exterior. Her drive helped him in his search for an appropriate occupational career as well as serving her own career development. Mrs Jarret's work was in the area of Mr Jarret's life-long hobby, drama.

For the wives it has been important that their husbands approved and facilitated their careers in various ways and, indeed, that they actually wanted them to work. This was crucial in transforming a wish to continue a career from something that was selfishly desired by one member into something that was wanted for the overall family benefit. Most of the dual-career wives in this series were first-born children and one of the characteristics of first-born children is the desire to please and the need for support and approval in their significant relationships. They often tended as a consequence to present this paradoxical picture of great determination combined with considerable dependence on those close to them.

Given the fact that both of the partners are engaged in the occupational world which is competitive in ethos, conflicts inevitably arise about precedence of work involvements. The conventional resolution of conflicts between the demands of two careers is in favour of the man, but for dual-career families this is not necessarily so. The weighing of advantages for the family as a whole may lead to the reverse conclusion in specific instances (as in the Kiley case), or it may involve a course of events in which now one and now the other has some particular advantage (as in the Harrises at one point in their career and it may happen with the Neals). The avoidance of excessive rivalry and envy which may accompany such situations seems to hinge on the individuals' capacity to take a joint perspective on the occupational situation, i.e., to see the work of each member as contributing something to the whole in which both have major investments. It takes a husband who is either very strong or very identified with the efforts of his wife to allow her to equal or exceed his own accomplishments without major disruption in the relationship, and most of the husbands in the series have some combination of these two attributes.

STRAINS

The families studied have shown a good many elements both of strain and satisfaction associated with the pattern of life they have evolved. Similar strains and gains might be found in more conventional types of families. On the basis of broad experience with families of different kinds, which serves as a kind of control, it is possible at least tentatively to pick out some of the strains and gains that do seem highly associated with the dual-career family. We have isolated five dilemmas which in their nature set up strains. They are dilemmas because of the choice element. The dual-career family, once chosen, entails particular strains; and sustaining the pattern means sustaining the strains.

Each family varies in the extent to which each of the dilemmas is problematic but the five selected dilemmas are common to all the couples and always entail some degree of strain. They are:

1. Overload
2. Environmental sanction
3. Personal identity and self esteem
4. Social network dilemmas
5. Dilemmas of multiple role-cycling

Overload

Sheer overloading is something that each of the families experienced, though they differed in the ways they handled it. Not having the wife at home to do the conventional 'back-up' work of domestic care or supervision, child care, social arrangements and so on, this work had either to be redistributed or neglected. Redistribution through the use of various domestic helpers is widespread, though rarely completely satisfactory. For one thing the calibre of help is not satisfactory for people with the level of standards shown by the dual-career families. For another thing, the intrusion into family privacy of the help personnel is often experienced as an additional strain, particularly where there are adolescent au pair girls who are acting out their own family rebellion problems on their temporary family substitutes.

In varying degree, the husband or the wife or both take up the slack to accomplish the tasks necessary for running the household at the standard they require. The actual pattern depends on the individuals and their situations. Doing so, however, usually involves a considerable strain because each sustains a demanding occupational role and needs support. Sometimes standards are deliberately lowered for the maintenance of the household, sometimes the children are pressed into helping roles. The latter tactic tends to be seen as a constructive socialization policy as well as an expedient in the overload situation. For the most part the additional load is simply absorbed, adding to the physical strains and diminishing the amount of free time which one often does not recognize as existing but which is present in most families' time budgets to allocate variously according to need. Most of the dual-career couples have to plan deliberately to create this kind of free time, even if only to be lazy or without immediate purpose. Sometimes they do it by having a weekend cottage retreat, as with the Bensons and the Jarrets; sometimes they make a point of *not* taking work home or of taking up a family hobby such as boating (Kileys). This kind of leisure is deliberately arranged in dual-career families rather than being 'there' as a matter of course, and families that do not work at creating and conserving it find that their 'work' at home and outside can consume all of their time and leave very little for other pleasures.

Environmental Sanctions

Times have changed in terms of the pervasiveness of negative sanctions in relation to married women working. The mass media and the more diffuse expressions of sentiment in this respect are, if anything, swinging in the direction of slightly disparaging the idea of women (particularly highly qualified women) being only housewives. On the other hand, continuous work at a highly demanding occupation and full participation on a competitive basis with men is another matter. The difficulties encountered at work are one thing, where women have to be particularly good and particularly careful (as in the experience of other minority groups in society) lest their deficiencies be reacted to stereotypically and chalked up to the expected shortcomings of their sex rather than (as with men and with dominant groups generally) an individual matter. While these aspects of environmental strain are present, they are known and accepted by women pursuing careers as part of what they must face if they wish to succeed; and there is a clear and definite tendency for this sort of strain arising from traditional sex-stereotypes to diminish. In part the improvement is due to the demonstration that blanket stereotypes are false in individual cases; partly it is due to the changing conception of work roles, 'de-masculinizing' them to some extent. The idea that work is physically arduous, dirty, ruthless and cut-throat may be partly true; but, aside from the fact that some women can participate in this on men's own terms, it is also clear that work nowadays is more a matter of intelligence, judgement, human relations and the manipulation of refined skills, all of which are attributes of both men and women.

The area of environmental disapproval that is less clearly manageable and less clearly changing to a more supportive situation has to do with child-rearing. If a family chooses not to have children, they not only face their own feelings of un-fulfilment as human beings as a possible hazard, but they may be considered odd by people generally, or at best unfortunate. If they choose to have children, as most families do, they are expected to provide conventional care, i.e., with the mother staying at home and exercising her 'natural maternal' instincts. Unless this is done, it is often assumed that irreparable harm may be done to the child, and this may at a later stage affect society through the development within it of a 'psychopathic' member, affectionless, dependent or aggressive. A good deal of information and misinformation from the writings of psychiatrists and paediatricians has come into popular usage through the mass media, and is applied indiscriminately to particular cases. Sometimes this indiscriminate application of a little knowledge is fuelled by envy. Women who have given up their own aspirations to take on the conventional housewife role may express their resentment at others who seem to be managing an alternative pattern by lashing out at them critically in social situations. They may indicate that they consider the dual-career wives to be bad mothers, bad wives, and perhaps bad and selfish individuals.

A balanced view of the matter would suggest that while extreme cases of maternal deprivation such as those experienced in wartime or under conditions of institutionalization in backward and old-fashioned care institutions contribute to pathological outcomes, the situation of a mother continuing to work has to be assessed in individual terms. If the mother is not particularly maternal she may not be doing her infant the best possible service by being confined to her home with it. This is particularly true if her main aspirations are in the world of work and she has the problem of frustration to cope with in addition to her own disinclination towards 'mothering'. The infant may be a scapegoat in such a situation, which as any clinician's casebooks will support, may produce greater problems than if good partial mother-surrogate care were arranged. This is an extreme case. Most of the dual-career mothers show considerable maternal wishes together with considerable interest in the occupational sphere. The challenge for them is how to distribute the care in such a way as to allow enough highly involved 'mothering' (by the actual mother *and* father) to take place along with filling the long hours of more routine care with competent ancillary people. Couples of the type studied here have gone to great lengths to assure that their help is reliable, stable and in harmony with their own outlook. In addition, in many cases of dual-career families, the husband's greater participation in domestic life has led to an increase in the children's exposure to their father than usual in conventional families and this may serve to correct an unfortunate imbalance in the conventional child-care and socialization situation in our culture.

An element that makes the child-care area more problematic than the sex-role stereotype problems at work is that, unlike the work situation, it is unclear in the child-care situation where the pattern is going or how it will be dealt with. While there have been a number of developments in child-care nurseries, housing facilities and industrial crèches which are known to many of the couples studied, they have not had institutional resources of these kinds available to them. The child care supplemental pattern is at a much earlier stage in its evolution than are the work role patterns.

One way of handling negative environmental sanctions is to avoid them by not associating with people known to be critical. Some insulation from others results automatically from the overload which leaves little extra energy available for casual sociability. In addition, the pressures of many career-demands are so great as to make it important to some people to have relative quiet and seclusion for their off-work periods. The Jarrets represent this pattern. Another way of handling it, perhaps best seen in the Kileys, is to treat it humorously. 'Most of the people around here think we're a bit mad' kind of attitude. The Bensons seem to have worked out a public dual personality so that they are considered part of the interesting scene in the world of art and architecture – a sort of professional Siamese twins – expected always to appear and perform together. As Mr Benson observed on this : 'Wouldn't you be irritated if you invited Richard Burton to a party and he showed without Elizabeth Taylor?' In still other cases there has been insistence that they be accepted as they are, different but worthy; but it has almost always been experienced as an uphill struggle against popular opinion and attitude. All of the couples developed friendships which supported them by providing positive sanctions and limited legitimation for what they were doing. Most wished that the positive sanctions were more diffuse and the legitimation felt on a more widespread basis.

Personal Identity and Self-Esteem

Most of the dual-career couples studied experienced dilemmas of personal identity and self esteem more or less autonomously of environmental sanctions. Issues as to whether the wife was being a good wife and mother, or more fundamentally a 'good

human being' when she chose to pursue her career involvements, and whether the husband was sacrificing his 'manliness'
in altering his domestic life to take on more of a participative
role were widespread.

The sources of this internal doubt and anxiety are clear
enough. The individuals in the study were socialized in terms of
norms and values of thirty years ago and more. While there
was enough of an egalitarian ethos at the time most of them
were growing up to make it possible for girls as well as boys to
develop high career aspirations, the pattern was not fully
worked through. Textbooks, cautionary tales, folklore,
aphorisms, role models and much of the detailed warp and woof
of culture was still woven in the old pattern. Even now, sex
role stereotypes are very pervasive in educational materials
and family practices. Boys have been and still are in many
schools considered 'normally' interested in machines and in
money, in fame and power, status and authority; while girls
'normally' are taken to be interested in beauty and the arts, and
in human relations and care functions. In fact, boys and girls
have mixtures of these attributes, and particular boys and girls
have individual mixtures which may vary from the stereotypes
without implying pathology. Variance from the stereotyped
sex-role interests and activities, e.g. girls showing -techno-
logical aptitudes and aspirations, tended in the past to arouse
negative reactions. This inevitably led to these internal doubts
and ambivalences persisting into adult life, giving rise to guilt,
anxiety and tensions of various kinds. At work, the individual
may hesitate to press herself at a crucial point, and thus may
be considered lacking in drive; at home, the individual may
react in various ways, for example, by being over-
indulgent to a child because of feeling guilty about being out
at work.

Feelings of concern, guilt, ambivalence and so on may take
different forms in familial relationships. A wife's defensiveness
about following her chosen career line may make her particularly sensitive to criticism or it may exacerbate periods of
self-doubt and depression. The husband may make great

personal and career sacrifices to help achieve the dual-career structure for its value to both parties, but he may show irritation or resentment at having modified his own personal identity in order to incorporate a successful wife into his pattern, sometimes in place of a more successful self. Most families develop what we have termed a 'tension line' which is set up more or less unconsciously between the pair and recognized as a point beyond which each will not be pushed. Compromises are worked out within the framework of this tension line.

While it has sometimes been asserted on the basis of clinical case literature that these difficulties undermine the intimate side of the marital relationship, we have no evidence that problems arising in this sphere are greater in dual-career families than in any range of complicated people with busy lives. Indeed, if anything there is some suggestion – still to be explored in more systematic research – that families of this kind are particularly good at working through problems that confront them. When these problems happen to arise in their intimate lives, they may handle these too with more communication and more purposeful decision-making than many other families.

The management of personal and interpersonal problems in the marital relationship is not only a matter of being purposeful and rational. Some couples manage by taking special care to provide the more affectionate components of the relationship – to deal with the sensitivities of their partners in a rather fundamental way, so as to balance the other's self esteem at points recognized to be vulnerable. Mr Benson, for example, emphasizes that criticism is important in any partnership if the work is to be maintained at a high standard, but where the partnership is a marital one as well and the partner may be vulnerable to the more general meanings of criticism from one's spouse, the criticism given in work matters must be done 'with love'.

Another way of managing these issues – more prevalent where husbands and wives are not work partners as well – is seen in the Kileys and Jarrets, where a very sharp segregation is made between work and home roles. When Mrs Jarret comes home she becomes 'cook' and 'my husband's wife'. When Mrs

Kiley leaves the office she attempts to hang up with her white lab coat her authoritarian mode of relating to people at work, and become a warm and sympathetic wife and mother.

Social Network Dilemmas

There are some special problems associated with the relationships of dual-career families with the social environment. All individuals and all families have a network of social relationships in which individuals or the family as a whole are regularly involved. These relationships may link the family to specific institutions – schools, medical facilities, work organizations – or they may be relationships of a more personal kind, such as with friends or with kin. It has already been noted that overload tends in most dual-career families to make serious inroads into leisure activities, though each couple had a social circle of friends whom they saw fairly regularly. In many conventional families, friends tend to be drawn from the neighbourhood and from the husband's occupational associates. In dual-career families there is a tendency not only for more friends to come from the wife's work environment, but also for the wife's friends to become somewhat more prominent than might be expected; this is because of the need for environmental supports to sustain the dual-career pattern as indicated above. If it were only the man's friends and the neighbours who served the potential friendship pool, the chances of having among them families who are at least sympathetic to the idea of a dual-career family are not usually sufficiently great. The wife's associates are therefore drawn into the social circle more than is perhaps usual in conventional middle-class families.

Most of the couples studied do not have a large number of relationships with kin. This stems partly from the fact that many were only children, partly from their age and the fact that many of their parents were deceased, and partly from their tendency to have been both geographically and socially mobile. While for many it would have been an advantage both psychologically and practically to have had kin close by, for most the idea of grannies, for example, as additional parental support figures was not an important element in their lives. For many, the high overload problem and the divergence from conventional norms which tended still to govern the lives of most of their relatives made for some drifting away. Occasionally this social distance with some relatives is deliberately arranged. Fulfilling the expectations of kins for sociability, hospitality and participation in family affairs may not be possible. The management of relatives' expectations as well as one's own sense of guilt about not fulfilling them is important, and most of the couples studied tried to find a way to deal with relatives so as to save feelings as much as possible over not being able to act in expected ways towards them.

In general, the dual-career families tend to make their network of relationships on a couple basis rather than an individual basis; their relationships with kin tend to diminish except where there are clear responsibilities and/or compatibilities, and they tend to increase the number of people in their networks who are in service relationships with them. The management of the service relationships takes up much of the spare energies of these couples and is an area that will be discussed in the next chapter as capable of improvement and rationalization in the interests of making not only the dual-career family more viable, but modern families in general.

Dilemmas of Multiple Role Cycling

In each of the major spheres of life people are engaged in a set of role involvements which make different demands at different stages of the cycle. When one enters a marriage, for example, the demands of family life are less, particularly for the wife, before children arrive. Similarly for work. When one enters an occupational role, particularly the career-type of occupation which involves a developmental sequence of roles, there are differences according to stage. Here the most demanding stages tend to be early on, when one is establishing oneself. Later, when a stable pattern is developed, a plateau may be reached from which functioning in work roles may be taxing but somewhat stabilized.

When one is dealing with the conventional form of family–work relationships, the family cycling may dovetail well with the work cycling in that many couples marry at the stage of the husband's entering into a regular occupational role. The high demands on him in his own establishment phases are supported by the relative non-turbulence in the family scene. Even if children arrive sometime during the occupational establishment phase, the fact that the conventional wife remains at home attending to their care tends to take the pressure off the husband where economic problems are minimal.

In dual-career families there is a wide range of variation. A common feature, however, is that the patterns differ importantly from the conventional one of the establishment phase of the husband's career coinciding with the wife bearing children. In most of the dual-career families in this study, occupational establishment for both husband and wife preceded child-bearing. In the Kileys' case, Mrs Kiley's occupational establishment preceded that of her husband, and she supported his preparatory and early establishment phases through her own occupational activity. This was assisted by his willingness to provide support on the domestic front. This pattern, while unusual for people of their background and circumstances, is less unusual among contemporary students. Marriage nowadays is earlier and there is widespread recognition that different opportunities for stipends, training, occupational entry and so on will make for different timetables between the marital partners.

The Bensons show another pattern, where they were jointly establishing their occupational situation and their family life at the same time. In this instance the incorporation of their office into their home provided the key structural arrangement making it feasible. They dealt with the dilemmas arising from high demands for both members in both spheres by overlapping the two as much as possible, allowing the children to 'be around' in the office and the office to intrude into the home setting.

The couples in this particular study tended to establish themselves occupationally prior to having children; they then had their children in a compressed period and the wives tended to interrupt their work minimally. By this time the couples had usually achieved a sufficient level of income so that they could support the domestic service side of the dual-career family's pattern. To some extent an occupational plateau was reached by most of the women before having children in terms of either position within an organization, reputation or clientele.

For younger couples, new patterns of role-cycling may emerge. Child-bearing may take place earlier and there may be a return to work at an earlier point in the occupational cycle. As will be discussed in the next chapter this will depend to some extent on how society deals with such issues as providing opportunity for mature student training and occupational re-entry.

GAINS

Aside fom the intrinsic gratifications that many couples have found in the sheer experience of mastering the numerous dilemmas in the way of making a dual-career family work well against many difficulties, there are a number of gains in the end product.

The financial gains are more important than are frequently acknowledged. Very often in writing about working women, the observation is made that highly-qualified women tend to work out of intrinsic interest while those with lower qualifications tend to work more for the money. Be this as it may, the financial return is an important element in the career development picture from several angles. First, the families emphasized how important it is for dual-career families to have a relatively high income, because they have relatively high standards for domestic living, child-care, clothing and transportation and so on. To pay out the extra that is involved in all this, their in-

Gains

come must be relatively high, particularly as help is more costly and tax benefits do not encourage the pattern. Many of the couples also indicated that the overloads experienced made it important to provide for leisure and holidays which may be relatively costly because of the need on such occasions to be looked after so that the marital pair can regenerate their energies. They work so hard in between that they often feel that they 'deserve' to be pampered a bit on holidays, which eats still further into the increase in family income that the extra worker provides.

In some of the families it is agreed that it is preferable to have both partners working somewhat less than 'flat out' rather than the husband, in order to get the highest possible income, giving himself so much to 'the rat race' that they sacrifice some of the family life that they might enjoy together. The Kileys expressed this sort of attitude.

Also present in some families is the issue of financial security against possible disasters. The accumulation of savings, independent pension rights, and so on are of some importance. The Harrises felt this way.

Some of the women in the study experienced early economic deprivation and are very much aware that this factor has been important in driving them towards a goal of economic security. By the time they were successful enough in their careers to have come to the attention of the study, they were sophisticated and secure enough to give less emphasis to this as a personal need than as a wish to give their children more security than they had had themselves. The husbands tend to support this, and in fact often obtain direct gratification from their wives' earning ability.

However, while money as such is more important than is sometimes recognized, it is by no means the most important element for the dual-career families studied. The crucial element for most of the families is something that can be subsumed under the general category of 'self-expression'. Mrs Benson would feel incomplete unless she were creating something – if not in architecture, then in creative art or writing; Mrs Harris would not feel fulfilled unless she were achieving recognition as a designer and producing tangible products of her work; Mrs Kiley feels that if she had to turn all of her managerial energies into the family she would be impossible to live with, and Mrs Jarret expresses a related idea when she says that even if she did not have her professional work (which is unthinkable) she would not want to be the sort of woman who confined her energies to her home and child. Mrs Neal, while protesting to some extent about the degree to which she is involved in her career, feels in her work major satisfactions of ideas and decisions. When she says that she would like to be able to work less, she means a thirty-hour week, which may become something like full time for many professions before long.

All of the women in this sample have as part of their personal identities a sub-identity associated with a professional work role. Many indicated that if the satisfactions from work were to be removed, they would experience a major loss. Though the particular jobs they do may represent compromises with their original idealized conceptions, in every case they are realizing in major degrees what they really want to do and feel is worth doing as human beings, making full use of their capacities.

The gains for their husbands are also more complex than is often recognized in writings about women and their careers. It is often observed that a husband who has a wife getting satisfactions from work has a happier wife; this may be true but not in a simplistic sense. The gains that most dual-career families derive from having the wife at work are part of a cluster of reactions to it. As well as satisfactions, the wives also experience strains, anxieties, conflicts, guilt and sheer exhaustion which may contribute to the difficulties in the marital relationship as well as to its enrichment. As has been indicated above, many of the husbands' involvement in their wives' careers derived from an interest which they as individuals have felt but have not realized in their own work. Mr Harris's interest in his wife's public recognition and her entrepreneurial risk-taking activities reflects elements of his own wishes which he has had to mute in order to press other elements of his aspirations. Mr Jarret's interest and sympathy with his wife's problems as a dramatic director express some of his own earlier interest in the theatre and keep that interest alive. Mr Kiley's interest in his wife's scientific work reflects his own earlier unfulfilled interest in research, from which he himself diverged. Though he has succeeded in another line of endeavour, the scientific interest is both alive and helpful to him. Mr Neal and particularly Mr Benson participate even more directly in the interests and problems of their wives. While these involvements may not persist through the entire life cycle of the marriage, they seem to be crucial in the establishment phase when the dual-career structure is being crystallized; and, as more than one dual-career husband has commented, 'Once they've tasted the dual-career pattern, it's difficult to settle for anything else.' This is untenable as a total generalization as is seen from the relatively large proportion of career-oriented wives who show the interrupted work pattern; but it would seem to be a tendency.

Finally, there are gains reported for the children in dual-career families. So much has been written to emphasize the deprivations that such children may experience – based mostly on institutional or traumatic experiences quite unlike those provided by professional women going to work – that some corrective statements are needed. A review of the research which has been done so far indicates that the case for damage to children as a direct consequence of mothers' working is unproven. Our data suggest that while there are indeed problems raised by mothers having careers, the kinds of competent individuals who are in dual-career families tend to make arrangements for child-care which compare favourably with what would have occurred had the mothers stayed at home. The parents report advantages deriving from the situation, e.g. that the children in the dual-career families show independence and resourcefulness. Helping with family tasks is seen as giving the children a sense not only of independence and competence but also of social worth. They contribute to the overall family needs and this legitimates their right to have a share in the family goods. Other perquisites of being in such families are a certain sense of 'special' merit, deriving from mother's work role. Often the children in these families show pride in their parents' accomplishments. This may take the form of tangible benefits – like Mrs Harris designing the school uniform for her daughter's school; or Mrs Kiley sending along bacteriological cultures for the science master to use. More often it takes the form of special interest and knowledge in the family that arouses in the child a feeling of competence and involvement in the wide range of interests that both parents have. The fact that both parents have interests allows a greater range of role models for children of both sexes, and this enlarges the area of occupational life and experience they can know at close hand.

Of course all these things can have pathological manifestations. Leaving children to be resourceful can fail and arouse greater-than-ever dependency; guilt over this may lead the parent towards overprotectiveness and the child may become unusually demanding. Poor or unstable staff may confuse the child and give it additional problems. Successful parents can be a burden for a child as well as a help. Multiple role models can confuse as well as clarify. The crucial points are likely to be how the situations are managed and what social pressures and sanctions are operating. However, these things occur in ordinary conventional families as well as in dual-career families, and our impression is that the positive benefits of the latter have been under-valued generally. The potential damages are real enough but may be exaggerated as specific to this type of situation. Furthermore, just as mental health interventions are possible to attempt to head off and work with the pathologies of conventional family structures, the same is true for dual-career families. Neurotic difficulties, confused identification, loneliness and disturbance seem to be products much more of bad management of child-care and sexual disapproval of variant patterns than of a particular family structure. The families studied differed in their talents in this regard, but the same individuals would not be likely to produce more psychologically healthy children if they sacrificed their own wishes and needs so as to operate the conventional family structure. In the next chapter we shall consider some of the issues raised by this study of dual-career families and what practical measures may be taken in a society to facilitate this pattern if it is seen to be of value by some of its citizens.

The Dual-Career Family and its Environment: Contemporary Issues

The dual-career families of today are, in a sense, pioneers for families of tomorrow. They had no role models or exemplars on whose patterns they could develop their own styles of life. Indeed, in most instances they had to struggle against the existing patterns in society to cut out for themselves viable niches in a social fabric that was woven with quite other designs for living in mind. To achieve their positions, they worked creatively, often under considerable tension and conflict. In so doing they had to overcome a number of obstacles, and the adaptive qualities that have won through in this process are a peculiar combination of determination and flexibility, not always available to most people. It is not as though they started off with a pre-conceived plan and worked relentlessly to implement it. On the contrary, for most the pattern that they evolved came into being through a series of happenings which make sense in retrospect. It was the unusual couple that knew what they were going to do and aimed purposefully towards it.

In future it may be that the proportions of dual-career families will increase. There are signs that this is likely. More women are pursuing further education; more are seeking part of their personal fulfilment in work; more may be incorporating into their informal marriage contracts the expectation that they will want to work; more organizations are allowing, even encouraging, women to rise into senior positions; many men expect that their wives will want to work and may even see this as a desirable means of enhancing the quality of their relationship. On the other hand it is not likely to be the pattern of choice for the majority of families in the foreseeable future. Many prefer, and will continue to prefer, a more conventional type of work–family structure. Most couples in the near future are likely to opt for mixtures of conventional and dual-career elements, depending on their circumstances, their personal desires and their relationships. If the dual-career model and its modified types that will inevitably emerge are to develop with less stress and strain, it is worth considering what complementary changes in the social environment could enhance this – whether by deliberate policy or by the ordinary processes of social evolution. To the extent that environmental changes facilitate the dual-career pattern, the costs of operating it are likely to diminish and the benefits to increase.

The environmental changes that will enhance dual-career or dual-worker family patterns can be considered under four headings :

1. Domestic reorganization
2. Changes in child care
3. Modification of the conventional bias in social planning and the built-environment, and
4. The legitimation of social variation.

DOMESTIC REORGANIZATION

One of the paramount values in contemporary society is the integrity of the individual household. In England where 'a man's home is his castle' the wish for an individual home as a bastion of comfort and privacy is very great. Leaving aside the masculine bias which this definition of a home includes, it would seem useful to consider whether, in the present cultural circumstances, there is a possible form of domestic reorganization which could preserve integrity for the private family residence while at the same time relieving the housewife from the heavy burden which thereby falls upon her shoulders to maintain such an establishment. Most changes entail a cost. In role relationships, where someone gains something the other usually has to give something up. On the other hand, with the changes that are under way, contemporary man's home is less and less like a brave knight's castle whether or not his wife goes out to work. If she does not, the castle may come to feel like a dungeon, for the wife at least.

However, not all changes going on are to the housewife's disadvantage. There are changes in sex-role conceptions that make it possible for the domestic division of labour to be reorganized on a more cooperative basis between husband and wife. This is becoming discernible, if not as rapidly as ardent feminist reformers desire. Many more men than ever before in Western society are washing up, cooking, doing housework, shopping, and caring for babies. The whole unisex movement in fashions parallels the trend towards convenience foods, convenience fabrics, etc. As a process of social evolution in men's and women's roles, the sharing and interchange of activities is clearly established as a major pattern, though by no means a universal one. On the whole this has not yet reached a stage where the participation of men in domestic activities is not only an act of good will towards the wife, who still retains responsibility, but an activity viewed as their own responsibility, at least in part. Most men who do things at home do so to 'help' their wives. They help with the washing up, they help with changing the nappies and so on but there is still a tendency to regard it as *her job* they are helping with. There are some couples who have reallocated responsibilities in a more fundamental way — either by defining them as their joint responsibilities or on the basis of a new division of labour between the husband and wife; but this is still rare even among the dual-career families in this study. To change this into a more widespread pattern — where both men and women have equal responsibility as well as shared participation in the life areas confronting them — or at least the option for dividing up the responsibilities in new ways which are individually rather than conventionally derived — is a contemporary challenge.

Before discussing the issue of how the challenge is to be met — an issue common to all of the environmental elements under discussion in this chapter — it is worth while discussing three approaches to the problem of reorganization of domestic roles.

Domestic Reorganization

The first approach is through the modification of sex-role stereotypes. There are a number of sex-role stereotypes current in our society which are based on Victorian cultural conceptions rather than scientific fact. These archaic conceptions are held unselfconsciously by teachers and parents and are passed along through the school systems without awareness of the implications. When a teacher takes a class of boys and girls out to London museums and separates them into two groups – boys for the science museum and girls for the Victoria and Albert – she reinforces archaic sex-role stereotypes. There may be some girls who are more interested in the science museum and some boys who are more interested in the costumes and art forms in the Victoria and Albert. By separating them *en bloc*, sex stereotypes are reinforced and individuals who have contrary inclinations are made to feel 'abnormal'. Boys to watch cricket, girls for the concert – Why? Interests and talents do not need to be channelled according to prescribed rather than actual individual inclinations. Yet this goes on as if it was the 'natural' expectation. Normative thinking is based on past patterns rather than an awareness of individual differences cutting across sex-lines in most areas of interest and participation. If the schools are preparatory institutions for adult life, let them prepare for the real characteristics of today's and tomorrow's life, rather than perpetuating outmoded conceptions based on past status conceptions and sex role stereotypes.

Once a family adopts the dual-worker structure, or wishes to adopt such a structure, what can be done to facilitate it? The individuals themselves in the pioneering phases have not 'bought' many conventional sex role stereotypes; or, if they had 'bought' them in their earlier socialization, they had decided to sell them or trade them in for something better for themselves. How to make it work when domestic help is dwindling in quantity and quality while the importance of a separate home remains as an ideal? The two further approaches deal with this question – first in terms of upgrading domestic helper occupations, and second by upgrading and improving more generally the whole range of service activities and occupations.

The drift of people out of domestic occupations seems to relate to several factors. First, the general upward mobility of the population through universal education and increased occupational opportunities means that lower-status occupations are continually drained, often to be replenished if at all by incompetent people or uneducated immigrants. In order to deal with this in relation to domestic work, it would seem that the occupations need to be reconsidered and new roles defined which will make them more attractive to competent people. The provision of competitive wages and conditions of work are only part of the picture.

On the other hand, the dwindling supply of good help must be attributable to other factors than merely economic ones. Any cursory examination of domestic employment and advertisement indicators shows the greater demand than supply, even at wages competitive with other work. The occupation has low status and is seen as something that women do only if they cannot do anything else. There is little in it of vocational pride or sense of exercising a set of skills. Added to this there is the individual connection with a particular household, in what may be too much of a servant relationship rather than a service relationship without implications of rigid hierarchy.

Servant vs. service is an important element in the definition of work roles. Being a servant is above all being in a form of relationship that was characteristic of the past and of a society which had rigid inequalities of status and all the rewards associated with it. This is out of keeping with contemporary ideas of how society should be organized, which stress individual achievement, the possibility of mobility and self-determination of the kind of life and role one will participate in. Service, on the other hand, is another conception. Service roles in society are increasing, and can include anything from domestic service to hairdressing to medical care or social work services; anything from recreational services to financial and banking services. This is a service society, and to provide service is a major form of occupational activity – dignified or not according to the way in which it is organized and conducted.

In order to increase the standing of a service occupation in the domestic sphere three elements seem necessary.

First it is important to give explicit recognition to the fact that this is not an occupation that people go into only if they cannot do anything else, but that the organization and management of household services is a highly skilled set of occupations, for which training and recognition for achievements may be provided. In the modern machine-laden household, this kind of work is not even tied as it was to prevailing sex-stereotypes. More schools of domestic science, and new kinds of school to foster the upgrading of domestic service roles should be supported. Both men and women should be encouraged to participate in such schemes, and to find careers in domestic service, perhaps organized in new ways.

Second, the characteristics of the service occupation which make it unacceptable to many – e.g. its loneliness and isolation – could be dealt with by providing a component of social interaction, perhaps by using pairs, couples or teams, perhaps by organizing associations, group activities or clubs for cadres of service workers, etc.

Third, the service worker and client relationship could be modified so as to lessen the sense that the service worker 'belongs to' a particular client in the way servants did in the past. If service is provided, say by a team of service workers in a given area who accept responsibility for the property and tasks which they take on, the workers will relate to their colleagues and bosses in ways comparable to other occupations rather than to their clients exclusively.

Aside from the upgrading of service occupations in the manner described above, the technology of service in the domestic area can be improved considerably, making it possible to run households with less effort. A good deal of this is, of course, continually going on with the introduction of convenience foods, convenience linens and clothing, all sorts of devices for cleaning, food preparation and so on within the household staff itself. However, there is considerable scope both for the rationalization of what is going on already and for the introduction of new products and techniques. New fabrics, new foods, new ways of packaging and delivering goods and services required for domestic work are wanted, and this is an area that has already shown itself to be of commercial interest to firms already involved in the production, sales and distribution of catering and other domestic goods. This is an area that will bear further development.

IMPROVEMENTS IN CHILD CARE

Child care has traditionally been the exclusive function of the family, ultimately the mother. It is jealously guarded by the family not only because of their legal responsibility but because of their moral responsibility in the face of dangers that threaten the dependent child in the hands of less caring figures and because children represent a major personal investment for most people. It is usual for people to vest their hopes and ambitions in their children and through them to realize the universal wish for immortality – whatever other more altruistic motives may be involved. The child-centred cultures of today put an onus on modern parents not only to feel responsible for their children's physical care, mental health and development, but also to enjoy it as a precious life experience. The non-maternal mother who does not idealize the full-time involvement with small children is either very backward in orientation or very advanced. Today's norms call for maternal behaviour from all mothers whether or not they are so inclined; tomorrow's may allow for a greater range of flexibility in mothering *and* fathering patterns.

At the core of modern civilization is a concern for the well-being of children, emotional as well as physical. *All* of the parents studied in the dual-career families had this as a major concern. They encountered practical as well as personal and inter-personal problems over this concern. Child-care facilities are inadequate for the implementation of their desire to find suitable supplementary care facilities. Each family somehow managed to make arrangements that fell short of disaster, and in many cases, even of the near-disastrous kind, the arrangements were felt to be better than what would have ensued had the mother been a full-time care agent herself. The practical problems were various : the relatively low calibre of people who offer themselves for care of children in the home, the virtual disappearance of the old nanny type (and the replacement by too few modern nannies), the mixed blessing of the adolescent au pair whose developmental problems often impose more trials and tribulations than she is worth, the uneven quality of day-care facilities and nursery schools, etc.

As with other service occupations, one thing that is clearly needed is a massive up-grading of the child care occupations and facilities. So long as the care of infants (beyond the basic familial care provided) is to remain a job for immature young people and obtaining able care figures is left to chance, this will remain the major impediment to married women with occupational competences using their talents effectively in the world of work.

Up-grading of child-care occupations means the provision of better facilities, better jobs and better training institutions for people in this field – in short, the professionalization of child-care work. It is important to develop a better image for this type of occupation generally. This is an occupation which might be attractive to some young men as well as young women. The idea that it is desirable to spend a period of one's life as a child-care agent is found in some Scandinavian countries. Working in a family is seen not only as a way of getting extra money or a trip abroad to improve one's language skills, but as an important part of one's education for life, and it is recognized by schools and universities.

The career of child-care agent need not only be up-graded for the young. It may provide a valuable point of re-entry for more mature people, particularly women who have interrupted their work to care for their own small infants. Some may discover in the course of this experience that they have talents in and derive satisfactions from child-care and would like to develop these in a vocational way.

Aside from the sheer manpower problems of finding sufficient help to provide child-care helpers for all the families that will be wanting them, there is the issue of whether this is the best solution to the problem. For each mother to try to arrange a helper who will specialize in child-care may not be best either from the manpower point of view or from the child development point of view. While it is generally acceptable that a stable person is necessary as the centre of emotional attachment for each child, this figure does not have to be the mother nor does it have to be there all the time. If it is the mother, the helping arrangements may be shared out in various ways for the periods of time when the actual mother is not there. Group care and play facilities seem to have worked out well in a number of societies, including Sweden and Israel, and there is no doubt in the child who the mother is or whether the mother is central – unless the mother does not wish to have it this way, a situation that can occur without care-surrogate facilities as well.

What seems to be generally wanted is some cooperation in child-care. It is not clear how this will emerge except that many different experimental forms are likely to occur in the near future. Precursors of this in the extended family, the three-generation family, the communal house, etc., will probably be taken up more systematically and built into housing estates and developments which are now entirely fragmented. It may not be 'children's houses' as in Israel, or 'family hotels' as in Sweden, but some form of cooperative nurseries or crèches are likely to be on the increase as ways and means can be developed to make them safe enough for mothers and fathers to feel that they can leave their children there regularly for relatively extended periods of time.

Innovations in child-care arrangements of this kind need not be limited to the public sector. Indeed, it may be that private sector initiatives will be more effective in the near future in our society in order to make better use of the manpower potentials available among married women with children. During national crises, such as the Second World War, the use of manpower resources by the nation made it expedient to nationalize child-care facilities in some countries so that young mothers could be freed of their burden of child-care to engage in productive effort for the economy. Lacking this national emergency, private manpower emergencies on selective bases may occur as the points of greatest leverage for experiments of this kind – particularly where there is decentralization of industry into areas thin in skilled populations.

MODIFYING CONVENTIONAL BIAS IN SOCIAL PLANNING AND THE BUILT-ENVIRONMENT

There is abundant evidence that a good deal of the social planning that has gone into urban development and redevelopment and into the construction of new towns has proceeded with a strong conventional bias. This has been reinforced by the fact that most planners have been men. The conventional and masculine bias favouring independent nuclear families with the assumption of a structure which keeps men out all day at work and women at home has been very pervasive up to the present day. The organization of services, transport, domestic facilities and so on fits logically into this paradigm, so at the present time the family that varies from the conventional norm experiences more strains than are necessary.

Assuming that the environmental institutions should serve family life as well as vice versa, it would seem important to plan for ways in which families can link to a range of external institutions more easily than they often seem to at present, particularly from the point of view of variant patterns like that of the dual-career family. With even the small sample of couples studied here, it is apparent that there are many possible patterns, ranging from the situation where both work at home to the other extreme where both work at a distance in opposite directions. Some have jobs that require travelling around, and most have careers that have involved changes of jobs or at least changes in the location of work. There are many possible implications of these different arrangements for the organization of housing in relation to work places. What comes through most clearly, however, is that the degree of segregation between workplace and residence that now exists as a result of historical separation of home and workplace that occurred in an earlier era is neither universally necessary nor desirable. A closer relationship between residence and workplace would seem desirable in many instances, and for women at the present stage of social evolution it may be critical for their participation.

Service occupations have already been mentioned in relation to the need for the reorganization of domestic work. In relation to planning it is the location of these service industries and provision for their circulation that is important if new ways for the organization of domestic service are to emerge. There are already in effect a number of experiments which have developed responsively to the strains and trends described. For example, housing cooperatives, industrial estates with attached residences and crèches, new service-centres in residential districts, and so on, all work towards relieving individual families of many onerous aspects of household management. What is needed is a greater development of these constellations of 'built-in' environmental supports on a systematic basis, building on evaluations of the 'natural experiments' now under way.

New kinds of houses, with variable sizes, numbers and shapes of rooms to serve families as their needs change throughout the life cycle is one development worth watching. Perhaps equally important is the idea of a community of housing units of different kinds, within which individuals and families can move about as their needs change, taking different kinds of units within the same housing community. New configurations of work, housing and service areas are being evolved and need study.

All these aspects need to be balanced so that the maximization of one does not preclude others. The issue is how much of one thing to sacrifice to obtain a measure of another. Total privacy precludes communal arrangement, but giving up a degree of privacy to obtain the benefits of cooperative domestic and child care arrangements may ultimately be worth the sacrifice for those who want it. So far the imagination of planners and builders has been limited on the whole to providing for different sizes and different economic levels of housing for the same basic family type – the conventional nuclear family. The need for developmental efforts in evolving new models, new designs for living, working and leisure is apparent, but solutions have only begun to be suggested. The solutions of the future are likely to emphasize variety and increased options for choice rather than standardization and crude efficiency alone.

THE LEGITIMIZING OF SOCIAL VARIATION

In complex metropolitan society there are trends both towards standardization – as in the mass media – and towards differentiation. Many more options are present in all areas of life than previously, and there is an ever-increasing range of choice available not only in material objects but in ideas, attitudes and behaviour patterns.

One of the issues confronting contemporary society is how to evaluate the various options available, both for oneself and for others. If anything is possible and everything is permitted, it is difficult to assess what is 'good' and 'right' as compared with an alternative possibility. Chaos and confusion are the ultimate dangers in such a situation, and irresponsibility an ever-present hazard. Just because there is a market for something – like copulating on the stage or taking drugs – this does not mean that there should be social approval for it. On the other hand, social disapproval, negative sanctions of various kinds, discrimination, criticism and so on, may impede the development of variations on conventional patterns which may be 'innocent' and have personal and social values. The dual-career family, where responsibly adopted, is such a pattern. It varies from the conventional one, and is adopted by its practitioners at considerable cost to themselves as they work out new structures without clear precedent. Yet nearly all of the dual-career families studied have indicated that in addition to the intrinsic problems of evolving and managing this difficult new structure of relationships they have had to face the further weight of social disapproval and criticism from others. Though they themselves were conscientiously responsible in their performances of both work and domestic roles they were often made to feel that what they were doing was reprehensible.

Looking at this particular part of the problem – the alleviation of social disapproval, or put positively, the legitimation of the variant pattern – how could the situation be improved? Clearly the recognition and even encouragement of a social pattern in laws and statutes is an essential element in the legitimation process. Formal legal legitimation is not enough. People seem to need to know not only that what they are doing is not illegal but that it is 'right', and their right as members of society. The issue of what creates social support and approval for a variant pattern is less clear from our own data and elsewhere than is the issue of what creates disapproval.

From the information in the interviews that we have conducted, there seem to be two overt sources of resistance to the idea of the dual-career family, and a number of less immediate impediments. While there is considerable reluctance both at work and in the family to relinquish elements of the conventional pattern which contributed to the comfort and security of the male, the primary over-resistances experienced by most of our dual-career families were by the wives in relation to other women. The bases for these resistances were in relation to possible effects on children, and to possible effects on the marital relationship.

The objective situation in relation to effects on children seems indeterminate. While there is solid evidence that traumatic institutional care for infants may be damaging to personality development, there is much less clear information about the effects of the alternative care patterns actually used by working mothers, particularly those in the more highly qualified and more remunerative types of work. From the evidence available to us and from prior studies, it would seem that families of this type are particularly conscientious about the substitutes and supplementary care they arrange for their families. In such instances it seems that there are no more grounds for assuming a higher than ordinary rate of disturbance for children as compared with those in conventionally organized families – the tensions in the latter adding up to no less a mental health hazard than the various arrangements engineered by the former. It is the quality of the available time spent with the children rather than the quantity that many would think the most important. The advocates of the alternative forms of arrangement might even argue, as some have, that there are improvements on the isolated nuclear family that accrue to the benefit of the child if the alternative arrangements are cunningly contrived. Why, then, the resistances on this score? Most people have a very strong distaste for experimentation, particularly with the lives of children, and though the existing system is recognized to be imperfect, its hazards are known.

Resistances to change in the conventional pattern seem to derive from a variety of sources – the feeling by those who enjoy satisfactions in the conventional pattern that what they cherish will be withdrawn; the feeling by those who do not enjoy satisfactions in the conventional pattern (but have succumbed nevertheless) of envy for those who do not conform. In such situations, negative images are generated – of the cold, masculine, competitive, unloving sort of woman who rejects society's definition of 'feminine' and 'good'.

As we have shown, couples have dealt with the perception of disapproval in their social environments in different ways – each with a certain psycho-social price – e.g. encapsulating the work and family relationships in a single set around the home; or treating the whole thing as a joke ('We're recognized to be very happy-go-lucky in our neighbourhood'); or withdrawing from social involvements outside work except on a very selective basis.

The issue at hand, however, is one for the future – namely, how can better resolutions be found for the paradox: in a society with vigorous values and morale there must be discrimination and sanctions on the one hand, and yet a great range and depth of tolerance is required for variant patterns to be allowed and even encouraged to develop. What seems to emerge from our own studies and observations is the importance of distinguishing between form and process. If there is a stereotyped reaction against a given social form simply because it is different – a common enough human experience – society will not be able to distinguish between new forms that are valuable and those that are not. Quantity and quality must not be confused. If only a small number of people practise a particular pattern, it is not necessarily unimportant. If a given pattern enjoys a widespread vogue, it is not *ipso facto* important. The fact that a family diverges from the conventional pattern is not enough to provide a guide to social reactions. The essential point is the processual one: how is it diverging? In adaptation to what special conditions? With what safeguards and attention to consequences for individuals? Is it being done responsibly or irresponsibly? etc. These are the most important questions, but they are not always the ones asked. Divergence is too often confused with irresponsibility, and this distinction must be made and kept in mind if the constructive 'divergers' are to be distinguished from the less constructive ones.

This set of principles is important in modifying critical orientations in the direction of more neutral ones. To provide more positive reactions to variant patterns one must face additional challenges.

One of the standard ways of dealing with the challenge described is through the use of mass-media – propaganda if you will. The merits of a given position are extolled, illustrious exemplars are highlighted and publicly acclaimed, and so on. One of the problems in such a programme is that the most relevant position for society of the future as we envisage it is a differentiated position. There is no single solution, but many solutions. The 'stars' in the social firmament in the future will not be out of a single mould, but out of many moulds, and the issue will be of how to help individuals to make the link between their own psycho-social needs and situation and the potentialities of specific patterns in an array open to them. There have for a long time been exemplars generally available of the dual-career pattern, but among the rather remote figures of 'stars' – the Oliviers, the Burtons, the Curies, and so on. One of the aims of the present volume is to present some more accessible role models – special enough to have pioneered the pattern in various fields, but ordinary enough to be identified as like a good many young people with qualifications growing up now and concerned with the issues of reconciling career and family life.

Legitimation comes here out of a sense of respect for those who have evolved and successfully managed the pattern, even in the face of adversities that may have been more severe than they will in future. Respect is for the way they have managed it rather than for the simple fact of having created a different pattern. The latter does not in and of itself merit respect, and therefore the positive aspects of social legitimation. In future, simple copying of the pattern will not merit respect, but the 'good' management of it, the respect and toleration of those who choose other patterns and similarly manage them well in relation to their own needs and the needs of others in their situation. This is what is to be legitimized in the wider sense, and the accomplishment of this kind of legitimation will, it is hoped, be enhanced by the twin contribution of the provision of information on which evaluations can be made, and the injunction to make the right kind of evaluation, one based on quality and not form alone.

APPROACHES TO SOCIAL CHANGE

This book puts forward a point of view rather than simply mirroring an aspect of social reality. It has a point of view that is put forward together with information which only partly supports it. Other social scientists and other people with different social ideals might read into the presented materials quite different implications and conclusions.

Dual-career families are clearly in the minority. From a study of its representatives one might feel that the people who have been able to make it work have been too unusual to be pace-setters for a larger population. Their talents may seem pro-digious, their situations fortunate, their strengths unusual, and as a consequence they may be seen by some to be anomalies of this historical stage. Our own feeling is different. We have felt that the dual-career families have indeed been different. All pioneers or creative innovators are. But their 'differentness' as individuals is not extraordinary. They have in most instances been more ordinary than we had expected and like many suc-cessful or prominent people sometimes a bit surprised by their own eminence. Also, though what they have done required skill, luck and determination, they seemed as a group to be the same mixtures of strength and weaknesses as others of comparable calibre and training.

Taking these impressions together wth our analysis of social trends in education, occupational life, sex-role conceptions and so on, we have come to the conclusion – as stated at the begin-ning of the book – that the dual-career family is no 'freak of nature' but a forerunner of things to come and therefore useful as experiments of nature, to be studied and learned from. While it may not be necessary in future for others to have diverged so much from the normal pattern (and therefore to have been divergent in motivation and behavioural tendencies) or for it to be such a stressful pattern to operate, nevertheless much of what these families have worked out for themselves provides contributions to the concerns of others. It was with this in mind that we and the dual-career families collaborating with us worked up what we could of their life patterns. What are the hoped-for effects?

First, this is a book for modern families where the husband and wife have valued, intended or thought about the idea of having something in the direction of a dual-career family struc-ture, but have not managed to do so. They may, in some instances, be able to take points or inspirations from the achieve-ments of others and make the extra effort required to operate the pattern. Couples may increasingly move from one pattern to another as they progress through the life cycle. Though it is difficult for the wife to be a high achiever occupationally after having withdrawn for an extended period, different degrees of occupational involvement for both marital partners are possible, and the balance within a person and within a family is sometimes rather tenuous as to which pattern will emerge at a given time. Increased information may swing the balance towards a more satisfactory solution for some.

For young people in particular, who have not yet formulated clear conceptions of the kind of family life they envisage and who are considering choices, this book may be useful in telling them something about what the interior of such families is like. The cases presented here are to be taken not as blueprints, but as suggestive jumping-off points for what may be quite different sorts of dual-career or dual-worker patterns in future.

For planners and housing administrators and others involved in the activities that bring about the 'built-in environment', it is hoped that this will stimulate a new dimension in their perspectives on family life and on the relations between work and family. Their awareness of some of the problems and some of the values of different kinds of families for which they must plan will, hopefully, be translated into facilities that may be operated more comfortably by families in future. Once again, this is not a blueprint, but a stimulus towards broader and deeper perspectives.

For educationalists and members of government bodies that affect educational policy there is a particular relevance in that it is this kind of programme that moulds the most fundamental preconceptions about the sex roles of men and women, and about the nature and place of family life in the larger society. Variations in family structures and styles of life should be recognized as legitimate, and to the extent that this is possible the contributions of some of the creative variants can be realized both for themselves and for their society rather than being diverted or 'hid under a bushel' for fear of being criticized. To the extent that planning and education for life in a complex society can include the possibility for recognizing and honouring increasing numbers of variant patterns of living with less conflict, the society is a humane and civilized one.

For directors and managers of the large organizations that play such an important part in modern society in relation to popular values and ways of life, the idea of dual-career families and their more widespread kindred types in dual-worker families may affect policies in various ways. Provisions may be seen as desirable for women workers in industry – such as crèches, altered work shift provisions, team work arrangements and re-entry assistance for mothers who leave their jobs on having children but wish later to return. From the consumption point of view, women who work and their families are likely to provide new kinds of markets – for convenience foods, clothing and services on a much more widespread basis than previously. The making available of such goods and services may in this case help not only the producer but the consumer as well. A long-term perspective is required here, and leadership from idealistic firms who may not obtain an immediate yield may in the long run make a very sound investment.

For the social scientist this is a study that aims to demonstrate the importance of informed case studies which, though very few and statistically unrepresentative, illuminate the dimensions intended in ways that might have been missed by more mechanical sampling and unidisciplinary methodological procedures. New issues and problems arising in a rapidly changing and complex society are best understood by a logic of inquiry tailored to the specific problem rather than merely the conventions of specific disciplines. In this case the mixture of sociological and psychological approaches used seems to have produced a better understanding of what these families were like than a unitary approach from the standpoint of either discipline alone.

Finally, for the much greater number of potential readers who are neither dual-career families, not even prospectively; nor are planners, industrialists, educators or social scientists, but ordinary people interested in how other people in the society which they share live and feel about the way they live, this book aims to contribute a degree of tolerance and understanding of others that contributes to a more humane society. The particular type of integration of work and family life, independence and interdependence among family members will vary from one family to another. However, it is important to recognize the need for interdependence and the importance of different balances in this as each couple and family work out what is best for them. Only in a society where such sympathetic insights are prevalent can a multiplicity of ways of achieving self-realization be achieved.

Appendix: Research Methods and Problems

In this study each family, with its networks of linkages with outside people and institutions, was perceived as a unique social system to be studied individually for its distinctive properties. To some extent we were attuned to the work of Oscar Lewis. In his detailed study of five Mexican families in the ethnographic style he illuminated not only Mexican lower-class life, but what he called 'The culture of poverty' generally. (Lewis, 1959.) Lewis' methods derived from anthropological field work, aided by modern technological devices, particularly the tape recorder. We felt that we could carry this type of work a step further by providing an explicit framework for analysing the materials. Lewis had selected and edited his materials, but only within the framework of the field anthropologist trying to produce a valid picture. We wished to produce a rounded picture of each family, but also to gather and analyse the data within a uniform set of categories so that systematic comparisons could be made among the families.

Another work that influenced us conceptually was that of Hess and Handel. These investigations of family life derived their orientations from clinical psychology – particularly the psychoanalytic and Gestalt schools. They sought to understand the dominant themes within each family much as one would within a personality, and to characterize each family by its ruling preoccupations (Hess and Handel, 1959). Hess and Handel gave more attention to the conceptual framework used but the system perspective was limited to the *internal* psychosocial organization of the family whereas one of our explicit interests was in the linkages between the family and external systems, notably work. In addition, we had had considerable prior experience with the intensive study of family processes (cf. Rapoport, 1961) which provided some methodological background for the particular approaches we selected.

As a consequence, we developed an approach which had several elements in its ideal formulation; but, of course, as in all field research, realization of the ideals was uneven. Ideally, we required that the information to be gathered from one family to the next should be comparable, and therefore an interview guide was prepared and every effort was made to gather information on all parts of it for all families. The guide was not a rigidly-applied questionnaire. We presented each couple with a copy of it at the outset of the interviews, and made the task of gathering information to fill in the required categories a collaborative one. We wanted to be sure that the studies did not suffer from the kinds of biases that arise from having only one interviewer, and one sex of interviewer, so we approached each family with a pair of interviewers, one male and one female. All of the interviewers were married though not all to one another. In order to get 'depth' information on a fairly frank level, it was necesssary to return to the families more than once, and we expected a set of interviews, some with the couple together and some with each member separately, which would run to a minimum of four contacts; the first to gather general information, the second and third to fill in specific missing information from the schedule, and develop impressions of differences of perspective as between husband and wife, a fourth after a preliminary case write-up had been completed to get the couples' reactions to it, where there seemed to them to be distortions, omissions etc. This minimum set was supplemented wherever possible with interviews with members of the couples' social networks, employers, colleagues, etc., to enlarge and improve the picture derived from the couples themselves. In the case of the couples chosen for case write-up in the present volume, at least one further session was required to check on the revision of the initial write-up for publication and to edit the write-up for acceptability to the family in published form.

These interviews were conducted at the convenience of the families – usually at their homes in the evenings, but sometimes at their offices or in our own offices (the latter mostly in individual interviews with one or another of the spouses). All interviews were taped and transcribed. The couples did not see the transcriptions, but where excerpts were used, intending to give a picture of how they saw things in their own words in the manner of the oral-history approach to social investigations, these were subject to editorial review and accepted as an approximation of what was said (subject to transcription errors, etc.) rather than evidence as in litigation.

In systematizing the information it was, of course, necessary to be selective. However, the use of an interviewing guide provided categories within which coding and selection of material could be made and the transcripts were scoured for all available information bearing on each of the categories. The initial write-ups which were fed back to the families were based on this schedule of categories, and were necessarily somewhat repetitious as information in any given category might be relevant and used for other categories as well – e.g. internal family decision-making processes and specific historical decisions as in the choice of schools, medical care facilities, or job changes. The fact that there were two interviewers who also shared the responsibility for the write-ups helped to assure as unbiased as possible inclusion of information for the categories recognized as relevant to the study. The feedback of the reports to the couples was regarded partly as an ethical requirement and partly as a validity check. For populations of the kind studied – 'ordinary', not psychiatrically disturbed, highly qualified and successful people who were often very insightful and articulate – we assumed that their own perceptions together with ours would provide the most valid approximation of 'the truth'.

Further about the use of two interviewers. Having a man and woman jointly interviewing the couple together and then the individuals separately was a procedure that we favoured on the basis of past experience with family research.

One member of the interviewer pair could act as technician (to keep the tape recorder managed unobtrusively), as observer of the interaction of the other (when one was more active than the other), as a reliability check on the subsequent analysis and interpretation of what was going on in the interview situation.

Sometimes this kind of check was simply used to keep the interview 'on the rails', sometimes to correct misperceptions or other errors.

In our past experience with interview materials involving highly-charged elements – sexual, financial, interpersonal – the checks that one interviewer can provide on the other are invaluable. Even experienced interviewers with considerable insight may have blocks in certain areas so that they are made uncomfortable by and consequently avoid gathering information in certain areas, e.g. conflicts or quarrels between husband and wife. Having a colleague on hand provides a useful corrective for interviewing errors both of omission and of commission.

Initially we assumed that when the time came for separate interviews the couples would prefer, as conventional couples would, to split up with same-sex interviewers. It was very interesting to note that in this situation, as in their lives generally, these couples did not follow the conventional expectations. Some preferred not to split up – handling the interviews as they handle their lives generally, jointly. Some, when given the choice, split up with cross-sex interviewers. Most indicated a willingness to do it either way. We found little reluctance to have the interviews taped, and in many cases we had help from the couples themselves in the management of the recording situation. Most of the couples went through a period of testing us out – to see how we handled them, how we handled the writing up of the materials and what disposition we made of the write-ups. Our contract with them was not to publish anything – even anonymous excerpts used to illustrate points made – without clearing with them.

There were two points of particular difficulty in the management of the course of interviews as described: the first feedback interview when the couples were presented with the picture of them that we had constructed from the interview materials; and the final write-ups (only for those who were selected for inclusion in this book). In particular families there were points of difficulty all along the way, but these were in the normal course of such interviewing, and required that the researchers exercise skill in making a relationship, inspiring trust and confidence, being aware of their own problems in the situation and sensitive to those of the respondents.

The initial feedback of the write-ups to the couples, ordinarily after the third interview, was a point of some tension. The couples had spoken freely – some said almost as though they were on a psychoanalyst's couch; many said more freely than they talk to their best friends – and what was put together from all this sometimes brought into the open elements which they had not quite made explicit to themselves. This was not only a matter of each finding out what the other thought and expressed privately in the separate interviews. We were very careful not to put anything into the write-ups from this type of source unless it seemed to be acceptable to the individual or was explicitly cleared as such. However, most people – even highly articulate and insightful people – lead their lives with a good deal of tacit avoidance of confrontations over all sorts of issues. The write-ups presented them with a third-party perception of the whole picture, and sometimes it aroused dormant disagreements that had to be handled if they came into the interview situation. As a matter of fact, from an ethical point of view we felt obliged to try to get them handled where we felt the write-ups had stirred them up so that we would not be guilty of having aroused trouble, or, in more ordinary terms, having made a mess of things without cleaning up afterwards. In all but one instance this type of difficulty was satisfactorily managed, though it called for the greatest 'therapeutic' type of skills available to us. In some instances the couples indicated that they had benefited by reviewing and reconsidering their positions in various ways through the medium of the write-ups. In one instance this was not true, and the couple indicated that they would have preferred to let sleeping dogs lie. The interviewers had, for them, simply added to the strain without the kind of resolution that reinforced their feeling that it was worth while, a feeling that had initially been formulated in terms of the aims of the research, but which eventually came to take on a personal-benefit dimension as well.

Appendix: Research Methods and Problems

Throughout the interviews and particularly at feedback point, it was considered important to provide supervision and support. Every interview was listened to from the tapes by one of the present authors, and problems were discussed with the interviewers. Case write-ups were reviewed by the authors before being typed and sent to the couples.

The second point of difficulty arose at the point of publication of full case studies as distinct from excerpts out of context and which therefore could have come from anyone. Here the fact that these were 'top people' came to be a liability. Most of them felt that even though pseudonyms were used and other devices making for confidentiality they might be identified. This brought some of them to exercise quite severely their right to review the write-ups and veto the inclusion of certain materials. From our side we had, of course, the option of not including them, and in two instances we were on the borderline about it because the cutting of materials had so truncated parts of the presentation. The reasons for reluctance from these couples were only partly personal – feeling embarrassed, or not wishing to be 'pompous' by having a biographical write-up at this stage of their lives. It was also to protect the feelings of relatives, or of children whose approval could not be meaningfully secured. In the end, though the cases presented here are quite different in length and depth of presentations, it was felt that they all provided enough of the essential picture to serve the purposes of the book. They are not total and complete in their scope, but they are believed to be valid in major outline and to represent an advance on presentations of this type now available.

References

Anderson, M. (ed.), *Sociology of the Family*, Penguin, 1971.

Bailyn, L., 'Career and Family Orientations of Husbands and Wives in Relation to Marital Happiness', *Human Relations*, Vol. 23, No. 2, 1970, pp. 97–113.

Bell, C., *Middle Class Families*, Routledge & Kegan Paul, 1969.

Bott, E., *Family and Social Network*, Tavistock Publications, 1957.

Bowlby, J., *Child Care and the Growth of Love*, Penguin, 1965.

Brozak, J., 'The Biology of Human Variation', *Annals of the New York Academy of Sciences*, Vol. 134, Article 2.

Dahlström, E. (ed.), *The Changing Roles of Men and Women*, Duckworth, 1967.

Epstein, C., *Women's Place : Options and Limits in Professional Careers*, University of California Press, Berkeley, 1970.

Fogarty, M., Allen, I., Allen, J., and Walters, P., *Women in Top Jobs*, Allen & Unwin for P.E.P., 1971.

Fogarty, M., Rapoport, Rhona, and Rapoport, R. N., *Woman and Top Jobs*, P.E.P., 1968.

Fogarty, M., Rapoport, Rhona, and Rapoport, R. N., *Sex, Career and Family*, Allen & Unwin for P.E.P., 1971.

Gavron, H., *The Captive Wife*, Routledge & Kegan Paul, 1966, Penguin Books, 1969.

Goode, W. J., *World Revolution and Family Patterns*, The Free Press, New York, 1963.

Hess, R., and Handel, G., *Family Worlds*, University of Chicago Press, Chicago, 1959.

Holter, H., *Sex Roles and Social Structure*, Universitetsforlaget, Oslo, 1970.

Hunt, A., *A Survey of Women's Employment*, Government Social Survey, SS 379, HMSO, 1968.

Jefferys, M., *Women in Medicine*, Office of Health Economics, 1966.

Kelsall, R. K., Poole, A., and Kuhn, A., *Six years After*, The University, Sheffield, 1970.

Koestler, A., *The Act of Creation*, Hutchinson, 1964.

Lewis, O., *Five Families*, Basic Books, New York, 1959.

References

Nye, F. I., and Hoffman, L. W., *The Employed Mother in America*, Rand McNally, Chicago, 1969.

Pahl, R., and Pahl, J., *Managers and their Families*, Penguin, 1971.

Rapoport, Rhona, and Rapoport, R. N., 'The Dual-Career Family', *Human Relations*, Vol. 22, No. 1, 1969.

Rapoport, Rhona, and Rapoport, R. N., 'Work and Family in Contemporary Society', *American Sociological Review*, Vol. 30, No. 3, 1965.

Rapoport, Rhona, and Rapoport, R. N., 'Early and Late Experiences as Determinants of Adult Behaviour', *British Journal of Sociology*, March 1971.

Rossi, Alice, 'Equality Between the Sexes: an Immodest Proposal', in R. J. Lifton (ed.) *The Woman in America*, Houghton Mifflin, Boston, 1965.

Riesman, D., 'Some Dilemmas of Women's Education', *The Educational Record*, 1965.

Sussman, M., *et al.*, 'Changing Families in a Changing Society', White House Conference on Children and Youth, Washington, 1970.

Toynbee, A., *A Study of Society*, Vols. 1–12, Oxford University Press, 1961.

Willmott, P., 'Some Social Trends', *Urban Studies*, No. 6.

Yudkin, S., and Holme, A., *Working Mothers and their Children*, Michael Joseph, 1963.

Some other books published by Penguins are
described on the following pages.

THE FAMILY AND MARRIAGE IN BRITAIN

RONALD FLETCHER

Pulpits, rostrums, and the more deeply entrenched batteries of press and radio still resound with lamentations about the decay of family life in Britain. Our modern society, it is said, is in a condition of moral decline. Immorality, divorce, delinquency stalk the land ... or so we are told.

Is there any truth in this murky picture? Or, on the contrary, do the facts quietly pronounce that the family is more stable and more secure today than ever before in our history? For history, when we survey all classes impartially, is largely a long tale of poverty, drudgery, desertion, and vagrancy.

In his systematic analysis of the subject, a sociologist discusses the extraordinary strength and resilience of the family group in the face of rapid and radical social changes and provides answers to questions which are often anxiously posed to us. Are married women working in industry neglecting their children? Has discipline within the family utterly disappeared, or is today's relationship between parents and children a new and fuller one? Have teenagers really so much money to spend? And, even if this is so, is it so deplorable?

The book arrives at encouraging conclusions and discusses the basis for further improvements.

'Deserves to be compulsory reading in all schools and theological colleges.' – *Times Literary Supplement*

'The fullest outline there has yet been of the social history of the family in Britain' – Michael Young, *New Statesman*

A Pelican Original

WORK

Two volumes each containing twenty personal accounts

EDITED BY RONALD FRASER

'These accounts are patently honest and the convictions they contain shiningly sincere. They are also remarkably lucid and, in some cases, vividly written' – *Daily Telegraph*

'Interesting, because any authentic, deeply felt piece of human experience, vividly reported, cannot fail to be so' – *New Society*

VOLUME 1

This collection of essays, originally published in *New Left Review*, is an imaginative attempt to show what it means in human terms to be doing a particular job, its satisfactions and frustrations, how it shapes lives. Twenty men and women in a wide variety of occupations write with feeling about the personal meaning of their work. They range from nightwatchman to policeman; bus driver to housewife; accountant to journalist; clerk to croupière; signalwoman to programmer; research scientist to man on the dole. The wider implications – beyond that of an individual in an individual situation – are commented on by Raymond Williams in a concluding essay.

VOLUME 2

What is it like to be a stockbroker, a bricklayer, a social worker, an actor? What patterns do jobs impose on lives, and how do individuals react to them? This volume, with twenty more personal accounts of occupations, makes the same imaginative leap into the lives of other people and invites the reader to draw certain disturbing inferences about the workings of our society.

SHAPE OF COMMUNITY
Realization of Human Potential

SERGE CHEMAYEFF AND ALEXANDER TZONIS

Technology is creating an ever-expanding environment which is becoming increasingly hostile to the natural one. The conflict between the natural and the man-made has reached a point of unprecedented crisis: life's total habitat is endangered. One of the most devastating threats is created by transport and communications which destroy meeting places and the sense of community.

Affluent societies in their narrow-minded preoccupation with quite material gains are losing sight of long-term consequences which, however, are tragic to man's survival. The simple remedial steps that are being taken now have become ineffective and obsolete.

Shape of Community is a manifesto urging the re-thinking of technology as a catalyst of human evolution, rather than simply as a blind destructive force. It proposes a design methodology and an urban model that may lead to a peaceful coexistence of man and nature, and man with man within community.

A Pelican Original

THE PELICAN ANTHROPOLOGY LIBRARY

The Pelican Anthropology Library is designed to introduce a rapidly changing and expanding subject to a wider public. It includes both reprints of modern classics of anthropological research and theory, and new introductory studies. Projected titles cover such subjects as primitive art, law, magic and religion, economics, and applied anthropology.

MARRIAGE *Lucy Mair*

Professor Mair casts an anthropologist's eye over the institution of marriage in its social context and as it is found in different societies throughout the world. In asking such questions as 'What are husbands for?' she finds some of the conventional answers inadequate and suggests some interesting new ones. Her book covers thoroughly such customs and practices as exogamy and endogamy, bridewealth and dowry, the levirate and ghost-marriage, mother-in-law avoidance, incest prohibition and divorce, as well as marriage ceremonies and symbolism. The book ends with a consideration of marriage in industrial and developing societies, with the new freedom of women and the atomization of kinship.

KINSHIP AND MARRIAGE *Robin Fox*

We are so accustomed to our own marriage and family customs that we tend to think of them as norms of human behaviour. But systems of kinship are not immutable; other cultures – both primitive and modern – have operated modes of determining kinship and controlling marriage and inheritance significantly different from ours. This volume in the Pelican Anthropology Library is the first introduction to these alternative systems of social engineering, many of them of a fascinating elegance and complexity. By analysing the pressures which mould each of them, Robin Fox gives us a fresh insight into the workings of our customs. He also suggests a tentative solution to the problem of the incest taboo. This is the first time that all the theories of kinship and marriage have been analysed within a single framework of argument in terms intelligible to the layman.